Preface

This volume is the product of research conducted under the Berkeley-Stanford Program in Soviet and Post-Soviet Studies. It was made possible by a grant from the Carnegie Corporation of New York, for which both the Program and the individual contributors are most grateful. It is an example of what we trust will be increasingly the pattern of future academic work in this area: the collaboration of several Russian with several North American scholars in joint seminars and conferences and the appearance of their papers between the covers of the same book.

We have made no effort to impose a single set of policy preferences or political judgments on our authors. Indeed, the diversity of responsible opinions in this book contributes, in my opinion, to its interest and value.

In addition to referring the reader to the Glossary for an elucidation of terms and names, we should indicate our general practice of using the names of places and institutions as they were at the time discussed; changes and variant forms are indicated in the Glossary.

I would like to express particular thanks to Edward W. Walker, who skillfully managed the complexities of international coordination needed to produce this volume and dealt with the many substantive and technical questions that arose along the way. His breadth of understanding of Russian politics and his diplomatic as well as editorial skills played an indispensable role in the success of this whole undertaking. We are also much indebted to Christine Shaff for managing to transform disorderly bits of paper and chaotic collections of bytes into a coherent manuscript. Alexander Dallin lent an experienced hand in planning, revising, and editing the volume. Bojana Ristich once again proved to be a superb editor. Gavin Helf provided us with wonderful maps, indispensable computer advice, and insightful substantive comments. Corbin Lyday spent many arduous hours rendering esoteric Russian into fluent English prose. Finally, Rebecca Ritke, on behalf of Westview Press, not only was a knowledgeable, understanding, and helpful editor but made important and valuable comments and suggestions on the whole manuscript.

Finally, I wish to thank all the contributors for their cooperation in producing this book. While it represents interim judgments that may well require refinement or reconsideration in the future, it was our conviction that the momentous events that have occurred in Russia since the collapse of the Soviet Union in 1991 demanded timely presentation and interpretation. We hope our readers will agree that it was well worth the effort.

Gail W. Lapidus
Chair, Berkeley-Stanford Program
in Soviet and Post-Soviet Studies

Introduction

Gail W. Lapidus

In the heady aftermath of the failed coup of August 1991, the Soviet system seemed destined for extinction and Russia appeared to be well launched on the path to political democratization, economic reform, and a cooperative partnership with the West. Flush with their victory and enjoying widespread public support, the defenders of the Moscow White House, under the leadership of Boris Yeltsin, had committed themselves to destroying the dissolving remnants of the Soviet party-state, creating a new democratic Russia in which individual liberties would be guaranteed in a new constitution, and undertaking far-reaching economic reforms and the creation of a market economy which Mikhail Gorbachev had contemplated but could never embrace.

Their victory promised as well a continuation and acceleration of the process of demilitarization that had begun during *perestroika*: not only sharp cutbacks in military forces and capabilities but a serious program of defense conversion and privatization that would turn Russia's vast military-industrial complex to meeting the urgent needs of the civilian population. New economic and political arrangements would also include a substantial decentralization of power, with new federal arrangements reversing decades of hyper-centralization by transferring significant responsibilities and resources to Russia's regions and republics.

In foreign policy as well, the Russian leadership sought to distance itself from the expansionist, confrontational, and autarkic features of its Soviet predecessor, building instead on the new orientations associated with *perestroika* and developed under Eduard Shevardnadze's leadership of the Soviet Foreign Ministry. Having defended the right of the Baltic states to regain their independence and having proclaimed the sovereignty of Russia itself, Russia's leaders played a crucial role in the dissolution of the Soviet empire. They now sought to bring together the former Soviet republics in a Commonwealth of Independent States based on respect for the sovereignty and territorial integrity of all. At the same time, the new Russian government held out the prospect of a still closer partnership with Europe and the United States, overcoming the legacy of the Cold War and the division of Europe while jointly addressing global problems. Toward Japan, there were intimations that the resolution of the longstanding conflict over the Northern Territories was finally at hand. All these hopes were symbolized by the reassuring presence of a pro-Western liberal, Andrei Kozyrev, as Foreign Minister.

Within two years, this vision of a post-Soviet Russia had been shattered. Russia's fledgling democratic institutions, crippled by political and institutional deadlock, failed to address adequately the country's avalanche of problems, a failure that was dramatized by President Yeltsin's decision to order a tank assault against the very White House that had been the symbol of the new political order. Political disillusionment was compounded by mounting economic hardships. Growing hostility to economic reforms and privatization, increasingly associated with social injustice, corruption, and crime rather than with yearned-for affluence, culminated in the repudiation of the architects of the reform program in the elections of December 1993 and an announcement by the new Prime Minister that "the era of romantic reform is over." The erosion of the popularity and influence of democratic reformers was also dramatized by the results of local elections, which returned to power a significant part of the traditional communist elite—the so-called nomenklatura. The new parliament's amnesty of the August 1991 coup-plotters, along with the challenge to President Yeltsin by the leaders of the 1993 resistance, appeared to signal a return to the political status quo ante.

The process of demilitarization also appeared to be stalling as the unfolding political drama in Moscow encouraged the contenders for power to bid for military support and gave the military and security forces an unprecedented and central—if not entirely welcome—role as guarantors of the political status quo. Moreover, hopes for the rapid conversion of the military-industrial complex were disappointed as the daunting obstacles to such a process became apparent. Indeed, pressures to stave off the collapse in defense production by increasing state orders to military enterprises were dictated as much by the concern to preserve the employment opportunities and welfare functions they provided as by the desire to preserve the sinews of military power.

Equally dramatic were the shifts in Russian foreign policy. Ever more strident assertions of Russian state interests and an increasingly confrontational stance toward the former Soviet republics, which earlier had been confined to the national-patriotic wing of the political spectrum, now characterized the statements of reformers and democrats. The growing resort to political, economic, and military leverage to influence the domestic and foreign policies of the new states was accompanied by efforts to consolidate the Commonwealth under Russian hegemony. A similar assertiveness complicated Russia's relations with Europe and the West. A startlingly uncharacteristic hard-line speech, which Andrei Kozyrev had delivered in Stockholm in 1992 to shock Western statesmen into realizing how a change in Russia's leadership could affect its foreign policy, had, by 1994, become a staple of official Foreign Ministry pronouncements; here as well, the era of "romantic Atlanticism" was proclaimed to be over. These unanticipated and disheartening developments had provoked a major debate in the West over policy toward Russia, and the assumptions on which that policy ought to be premised.

The time seems especially propitious, therefore, for a scholarly review and assessment of the development of post-communist Russia and of its implications for broader theories of post-communist transition. The burgeoning literature on the subject has focussed on three features of transitions in post-communist states that distinguish them from previous transitions from authoritarian rule in Latin America and Southern Europe.

The first major difference lies in the scope and depth of the needed transformation, as the consequence of a communist legacy that had entailed a more far-reaching eradication of civil society and destruction of the institutions and behaviors associated with market economies than was characteristic of non-communist authoritarian regimes.

A second difference is the need to engage in state- and nation-building simultaneously with radical political and economic transformation, a challenge that threatened to overwhelm the relatively weak post-communist governments of East Central Europe and the Soviet Union.

Yet a third complicating factor is the presence of severe ethnic conflicts and tensions in this region on a scale not present in previous transitions, tensions that were further aggravated by the dynamics of political competition and economic redistribution.

The case of the Soviet Union (and to some degree of Yugoslavia and Czechoslovakia) was further handicapped by the absence of well-established and legitimate political identities and boundaries in advance of the initiation of democratization, a condition that Dankwart Rustow had earlier argued was essential to its success. In view of the fact that there is no democratic way to settle such issues, the contestation over these issues could not but complicate already intense struggles for power and resources. Thus, the major consequences of the process of liberalization were a growing challenge to what were viewed as the imperial features of the Soviet system and the concomitant emergence of centrifugal forces, which resulted in the dissolution of the Union—in effect, a process of decolonization.

This pattern of development also had two consequences that decisively set off the Soviet case from all other examples of transition. First, the process of transition that was initiated in the USSR culminated in the dissolution of the Soviet state, making the subjects of transition the fifteen new states which succeeded it. To the extent that the majority of them represent completely new political entities on the international scene, state-building and nation-building may prove a more useful conceptual framework than the customary axioms of transition.

Second, the dissolution of the Soviet Union represented not merely a return to the status quo ante as of 1917; it involved the loss of territories and populations that had long been a part of the pre-Soviet Russian empire. The political and psychological trauma of this development, necessarily turbulent under any circumstances but especially so in a country accustomed to perceiving itself and being treated as a great power, forced issues of identity to the center of attention. Not surprisingly, this entire development has been highly contentious and divisive, and the source of serious political cleavages. The question of "who was guilty?" has gradually overwhelmed all other issues of economic and political reform, and it is increasingly the "democrats" who are blamed not only for the economic and social crisis but also for the destruction of an idealized Soviet state. These are but some of the circumstances which make the Russian case so exceptionally complex and in many respects different from transitions from authoritarianism elsewhere in the contemporary world. They deserve our thoughtful study.

1

Russia's Post-Communist Politics: Revolution or Continuity?

Lilia Shevtsova

To many, Russia's path after the fall of communism and the collapse of the Soviet Union has been little more than a conglomeration of dramatic and chaotic events. In many ways, these new developments beggar easy description—the convulsions of the political fabric, the about-faces and zigzags of political leaders, the chaotic nature of conflicting social tendencies. But in the midst of this confusion, and the apocalyptic pronouncements it has inspired, a certain pattern can be discerned: a new political reality is emerging in post-communist Russia.

Boris Yeltsin's "Revolutionary Liberalism"

The first stage of Russia's post-communist development began in December 1991 with the abolition of the USSR and ended in September 1993 with Yeltsin's dissolution of the Russian parliament. The period witnessed a transfer of power from traditional Soviet institutions to a new Russian center headed by Yeltsin and his advisors. (See Figures 1.1 and 1.2.) Hoping to transform Russia's state-run economy into a market-based system "in a single bound," Yeltsin launched a program designed to transform Russian society radically. At the same time, he adopted a foreign policy aimed at preserving Russia's status as a superpower and securing Moscow's position as an ally, not simply a partner, of the United States.

It soon became clear, however, that Yeltsin's program was deeply flawed. Economic reforms were launched without adequate knowledge of how marketization was to be accomplished and without the benefit of

6

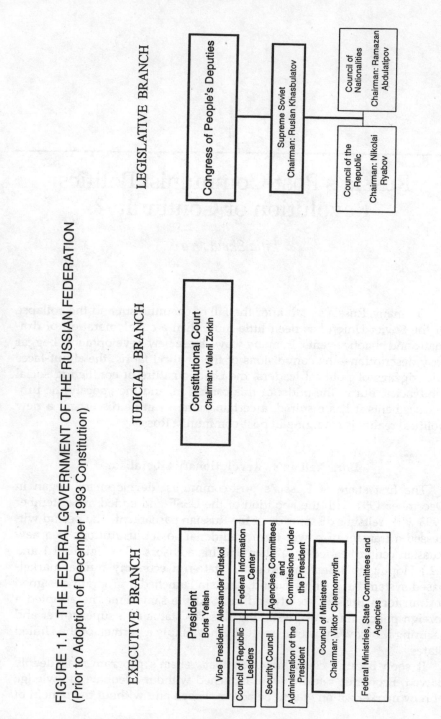

FIGURE 1.1   THE FEDERAL GOVERNMENT OF THE RUSSIAN FEDERATION
(Prior to Adoption of December 1993 Constitution)

LEGISLATIVE BRANCH

Congress of People's Deputies

Supreme Soviet
Chairman: Ruslan Khasbulatov

Council of the Republic
Chairman: Nikolai Ryabov

Council of Nationalities
Chairman: Ramazan Abdulatipov

JUDICIAL BRANCH

Constitutional Court
Chairman: Valeni Zorkin

EXECUTIVE BRANCH

President
Boris Yeltsin
Vice President: Aleksander Rutskoi

Council of Republic Leaders

Security Council

Administration of the President

Federal Information Center

Agencies, Committees and Commissions Under the President

Council of Ministers
Chairman: Viktor Chernomyrdin

Federal Ministries, State Committees and Agencies

FIGURE 1.2   THE FEDERAL GOVERNMENT OF THE RUSSIAN FEDERATION
(After Adoption of December 1993 Constitution)

LEGISLATIVE BRANCH

Federal Assembly

| Federation Council (178 Seats) | — | State Duma (450 Deputies) |
| Chairman: Vladimir Shumeiko | — | Chairman: Ivan Rybkin |

JUDICIAL BRANCH

Constitutional Court
(Not Yet Constituted)

EXECUTIVE BRANCH

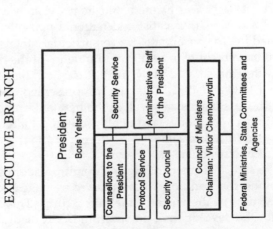

President
Boris Yeltsin

Security Service

Administrative Staff
of the President

Counsellors to the
President

Protocol Service

Security Council

Council of Ministers
Chairman: Viktor Chernomyrdin

Federal Ministries, State Committees and
Agencies

a stable political order. Moreover, the attempt to preserve Russia's super-power status interfered with the demands of democratization and complicated Moscow's efforts to establish good relations with the outside world, particularly with the other Soviet successor states. The new elite, like the old, continued to approach politics as a Manichean struggle that could lead only to the unconditional victory of one side over the other.

Russia's post-communist transformation was uniquely difficult. In most of the post-communist countries of Central Europe, the collapse of communism did not bring with it the total collapse of the state. Russia, on the other hand, was forced not only to build a new economy and a new regime but to reconstruct at the same time the state structures needed to carry out these tasks. Moreover, the USSR's superpower status, Russia's military-oriented economy, the multinational character of its federation, and the deeply-rooted hegemonic and messianic sentiments of both elite and society further complicated the transformation process in Russia.

The lack of elite consensus about the principal agenda of reform also differentiates Russia's transition from that in other countries. In most post-communist states in Central Europe, political elites agreed upon basic priorities and developed mechanisms for peacefully negotiating the early stages of the transition. The economic and political pragmatism of former communists also contributed to stability and support for reform from below. In Poland and Hungary, for example, old and new ruling elites succeeded in working out "roundtable" agreements on power-sharing and reform priorities that were backed by a coalition of the most powerful political forces in each country. As a result, responsibility for the consequences of reform was shared by all signatories to the agreement.

Russian political society, in contrast, was far more divided from the very outset. In the aftermath of the failed August 1991 coup, the Russian Communist Party was banned, and its activists became completely disoriented. Conservative statist and national-patriotic forces, on the other hand, had yet to consolidate or even articulate their programs. The only political movement with significant influence at the time was Democratic Russia, the mass-based movement that had helped bring Yeltsin to power in 1990 and 1991. Although it represented liberals and democrats among the intelligentsia as well as the new entrepreneurial class, Democratic Russia's support was mainly limited to large cities. As a result, Yeltsin was forced to launch his reforms without a coherent opposition with which to negotiate.

To be sure, a segment of the anti-communist opposition and pragmatists among the traditional *nomenklatura* managed to conclude a shaky, informal pact in the wake of the failed coup. This "August Pact" provided for the devolution of power from USSR institutions to those of the

RSFSR (soon to be renamed the Russian Federation). The pact was worked out, however, by a small group of people and without public discussion. Moreover, it left few of the participants with a role, and hence a stake, in the future order. Lacking unified political support, clear obligations for participants, and incentives to fulfill the agreement, the pact quickly collapsed. Russia's political elite was therefore unable to reach a consensus on the character of the new Russian state or the model of post-communist transformation.

Of equal importance, Yeltsin failed to build broad social support for reform. Instead of using Democratic Russia to build support at the grass roots, Yeltsin chose to rely on a narrow circle of close advisors, most of whom were pragmatic members of the old *nomenklatura*.[1] At a critical moment in late 1991, Yeltsin refused to hold pre-term elections to legislative and executive bodies, both in Moscow and in the provinces. He also missed the opportunity to create a new, more coherent institutional order with clearly defined spheres of responsibility for different branches of power. Finally, he gave no attention to establishing a well-functioning party system. In the absence of mass-based parties or social movements, corporatist groups rooted in the old ruling class proved better at articulating their interests and influencing policy.[2] Instead, Yeltsin concentrated on building a vertical system of presidential power through the appointment of loyalists as "presidential representatives" (*predstaviteli prezidenta*) and "heads of administration" (*glavy administratsii* or *gubernatory*) in the provinces. The end result was a collection of ill-designed institutions with few social roots, which immediately became a source of constant conflict.

In short, Yeltsin embarked on a course of "revolutionary liberalism" from above in a style characteristic of many authoritarian rulers. He relied not on society but on the administrative apparatus of the *ancien régime* to implement his program. Ironically, his "revolution from above" was reminiscent of Soviet-era "campaigns," while his strategy of reform resembled Gorbachev's—the use of charisma to personalize the political process; reliance on a vertical system of presidential power to implement his policies; and improved relations with the West in the hope that a new "Marshall Plan" would rescue the country. Also like Gorbachev, Yeltsin chose many policies at random, "winging it" rather than operating from a well-chosen, carefully considered plan.

Despite these similarities, there were also important differences between Yeltsin and Gorbachev. Gorbachev attempted to transform the communist system, not destroy it. Yeltsin's primary political goal, in contrast, was the obliteration of the old power structures and the state that supported them, while attempting at the same time to build entirely new political institutions.[3] This simultaneous attempt to destroy and create accounts for the revolutionary nature of Yeltsin's policies and distinguishes him from Gorbachev.

In retrospect, however, it is clear that Yeltsin failed to break with the style of governance and the mentality he had acquired as a Communist Party *apparatchik*. His tendency was to purge supporters when doing so served his political interests. This flexibility helped him maneuver on the highly polarized Russian political scene. But it also made it impossible to elaborate a stable and viable policy, to strike stable alliances, or to secure a power base. Yeltsin's reform government was therefore doomed to be a cabinet of loners—of "kamikazes," as former Prime Minister Yegor Gaidar once described himself. Yeltsin's revolutionary style was thus contradictory and inconsistent. He would attempt to make a radical breakthrough on one issue and ignore the price this breakthrough would exact on his program in general. He also allowed himself to become involved in haggling over details and would make sudden and unjustified concessions.

In the final analysis, Yeltsin proved unable to meet the new challenges he had himself helped create. His decision in late 1991 to forego political reform, his failure to force his allies in the democratic movement to be more accommodating, and his unwillingness or inability to present society with a clear vision of reform, all contributed to the political crises that deepened over the course of 1992 and 1993.

Conflict at the Top: Elite Opposition to "Shock Therapy"

Almost immediately after the August coup, groups that had previously supported Yeltsin began to splinter. The "democrats" crystallized into two competing factions: "functionaries"—those at the upper strata of power whose loyalties lay wholly with Yeltsin—and "ideologues"—representatives of the liberal intelligentsia who remained outside the inner sanctum of power and became some of its most vocal critics. In turn, the president's inner circle also splintered. An increasingly visible struggle for power and the ear of the president was waged by a "second echelon" of political leaders—Vice President Aleksandr Rutskoi, State Secretary Gennadii Burbulis, and Chairman of the Supreme Soviet Ruslan Khasbulatov. By early 1992, Rutskoi and Khasbulatov, key allies of Yeltsin during the events of August 1991, had become his most vocal critics and powerful rivals.

At the same time, other groups with a specifically anti-democratic orientation and an even deeper antipathy to Yeltsin's reform program began to coalesce. In contrast to Central Europe, where opposition forces formed to the left or the right on the basis of socio-economic issues, Russia's opposition united around the theme of Russia's lost great-power status. A loose alliance formed between three somewhat dissimilar groups—"national-patriots," former communists, and advocates of a strong Russian state (*gosudarstvenniki*), who demanded above all that the state vigorously defend Russia's national interests.

This coalition made its presence felt for the first time during a vociferous public demonstration in February 1992. Although neither side of this "right-left bloc" succeeded in galvanizing public opinion, the event constituted a turning point in Russian political life. It dramatized the growing popular disappointment with Yeltsin's radical reform program and an increasing popular apathy that threatened to make politics the exclusive province of back-room deals and secret "sweetheart" agreements.

Sensing the popular disillusionment with his program, Yeltsin appeared to agree to ameliorate the harsh consequences of the January 1992 price liberalization—the first element of Economic Minister Yegor Gaidar's program of IMF-approved "shock therapy." Nevertheless, a previously muted struggle for power between the executive and legislative powers in Moscow began to intensify and quickly became the decisive factor in Russian political life.

The roots of this confrontation were complicated. It was only partly the result of the lack of a clear division of powers and the incompatibility of the institutions of the new Russian presidency and the remnants of the old political system represented by the Supreme Soviet and the Congress of People's Deputies. More important was the fact that every faction in this struggle felt compelled to monopolize power. Moreover, the impasse was made even more dangerous by the zealotry of its main actors—President Yeltsin, Supreme Soviet Chairman Khasbulatov, and those around them.

Accompanying this executive-legislative conflict in Moscow in early 1992 was a deepening struggle between the federal "center" and local officials and institutions in the provinces. A chain reaction began as one after another of Russia's ethnic republics declared "sovereignty," a process that met with growing dissatisfaction from Russia's non-ethnic regions. Increasingly, edicts passed in Moscow were ignored in both the republics and the regions. Tuva, Sakha-Yakutia, and Checheno-Ingushetia passed laws asserting that their constitutions legally superseded the federal constitution. Russian regional elites, unhappy at the perceived privileges being afforded the ethnic republics in the Federation Treaty signed in March 1992, also tried to "extort" greater financial benefits from the central government. Again, these center-periphery tensions were driven only in part by the lack of a well-established division of powers between Moscow and the provinces—equally important was the unwillingness of elites both in the capital and in the localities to compromise.

Lacking a clear vision of a new federal structure, the Yeltsin team chose the worst possible strategy for dealing with the challenge from the provinces: individual arrangements, conducted in secret, negotiated alternately with republics and regions, that promised inordinate financial advantages to some and temporary compromises to others. Federal-republic and federal-regional relations were thereby transformed into a process of endless haggling. This only weakened the embryonic structures of the new Russian state and distracted attention from the critical issues of economic reform and the cleavages that lay behind Moscow's problems with the provinces.

The president's vertical system of power was designed to serve as a yardstick by which Yeltsin and his lieutenants could judge provincial leaders. Nevertheless, Yeltsin soon found that his edicts were being contradicted or ignored by local leaders who were angered by what they perceived to be Yeltsin's usurpation of their power. A dual system of power *(dvoevlastie)*, already established in Moscow, began to find its way to the provinces. Indeed, an openly anti-Yeltsin orientation emerged in some regions with both branches of power united in opposition to Moscow.[4]

Controversy also developed in early 1992 about where the reforms should be carried out—in the Russian Federation only, or throughout the Commonwealth of Independent States (CIS). For a period, Yeltsin wavered between an isolationist, Russia-only policy on the one hand, and one geared to the CIS on the other. As a result, the adoption of a reform program specifically tailored to Russia was postponed. Ukraine's open rivalry with Russia eventually forced policy makers in Moscow to focus on Russia's national interests. Nevertheless, opposition from "old believers" committed to Soviet-style hegemony delayed the emergence of a consensus in Moscow about Russia's national interests as distinct from those of the other post-Soviet states. Only in 1993, under the influence of deepening economic crises in most of Russia's new neighbors, did a painful and contradictory process of economic reintegration begin in the former Soviet Union.

The Emergence of the Anti-Democratic Opposition

In April 1992, the deepening polarization of Russian politics, and particularly the intensifying struggle between the president and the legislature, came to a head. Thereafter, the great demarcation in Russian political life became whether to support Yeltsin and the executive or Khasbulatov and the legislature.[5]

The precipitating event of the confrontation was the Sixth Congress of People's Deputies, which convened in April 1992. The Congress itself, with its over 1000 members, was more a political rally than a civilized parliament. On the eve of the session, the radicals in Yeltsin's entourage, Secretary of the State Council Gennadii Burbulis and State Counselor Sergei Shakhrai, recommended that the president try to circumvent the Congress and Yeltsin's many opponents in the legislature by turning to the people directly. Their suggestion was that a referendum be held on a constitution that would establish a presidential, rather than a parliamentary, republic. Approval would have meant the end of the Congress of People's Deputies and possibly the establishment of a Fujimori-style authoritarian regime in Russia.[6]

On this occasion the president's attack forced the parliament to back down. Despite strong opposition to Gaidarnomics at the Congress, Gaidar's government was preserved. But Yeltsin's victory was not followed by an acceleration of reform. On the contrary, Yeltsin seemed to lose the political initiative. It was seized instead by conservatives—representatives of the "directors' lobby,"[7] regional elites, and representatives of agrarian interests, all of whom favored a more moderate and controlled approach to reform. As a result, Yeltsin was forced to bring three members of the directors' lobby into the cabinet: Vladimir Shumeiko, Georgii Khizha, and future Prime Minister Viktor Chernomyrdin. Shortly thereafter, Viktor Gerashchenko, former director of the USSR State Bank, was appointed head of the Russian Central Bank. Gerashchenko's appointment in effect marked the end of "shock therapy" in Russia, as the government soon adopted a more moderate policy on economic reform.

Yeltsin reacted to the growing opposition he faced from the legislature by creating a new presidential structure—the Security Council—headed by conservative Yurii Skokov, to monitor the activities of all other executive organs, particularly the military services, the Ministry of Security (the former KGB), and the Ministry of Internal Affairs (MVD).[8] The decision reflected Yeltsin's style—inconsistent in details, but consistent in his stubborn efforts to concentrate control of key administrative and political instruments in his own hands. In practice, however, the new structure only increased the growing chaos within the government and weakened Yeltsin by making him hostage to his powerful administration.

Indeed, Yeltsin continued to rely on top-down "campaign" methods, thereby alienating the democrats. Their unhappiness with Yeltsin, as well as their general disarray, in turn helped the political fortunes of the anti-democratic opposition. At the same time, it became evident that the majority of political and social groups in Russia were opposed to the way Yeltsin was pursuing the goals of marketization and democratization.[9]

Indeed, in June 1992 the first organized activity of the extreme opposition took place in the post-Soviet era in Russia. A united right-left bloc, called "the National Salvation Front," was formed.[10] The Front brought together three different groups—former communists fighting to regain their positions, increasingly active and aggressive nationalists, and former democrats who had come to the conclusion that Russia needed not democracy but a strong state and an iron hand.

Offsetting this polarization of the Russian political spectrum somewhat was the formation of a centrist organization, the "Civic Union," that same month. Led by Arkadii Volskii, the Union was formed from a merger of Volskii's Union of Industrialists and Entrepreneurs, the People's Party of Free Russia under then Vice President Aleksandr Rutskoi, and the Russian Democratic Party of Nikolai Travkin.

The significance of the Civic Union was that it marked the return of the previously slighted *nomenklatura* to the political arena. In this respect, the Civic Union resembled the "Movement for Democratic Reforms" launched by Gorbachev some years earlier. Unlike the "Movement," however, the Civic Union was able to garner support from a wide spectrum of political groups, including the directors' lobby, various regional organizations, and those who saw it as a political instrument that could combat "Gaidarism" and even Yeltsin himself. The birth of the Civic Union thus reflected the conservative drift of Russian politics.

Indeed Gaidar, the architect of the economic reform program, soon found himself under heavy fire from both sides of Russia's political spectrum. On the one hand, he was criticized for being too radical by those opposed to economic liberalization, even though by this time there was scarcely anything remaining of "Gaidarism." On the other hand, he was criticized vigorously from the left for being too conciliatory to conservatives, and above all to the directors' lobby.

As the summer of 1992 progressed, the anti-democrats began to warn of an imminent disaster with predictable vitriol and frequency. Gaidarism, they argued, was leading the country to ruin, and something dramatic would have to be done to stop it. Fears arose of another coup, this time directed against Boris Yeltsin. Even the Chairman of the Constitutional Court, Valerii Zorkin, warned that the threat of armed conflict should not be taken lightly.[11]

Was there, in fact, a genuine threat to Yeltsin that summer? Even if there was, nothing was done to carry it out. Nevertheless, the constant warnings from those close to the president of an impending anti-democratic coup served a dual (if ambiguous) purpose. They not only discouraged conservative attempts to solidify the opposition, but also offered a pretext for declaring presidential rule, which many of Yeltsin's closest aides were by then advocating.

From that time on, Russian society lived in a state of permanent anxiety amidst predictions of a military solution to the political crisis. The two branches of power in Moscow had, it seemed, become substitutes for traditional parties. Each represented different, antagonistic interests: the executive power representing liberals and technocrats, and the legislature representing nationalists and populists. With every new failure of Yeltsin's liberal revolutionary program, the confrontation intensified, forcing a split in society at large. Moreover, the standoff soon brought reforms to a halt. By the end of the summer, then, the president found himself facing a host of profound political challenges: the growing strength of the opposition; the increasing assertiveness of provincial elites; and an accelerating decline in social and political support for his policies.

Russia Changes Course

Thus the fall of 1992 witnessed preparations by Russia's main political forces for a decisive showdown in November, when the next session of the Congress of People's Deputies would convene. Convinced that their time had finally arrived, the Civic Union and its allies began to issue ultimatums to the president.

Yet the newcomers—the Civic Union and the "right-left" bloc—failed to take advantage of the executive-legislative impasse. Both made alliances with representatives of the executive as well as the legislature (although clearly the National Salvation Front was ideologically more comfortable with Khasbulatov and his supporters); but the two groups had different goals. The right-leftists sought to impeach Yeltsin and disband all structures of power in order to restore the Soviet state. The Civic Union, in contrast, hoped to win a share of political power, or at least to force the government to adopt a more moderate economic policy of "state capitalism" that would serve the economic interests of its constituency—the pragmatists in the traditional ruling class.

Aware that his political support was shrinking, Yeltsin made a sudden change of course in September. Throughout 1992, he had attempted to avoid needless fights with the Supreme Soviet and the Congress. He had tried, albeit with limited success, to court political groups within the legislature to prevent a unified opposition from forming. In September, however, he threw down the gauntlet, demanding that the deputies "desist from pointless activity." However, he offered them and also the administrative heads in the regions a two-and-one-half-year extension to their terms of office. To further sweeten the deal, he reshuffled some of his key advisors, pointedly dismissing Burbulis, who had always been a lightning rod for the opposition, and elevating several of his more conservative and uncompromising advisors—Yurii Skokov, Yurii Petrov, and Oleg Lobov. His hope was that by doing so he would neutralize some of the conservative opposition to his policies.

In October, however, Yeltsin again appeared to yield to growing demands for a softening of shock therapy. For the first time, he criticized Gaidar publicly. Public speculation centered on the likely departure of a new "sacrificial lamb" from the presidential team—if not Prime Minister Gaidar himself, then someone close to him. Yeltsin also created two additional organs—the Council of the Heads of Republics and the Council of Governors—to attract provincial elites to his side from both the regions and the republics. Finally, he struck at the extreme opposition, banning the National Salvation Front. Of questionable legality, the move was in any case meant for the Supreme Soviet, not the Front—Yeltsin was in effect telling the deputies: "Don't burn your bridges; I am capable of decisive measures!"

When the Congress finally convened in November, Yeltsin's camp was divided but not without its strengths. Radicals around him favored a decisive showdown between the executive and the legislature, and advised Yeltsin to play his final trump card of a plebiscite—the "appeal to the people." Yeltsin's moderate advisors, on the other hand, favored a continuation of the uneasy armistice between the two branches, though they clearly understood that executive-legislative relations were rapidly deteriorating. Both groups anticipated a new threat to the power of the executive—an effort by the Congress to impeach Yeltsin or a constitutional amendment that would make the presidency a purely ceremonial post, like the British monarchy. In their minds, the political struggle had already become a matter of survival. They preferred that it be waged by peaceful means if possible, but they were very willing to resort to other methods if necessary.

As the Congress progressed, Yeltsin attempted to distract the deputies by offering them yet another "human sacrifice." Yegor Yakovlev, the liberal-thinking head of state television, already a marked man on the conservative hit list, was dismissed from his post. So too was Vice Premier Mikhail Poltoranin, another favorite whipping boy of the opposition. But the Congress was in no mood for compromise. It staked everything—even its very existence—on the attempt to dethrone Gaidar and prevent the president from having any influence over government policy or cabinet portfolio.

Yeltsin responded by announcing a national referendum on a new constitution. The deputies in turn declared that any attempt to hold a referendum would be anti-constitutional. Attempting to play the role of arbiter, the Chairman of the Constitutional Court, Valerii Zorkin, came up with a way for both parties to overcome their deadlock—the "December Compromise." The agreement called on the Congress to permit a national referendum in April 1993. In turn, Yeltsin was persuaded to sacrifice his two most trusted advisors—Burbulis and Gaidar. Gaidar was replaced as Prime Minister, with Yeltsin's consent, by a man who appeared to be an archetypical Soviet industrialist and a former minister in Gorbachev's government—Viktor Chernomyrdin.

In theory, of course, the agreement to hold a referendum was supposed to answer, once and for all, who would have the upper hand—Yeltsin or the Supreme Soviet. But the attempt to frame the debate in these oversimplified terms only underscored the absence of a complex model of political development for the new state. Presenting the issue as an either-or choice once again manifested the Russian elite's traditional way of thinking of political power as something to be monopolized by a single force. Thus rather than displaying the strengths of the two sides, the compromise only exposed their inadequacies.

Unlike the compromise reached earlier in April, however, Yeltsin suffered a genuine defeat on this occasion. For the first time, the president was widely seen as weak and frustrated, struggling unsuccessfully to break a vicious cycle of events that were spinning out of control. Not only did he suffer the indignity of having his democratic advisors whittled away one by one, but he also appeared to have lost the support of the heads of his security services—the Ministers of Defense, Internal Affairs, and State Security.

The departure of Burbulis and Gaidar also convinced the public that a change of course was taking place—"revolutionary liberalism," it seemed, was being abandoned. It turned out, however, that the December Compromise was only one in a long series of temporary armistices.

In fact, a referendum could not decide the kind of government Russia would have—a plebiscite is too blunt an instrument for deciding complicated issues of state-building. And neither could it end the confrontation between the two branches of power. Not one of the issues facing Russia—economic, political, or constitutional—had been resolved by the compromise, and not one would be resolved by a referendum. What had come to a conclusion in December, however, was the first phase of Russia's post-communist political development—the stage of revolutionary liberalism.

The Executive-Legislative Impasse

By late 1992, the failure to create a durable legal and institutional basis for the Russian state was having profound effects not only in

Moscow but in the provinces as well. The blocking of reform at the center was stimulating centrifugal forces at the regional level, encouraging polarization along ethno-territorial lines. The bloody Ingush-Ossetian conflict had already brought civil war to Russia's hinterland, and the disintegration of the federation now seemed quite possible.

Despite the accord reached by Yeltsin and Khasbulatov at the Congress in December, a wide spectrum of leaders in the republics and regions began to agitate against a referendum. Some feared that its results would cost them their positions, while others believed it would only accelerate the disintegration of state power.[12] Regardless, their opposition to the referendum highlighted the rise of the provincial elite to an unprecedented position of influence.

In fact, the interests of the regions and republics differed sharply, and the center's attempt to strike ad hoc bargains with each only undermined an understanding of Russian sovereignty that would be binding on all parties. The republics, for example, were demanding a new federal arrangement that would have given them a privileged status in a loose Russian confederation. At the same time, however, the increased emphasis on decentralization and local models of development also strengthened the network of horizontal arrangements between regions and republics, reconciling, to some extent, their diverse interests.[13]

As January progressed, it became clear that the December compromise would soon collapse and that a new round in the executive-legislative crisis in Moscow was approaching. In the hope of avoiding a clash, the Civic Union proposed that a "roundtable" be convened and attended by all influential political groups, to adopt a new governmental structure. This suggestion was rejected by the president and his team, however. They preferred instead to declare direct presidential rule for an unspecified period. Both the president and Supreme Soviet suggested new elections as a way out of the deadlock. Yet predictably, the president demanded parliamentary elections, while the legislature insisted on simultaneous elections for both a new legislature and a new president—termed the "zero-sum option."

By February, all major political actors—the Supreme Soviet, the Constitutional Court, and a majority of republican and regional leaders—had publicly rejected the December Compromise. Yeltsin suggested another option—a provisional agreement to regulate the responsibilities of the various branches of government and provide for sanctions in the case of violations by any of the signatories. Yeltsin would in turn pledge not to push for a referendum or force the adoption of a new constitution. However, he also let it be known that should the Supreme Soviet *not* sign the accord, he might have resort to a "third path"—i.e., a resort to force.

Yeltsin's Sleight of Hand

The anti-Yeltsin forces achieved their greatest degree of political influence in the legislature in spring 1993. The Congress of People's Deputies convened in extraordinary session on March 10, 1993, and promptly passed a declaration, "Measures for the Realization of Constitutional Reform in the Russian Federation," that deprived Yeltsin of the plenipotentiary powers accorded him earlier. The Congress also voted against holding the previously agreed to April referendum, strengthened the powers of the Constitutional Court, enhanced the independence of the government from the president, and gave the Supreme Soviet added authority to overrule or modify orders from the executive branch. Thus the Congress completely reversed the tactical victories that Yeltsin had achieved at the previous Congress.

When the Eighth Congress adjourned, Yeltsin faced a dilemma: either continue the struggle or resign himself to losing his battle with the legislature. Again influenced by radicals in his entourage, he chose the former. On Saturday, March 20, 1993, Yeltsin announced a "special regime" in a television broadcast to the nation. Only the most radical segment of the democrats reacted favorably, while most political forces, including most democrats, expressed embarrassment, even shock: the vice president, the chairman of the Constitutional Court, the state prosecutor, and, naturally, the speaker of the Supreme Soviet, and provincial leaders immediately and predictably denounced the president.[14]

Yeltsin's move did not catch the leaders of the Western democracies unaware; they were informed in advance by German Chancellor Helmut Kohl, who was meeting with Yeltsin in Moscow. The West reacted favorably, no doubt spurring him on. The major surprise came from Yurii Skokov, Yeltsin's close advisor and the powerful secretary of the Security Council, who joined in denouncing the move. The Constitutional Court immediately began hearings on the legality of the president's decree, despite the fact that the text of the decree had not yet been circulated. The Supreme Soviet, after the briefest of deliberations, called for a special session of the Congress of People's Deputies to impeach Yeltsin.

Faced with a threat of being unseated, and lacking the support of either the "power ministries" or the regional elite, Yeltsin retreated. In the version of his announcement that appeared on Monday (newspapers in Russia are not published on Sunday), no written mention was made of any "special regime." Some observers speculated that the television address may have been a bluff, while others felt it had been a serious attempt to institute a presidential dictatorship. Although Yeltsin claimed at the time that his television address had been misunderstood, it would later become clear that he had been serious indeed, for he would soon try again.

As both sides prepared yet again for a decisive confrontation, Yeltsin and Khasbulatov unexpectedly announced that they had reached an agreement. Yeltsin would retreat from his plans to hold a referendum, and would agree to the zero-sum option of holding simultaneous elections for both the executive and the legislature. Khasbulatov in turn announced his willingness to disband the Congress and replace it (and presumably the Supreme Soviet) with a newly-elected bicameral legislature.

The agreement would have meant political suicide for the deputies of the Congress and Supreme Soviet.[15] Outraged at a back-room deal made without their consent or knowledge, the deputies tried to remove both Yeltsin and Khasbulatov. Yet another session of the Congress convened, at which a motion to impeach Yeltsin failed by only 72 votes, just short of the required 689. Khasbulatov fared better, winning 558 votes against impeachment, with only 339 for. Despite their open dissatisfaction with the speaker, then, the deputies had decided that no one was better qualified to advance their interests.

The Congress marked the beginning of an even more complicated stage in Russia's post-communist political development. Both sides understood that the existing institutional order was unworkable, but neither side could offer a solution. Having painted themselves into a corner, the deputies at the Congress were compelled to agree to Yeltsin's proposal to hold a nationwide referendum in April 1993. They did, however, manage to reword the questions in the referendum significantly, to the disadvantage of the president.

The four questions Yeltsin had wished to put to the electorate were: Do you agree that the Russian Federation should be a presidential republic? Do you agree that the Russian Federation's supreme legislative organ should be a bicameral parliament? Do you agree that the new Constitution of the Russian Federation should be adopted by a Constituent Assembly? And, finally, Do you agree that every citizen is entitled to possess, use, and dispose of land as an owner? The Congress, however, insisted on the following: Do you trust the president, Boris Yeltsin? Do you support the socioeconomic policies of the government? Do you favor early elections for the presidency? And, Do you favor early elections for parliament?

The conventional wisdom in Moscow and elsewhere was that Yeltsin would suffer a significant defeat in the referendum. The results therefore came as a great surprise. Out of a total electorate of 107.3 million, 69.2 million (64.5%) went to the polls, with 58.7% of those voting supporting the president, and 53.0% supporting the government's controversial socioeconomic policies. At the same time, less than half (49.5%) of those voting expressed approval for early presidential elections, while 67.2% favored early elections for the legislature.

Yeltsin had clearly won a moral and a political victory. Nevertheless, 38 million had not voted in the referendum, and in two republics it was not even held. Yeltsin failed to win a majority in 12 out of the other 19 republics, as well as in a score of Russian regions. Most voters, it seemed, had not voted *for* Yeltsin as much as they had voted *against* the extreme opposition. Thus many moderate political observers, taking into account not only those who voted against the president and reform but also those who did not turn out for the referendum, interpreted the results as a vote against a dramatic change of course and for the retention of both branches of power.[16] In any case, the referendum was a purely plebiscitarian act of opinion sampling; its results were not legally binding.

In the aftermath of the referendum, Yeltsin's team submitted a new draft constitution that greatly expanded the powers of the president and subordinated the other branches of government to the executive.[17] After much discussion, Yeltsin agreed on a forum to debate the text of the draft—a constitutional convention *(konstitutsionnoe soveshchanie)*.

Russia's sole previous experience with a constitutional convention had been in January 1918. A nationwide election to a Constituent Assembly had led to a clear victory for the Social Revolutionaries, an anti-Bolshevik party. Unhappy with the results, Lenin promptly dismissed the Assembly after a single day of deliberations. Yeltsin's convening of a "second" Assembly was widely interpreted as an effort to reconnect Russia's political present with its pre-revolutionary past.

In essence, the Assembly was to be a counterweight to the recalcitrant Supreme Soviet. Representatives of republics, regions, the major sociopolitical movements, and the new economic groups were invited to participate. The convention began its work on June 6, 1993 in a genuinely inclusive fashion, even debating a different draft constitution that was submitted by the Supreme Soviet.[18]

The ensuing political debates defined the contours of future conflict. If before the Convention the main drama had been the power struggle between executive and legislature, the convention itself highlighted the disagreements between the center and the regions over the federal structure of the new state.

By the summer of 1993, the Convention managed to come up with a draft that was in turn submitted to Russia's provinces for discussion. The draft departed from the earlier hard-line, authoritarian proposal of the president, and attempted to equalize power between the republics and the regions. The Supreme Soviet, meanwhile, adopted a measure on the procedures for adopting a new constitution, hoping to influence the constitutional discussions. It even tried to set up a commission to prepare another draft to be submitted for approval to the next session of the Congress of People's Deputies.

Two contradictory proposals were therefore sent out to the regions and republics, thus intensifying the legal problems associated with the ratification process. But again the regions and republics refrained from endorsing either side, hoping to benefit from recognition of their political importance. Predictably, the level of political intrigue began to increase as all parties grew aware of the stakes involved.[19]

By the middle of August, Yeltsin realized that he had failed to neutralize the legislature with the help of a new constitution. The regions and republics were not responding positively to his draft. Moreover, it had become clear that there was no legal way to adopt a new constitution. Yeltsin therefore decided to seek another way to rid himself of the parliament. On August 13, 1993, he organized a meeting of regional and republic representatives in Petrozavodsk to create yet another organ of state power—the Council of the Federation. In doing so, he was going over the heads of the Supreme Soviet and the Congress of People's Deputies. Nevertheless, the move seemed risky: in principle, the regions and republics could use their new-found power to oust Yeltsin himself.

Yet the Petrozavodsk meeting did not destabilize the political situation, as many had feared. Rather the political stalemate continued. It had become clear that even if one group proved victorious, it would be faced with the question of what to do with its power. And since neither the president nor the Supreme Soviet had an answer to that problem, the stalemate allowed both to gain needed time.

The "Second October Revolution":
The Soviet Era Comes to an End

The summer and early fall of 1993 found Russia deeply dispirited. The political stalemate, while granting a breathing space to the main contenders for power, only increased the general malaise. It had become clear that the new regime had not made good use of the post-August 1991 period, had failed to adopt a coherent political and economic agenda, and had contributed to the disenchantment of the average citizen with politics. Even the referendum had resolved nothing, while the constitutional convention failed to produce any substantive results, only creating a new round of intrigue and impasse.

Perhaps sensing this mood, the presidential staff felt it could wait no longer. The Supreme Soviet was continuing to issue counter-edicts to every presidential decision, and the ensuing deadlock threatened to destroy the regime. The best solution would have been to call for pre-term elections for both the presidency and parliament, and to give newly elected representatives the opportunity to adopt a new constitution and seek a solution to Russia's deepening economic and political crises. But this zero-sum option solution was rejected by the president and his advisors. Instead, the president took a fateful step. On September 21, 1993, Yeltsin issued Decree 1400, dissolving the Supreme Soviet and calling for new legislative elections on December 12, at which time the electorate would also decide the fate of Yeltsin's draft constitution. Direct presidential rule had finally come to pass.

Whether Yeltsin clearly understood the reaction his decree would provoke remains a subject of bitter controversy. In any case, the Supreme Soviet chose not to leave the political stage gracefully, as the USSR Supreme Soviet had done two years earlier. For two weeks, supporters of the parliament, including many deputies, occupied the White House, refusing to leave despite being isolated by the militia and despite having their electricity and water cut off. Finally, on October 3, supporters of parliament, catching the Moscow militia and MVD off guard, broke through police barricades, reaching the White House and then, at the urging of Rutskoi, moving on to storm the Moscow mayor's office and the Ostankino radio tower. These acts began the bloodshed.

Yeltsin reacted swiftly and brutally the next day. After a period of apparent indecision and disorder, the president managed to convince the military to storm the Supreme Soviet building. After firing on the White House with tanks, the military forced the few hundred deputies and their supporters left inside to surrender. The White House was charred black with fire, and over one hundred people were killed. Both the vice president and the speaker were led to prison in handcuffs, although neither was charged with treason—a crime which would have necessitated the death penalty.[20]

Thus ended the period of peaceful political development in Russia. In the final analysis, both sides shared responsibility for the tragedy, though to what extent remains debatable. The upshot was undeniable, however: "soviet power" had come to a decisive end in Russian history even as the taboo on violence in Moscow had been breached. Having adopted the principle that "the end justifies the means," Yeltsin had opened the door for an even more ruthless and cynical round of politics in Moscow. But the ideological contradictions between his goals and the use of means drawn from the traditional arsenal of communist politics were too great to bridge. As a result, Russia entered a new, even more turbulent period of political development.

In the wake of the October tragedy, the presidential team drafted a revised constitution that greatly increased the executive's already consid-erable powers. The draft created the basis for an authoritarian regime with little counterbalance to presidential power.

A pro-presidential political movement, Russia's Choice, was quickly created. Led by Gaidar, the party was given preferential treatment by the state-controlled media in a two-month, orchestrated election campaign designed to deny other political groups time to consolidate and cam-paign on an equal footing. The idea was to organize elections as rapidly as possible, making use of the time bought by the devastation of the extreme opposition. A significant part of the governmental apparatus put itself up for elections to the legislature, thus guaranteeing the fusion of the two branches and preventing the legislative branch from embarking on another confrontation with the executive—a practice taken from the pre-*perestroika* period when such appointments were routine.

Having gone to such lengths to secure their positions, the democrats expected that their problems would be over. But the confidence of Yeltsin and his staff proved excessive, and the results of the December 12, 1993 elections came as a profound shock. According to official (and still con-troversial) results, the constitution was approved by 58% of those voting. However, only 54.8% of the electorate took part in the referendum. In the party list elections for the State Duma (the new lower house of the parlia-ment), Russia's Choice won only 15% of the vote. Shockingly, Vladimir Zhirinovsky's Liberal-Democratic Party—with its openly fascist tenden-cies—won 24% of the party list vote. The Russian Communist Party, together with its allies in the Agrarian Union, won a combined 19% of the party list vote. The elections clearly showed that what the electorate wanted, more than anything, was order.

Once again, then, Russian politics showed an uncanny disposition toward ironic paradoxes. Not only were the majority of its seats won by an anti-presidential bloc, but it was now a new, post-communist legisla-ture with even greater legitimacy than the president, who had been elected in June 1991 during the communist era. Moreover, Yeltsin found himself facing a serious political challenge not only from Aleksandr Rutskoi, who had often been a reckless and clumsy politician, but also from Vladimir Zhirinovsky, a demagogue whose behavior was com-pletely unpredictable. Compounding Yeltsin's political difficulties was a split within Yeltsin's entourage, as a result of which some of his former lieutenants, such as Sergei Shakhrai, entered the race to replace Yeltsin in the next presidential elections.

Democratic groups seem not to have understood that by resorting to force to crush the opposition in October, they had dug their own graves in December. Relieved of most of their responsibilities, the liberals and radicals were left with a single task—to form a minority opposition in the lower chamber of the new parliament. At the same time, the election allowed regional elites to reconsolidate on a sharply anti-reformist platform.

Sensing the growing populist and statist sentiments of both the elite and the electorate, Yeltsin formed a government in January 1994 headed by a new centrist Prime Minister, Viktor Chernomyrdin. Neither Gaidar nor another key representative of radical economic reform, Boris Fedorov, was included. The generally conservative character of the new government was reflected in the large representation of members of the Agrarian Lobby and the military-industrial complex, the real winners of the "September Revolution." Particularly important were the appointment of Oleg Soskovets as First Deputy Prime Minister and Aleksandr Zaveriukha as Deputy Prime Minister in charge of agriculture—both were friendly to the industrial and agrarian lobby, and both were hostile to radical economic reform.

By 1994, then, the period of "great leaps forward," revolutionary phraseology, reformist utopianism, and irrational expectations of financial assistance from the West had come to an end in Russia. Left-center and extreme right-wing groups, whose sole political orientation was an unremitting hostility toward the pro-Western orientation of the radical-liberals, now dominated the new politics, and their views shaped not only elite behavior but also the discourse of society at large.

As for Yeltsin, he had become entirely distant from society, obsessed not so much with finding a "kinder and gentler" social contract as with reconcentrating political power in his own hands. Under the new constitution, the broad range of powers granted the president enabled him to interfere constantly in the business of other institutions. This not only prevented mid-course policy adjustments, but narrowed the possibility of dissent within the government. Most importantly, it undermined the executive branch by making it appear responsible for every political blunder regardless of whether it had occurred in Moscow or in the provinces.

At the same time, the executive branch had divided into two functioning governments. The first, the "political government" of Yeltsin, controlled the activities of the Ministries for Security, Defense and Internal Affairs, and Communication, as well as the press, radio, and television. The second, the "economic government" of Prime Minister Viktor Chernomyrdin, managed financial and budgetary affairs. The division created new conflicts between a powerful presidential apparatus and a weak cabinet deprived of real control over the machinery of state. As a result, state and society continued to lack an effective communications link, despite the new constitution.

The key question remained whether Chernomyrdin and the industrialists would use their victory to solve the deepening political and economic crisis. Alternatively, they might seek merely to strengthen their own positions. If so, it might once again turn out that the seeming winners in the political struggle were the real losers.

The Mixed Legacy of "Revolutionary Liberalism"

The results of the 1993 election, troubling though they were for the president, should be understood in the context of the nearly three years of his tenure. During the first three years of his presidency, Russian society undeniably grew more comfortable with democratic ends and means. What is unclear, however, is whether this change occurred because of, or in spite of, the actions of the president.

Without doubt, Yeltsin can take credit for the final collapse of communism. He was also responsible for overcoming the heady romanticism of the early post-coup period. During his tenure, Russia's statehood was consolidated and the first steps toward marketization were taken. The force of his personality not only kept extremist elements from triumphing, but also was the overriding—and occasionally the only—stabilizing element in a fragile new society.

Nevertheless, there have also been many failures for the president. When the need for genuine radical change in both the economic and political spheres was most acute, neither the president nor his inner circle had a clear notion of how to proceed—although in all fairness, neither had anyone else. Instead of working out a clear strategic plan, they chose to govern by intuition, reacting to events and finding themselves always one step behind. Yeltsin also proved a master of confrontation—he clearly reveled in a charged political atmosphere and performed best in crises. Indeed he often seemed to provoke conflict deliberately. He thus lost the opportunity to become a leader of national unity, as Lech Walesa and Vaclav Havel had during the first stage of the post-communist transitions in Poland and Czechoslovakia, and as Alfredo Suarez had during the democratic transition in Spain.

Perhaps Yeltsin's greatest failing was his poor sense of timing. Unwilling to construct a new political system immediately after the August 1991 coup, he helped create the political standoff that would eventually force him to take the violent measures of October 1993. And like Gorbachev, Yeltsin too chose many policies at random, in effect "winging it" rather than operating from a well-chosen, carefully considered plan.

Still, it would be unfair to characterize Yeltsin's policies as merely destructive. At times he displayed traits of genuine transformative leadership. Moreover, it was inevitable that a series of dramatic and painful changes would come to Russia after the end of 1991. Indeed, the inescapable lesson of the failed August 1991 coup was that the communist system could not be saved. Yet the contradictions between his goals and the means chosen to realize them, often drawn from the traditional arsenal of communist thinking, were too great to bridge.

The liberal-revolutionary period was thus a time when myths that took root during the excessively optimistic Gorbachev era, as well as immediately after the August coup, were overcome by force. The greatest myth of all was the notion that the August 1991 coup failed because of a popular uprising "from below." In reality, bureaucrats "from above" played at least as important a role, and their "coming of age" did not easily translate into a victory for democracy. A second myth was that Russia could somehow transcend the vast space between a socialist authoritarianism and a capitalist democracy in a single leap. Yet another was that the West—particularly the United States—would come to Russia's economic rescue.

There was, however, an important advantage in realizing that all these were indeed myths: many came to understand that the new Russia could not mechanistically recreate itself in some standard, Western image. Instead, it would have to find its own way. Whether such a forced sobriety eventually discredits the very concepts of reform and democracy remains to be seen.

Unfortunately, the new era required a painstaking approach to consolidating a fragile society, to creating a new ideology of statehood, and to building a new infrastructure of political power. Here the behavior of Russia's new political elite has been particularly disappointing. Admittedly, the tendency to employ revolutionary phraseology and combat tactics were not simply the failings of Yeltsin or his inner circle—they were characteristic of the entire generation that came to political power in the wake of the Soviet collapse. Schooled in the traditional paradigm of domination, their communist mind-set was perhaps the chief reason for the extended crisis of power during the first three years of the post-Soviet era.

Resolving Russia's economic and political crises will depend on whether a new generation of leaders enters the political arena, and whether this new generation can offer Russia a genuine alternative to past policies. In this regard, the results of the December 1993 elections were particularly disappointing. The need for new political parties and interest groups that can articulate wider societal needs has never been more urgent, for a genuine ideological vacuum threatens the few concrete achievements of the past three years.

As to why this vacuum proved so critical so soon after the Soviet collapse, the answer can be found in the paradox of revolutionary liberalism. The name captures the ideological intent of the reformers, but the careful reader has no doubt observed that Yeltsin's policies have been subject to constant compromise. How, then, can we characterize them as truly revolutionary?

The answer is in the content of those policies, not the rhetoric. The vast majority of Yeltsin's promises to soften his economic program, replace key personnel, or compromise with the legislature, were tactical in nature. At no time did he depart from the radical orientation of his reforms. And tactical compromise, as Lenin had understood, is not necessarily a departure from ideology.

A second objection to the description of Yeltsin's program as "revolutionary" is that his reforms achieved little of substance. Russia's precipitous economic decline continued, and Russia's superpower status was not restored. To some extent, this was due to individual incompetence and inexperience. But to a greater extent, it resulted from the inability of revolutionary liberalism to solve Russia's problems. Revolutionary liberalism did not offer a method by which any of the goals of the new state—whether economic recovery, the restoration of global prestige, or the consolidation of new political structures—might be met.

It was where politics intersect with economics, however, that the deficiencies of revolutionary liberalism were most glaring. Gaidar's economic policies were a giant laboratory experiment carried out in Russia in order to fulfill the grand designs of someone else. As a result, the experiment was undertaken without regard for the sociological, psychological, and political conditions of the laboratory itself—in short, without regard for the welfare of the "animals" being experimented upon. Indeed, the IMF-approved economic reform program ignored the fact that the government had an obligation to meet its responsibilities under Russia's post-communist social contract, however informal that contract may have been.

The Dilemmas of Russian Statecraft:
Reform and Continuity

By the end of 1993, then, revolutionary liberalism had been abandoned and the pragmatic wing of the old Party *nomenklatura* had reasserted control of the government and governmental policy. At the same time, privatization was turning other elements of the traditional *nomenklatura* into property owners. Yesterday's *apparatchiks* had thus become today's entrepreneurs, and these new entrepreneurs were making every effort to use their economic muscle to achieve political ends.

It is the extent of this elite continuity that distinguishes Russia's political transformation from those of Central Europe. In the latter case, the non-communist opposition and leaders such as Lech Walesa and Vaclav Havel arose from outside the established political order. In Russia, by contrast, the opposition emerged from *within* the ranks of the existing elite, indeed in many cases from within the Central Committee itself. Members of this traditional elite, including both Gorbachev and Yeltsin, led the transformation effort, and were predictably reluctant, and in some respects unable, to carry out a broad-based purge of the elite to which they belonged.

This staying power of the *nomenklatura*, along with other continuities between the Gorbachev and Yeltsin eras, have led some Russian radicals to conclude that Russia has not been transformed at all—rather it has been "modified," and only partially at that. Yurii Burtin, the well-known correspondent, has concluded that out of two possible scenarios—the "popular" and the "bureaucratic"—the Russian apparat was able to secure the latter, the essence of which was the preservation of traditional positions and relationships in the guise of a new political-ideological framework. As Burtin put it,

> For the time being it seemed to us that the stagnation and economic inef-
> fectiveness of the state-party system went hand in hand with its precari-
> ous instability. Whether the reverse is now true—that our seeming
> inability to get on with the business of progressive development is
> connected with a highly developed skill on the part of our ruling class to
> ever change its outward appearance—remains to be seen. This system is
> like a werewolf—it changes its external hide whenever it pleases, but its
> essence remains the same. [21]

Have the modifications to the old communist system meant the reten-
tion of the essential qualities of the old regime, or have reforms changed the system's essence? If the latter, then a *nomenklatura* "renaissance" may be indispensable to post-Soviet transformation, particularly for a regime that never experienced its own Prague Spring or Hungarian version of reform.

Indeed, many observers claim that the scenario that unfolded in Russia after August 1991 was a classic case of counter-revolution—the victorious "democrats," they argue, in fact adopted a program little different from the agenda of the coup leaders. As one analyst put it, "Who can play dumb to the fact that had the notorious State Committee for the State of Emergency emerged the victor, it would have done exactly what the victorious democrats have?"[22]

A different interpretation has been offered by Gavriil Popov, the former mayor of Moscow and one of the leaders in the democratic movement, who has argued that the bureaucracy has triumphed, but only in part. "We [democrats] did not have the strength needed to steer the tran-

sition," he has admitted.[23] The *apparat* was therefore not destroyed, but "its power was instead redistributed among its various factions."[24] Moreover, the democrats wasted an opportunity to share power in a coalition with more moderate, reform-oriented members of the apparat. Thus, even though the pragmatists in the *nomenklatura* have yet to exhaust their capacity to carry out reforms, the democrats must constantly push them down the reform path.[25]

Among those who emphasize the continuity between the old and new eras, some feel that possible scenarios are not limited to the popular and bureaucratic. Former dissident Lev Timofeev has concluded that choices boiled down to "either the [continued] power of the upper echelons, or the threat of civil war should someone attempt to remove those [echelons] forcefully." Yet he adds, "There does not appear to be anyone who could remove them—therefore, strictly speaking, the choice does not really even exist."[26]

A third interpretation emphasizes the singularity of the 1991 experience. Vitalii Tretiakov, senior editor of the liberal *Nezavisimaia gazeta*, has written: "Since the autumn of 1991 we have witnessed the successful maturation of two contradictory political processes: the reform of the state regime and the restoration of the state-party structures of the [former] USSR."[27] The former Minister for Regional Affairs, Sergei Shakhrai, has alluded to a "hypothetical scenario" supposedly formulated during the Gorbachev period, calling for the Party to relinquish power but to hand over the reigns of state to the directors' lobby and the middle echelons of the military-industrial complex, making their eventual reinstatement seem fully predictable.

Yet this is clearly a vast oversimplification. The notion that Russia's transformation was the design of the apparat or the KGB ignores the fact that it resulted from many interrelated factors. The apparent predominance of the apparat does not mean it was the sole, or even the most decisive, influence. Most important, no matter what the designs of the powers-that-were, the evolution of society has extended far beyond their control.

Future Prospects:
Liberal Authoritarianism and Regime Stability

In post-communist Russia, as well as in the other Soviet successor states and the post-communist states of Central Europe, the transformation of the old regimes was initiated by the Communist Party from the top down. On the one hand, this has limited the threat of widespread social turbulence that has accompanied revolutions elsewhere. But on the other, it has steered the transformations in a highly bureaucratic, "administered" direction.

The administrative tendencies of Russia's new ruling elite indicate just how strongly traditional beliefs that democracy and marketization must somehow be "constructed" are embedded in Russian political culture. One of the most serious obstacles to Russia's normal development is the assumption that one can "liberate" a country from communism by communist methods. Nevertheless, it is difficult to deny that without a shove, society will be unable to build its own self-regulating mechanisms.

As a result, it seems clear that the transition period requires a strong state—not only to set up new procedural rules, but to guarantee the stability those rules require if they are to be implemented. Russian experience has already demonstrated that a weak state will itself contribute to new instability. But can a strong state voluntarily limit its power after having created new rules? Will the first "shove" mean another round of authoritarianism? If so, it may turn out that a liberal authoritarian state is no better than a communist one at safeguarding social and individual freedoms.

What may prove decisive in preventing authoritarianism in Russia is a newly forming property-owning class. Currently, this embryonic social stratum suffers from deep internal rifts stemming from whether the new "capitalist" comes from the old *nomenklatura*, and in which region of the country or sphere of economic activity each is involved. Differences also exist between those who favor democracy and those who advocate an "iron hand" to guide the country; between those who want the state to follow a more independent economic course and those who would reinstate the ties between Russia and other former Soviet republics; between those who want a Western model of development versus those who argue for a "Eurasian" variant; and finally, between those who continue to press for "shock therapy" and those who agitate for a "tiptoe" approach to marketization.

The relationship between these new entrepreneurs and the government has contributed greatly to skyrocketing corruption. As a well known Polish social scientist has correctly noted, "[capitalism] simply permitted the Communist *nomenklatura* to retain its positions of privilege, regardless of the changes in political power."[28] Ideally, an independent, property-owning class could help prevent a return to authoritarian political means. In the Russian case, however, this class's origins in the old state bureaucracy make it far more comfortable doing business under the shadow of a corrupt, authoritarian state and in a semi-legal atmosphere than in an open environment characterized by clearly defined rules of the game.

The intelligentsia will also be very important to Russia's future political development. The intelligentsia, which played such a critical role in the dissolution of the USSR, does not seem to have an economic interest in further democratization. Its continued support for democratization, therefore, will have to be based on altruism. In contrast to Central Europe, where the intelligentsia has been very supportive of democratic reforms, in Russia the intelligentsia has often been disdainful of, and disdained by, the new regime, and this has only helped to reestablish the *nomenklatura*. But this is neither terribly surprising nor entirely discouraging. As Staniszkis points out, the "tendency toward authoritarianism [even] among those who constituted the democratic opposition" has characterized the intelligentsia's behavior throughout the post-Soviet era.[29]

With regard to the troublesome issue of regime stability, generally accepted Western definitions do not seem applicable. The standard criteria—regime longevity, legal and constitutional continuities, and the absence of violence—are not appropriate for countries experiencing rapid and profound institutional change. Indeed, in the short run, stability requires a reliance on old structures and concepts, yet "transformation" entails their elimination. How, under these circumstances, can society remain stable?

As for the type of political regime Russia has today, Western categories of "democracy" and "authoritarianism" also seem deficient. Most post-communist regimes today do not lend themselves to being pigeonholed into categories taken from other historical experience. Philippe Schmitter may be right to characterize post-communist societies as "transitional," but by the same token, Russia is not merely an "unconsolidated democracy."[30] And neither is it sufficient to describe it simply as "populist."[31]

Today, the political elite in Russia can be divided into two categories: revolutionaries and functionaries. The first group spearheaded the democratic movement and became the first generation of Russia's new counter-elite. Not all were anti-communists or dissidents before they came to power; and perhaps even the majority came from a *nomenklatura* background. Coming to power during the heady days of Gorbachev's *glasnost* and *perestroika*, the revolutionaries all too often allowed passion to substitute for professionalism, and as a result, their political domination proved short-lived.

Within a single year, then, the revolutionaries had been displaced by the functionaries, who were far more adept at the day-to-day affairs of state. Indeed, the *nomenklatura* quickly managed to return to its former positions of administration. Their weakness, however, was their inability to create a new political and social system.

Thus a third generation that displaces both the revolutionaries and the functionaries will have to decide whether the post-Soviet transformation proves a genuine breakthrough or merely a reconsolidation of traditional forces.

Tentative Conclusions:
The Uneasy Development of a New State-Society Relationship

Without exception, post-communist societies have shared the following characteristics: a poorly developed system of party formation; fragile coalitions among the ruling elite, which break down and are then recreated with frequency; continuous confrontation between the executive and legislature; periodic clashes between the president and the government; the pursuit of unregulated emergency powers by the executive, relying on a plebiscitary appeal and based on personal charisma; and an ideological vacuum caused by the wholesale repudiation of Marxism-Leninism. In no country has a successful model of political development been carried out. In all countries political clashes have occurred between half-baked new ideologies— "westernism" versus nationalism; democratization versus an iron hand. Even more confusing, yesterday's radicalism has become today's pragmatism, and indeed may well become tomorrow's conservatism—or vice versa.

Clearly, the changes taking place in post-communist states cannot be looked at through the prism of classical models of political development. Neither can they be pigeonholed into simple, neat categories. The sequence and nature of the events involved are far too complicated. Moreover, generally accepted conditions for gradual democratic evolution are usually absent: the middle class is still in its formative stages; the severity of ethno-national problems complicates state building; the legacy of communism, particularly the severity of economic crisis, prevents speedy problem solving; historical traditions are inconsistent with liberalism; and offers of international assistance to the new governments are few and far between.

Less noted, however, are important obstacles to a return to authoritarianism or dictatorship in Russia. These include:

- the failure of all sides to monopolize power, and the gradual realization that compromise is essential;
- the ongoing development of a genuine civil society independent of the state;
- the steady decentralization and regionalization of the country, which acts as a highly effective counterweight to over-centralization;

- the gradual weakening of paternalistic attitudes, both within the elite and within society;
- increased ties to the larger global community.

Together, these obstacles to a rapid and successful reform as well as the obstacles to a return to dictatorship will likely generate a mixed regime in the near future, neither authoritarian nor, strictly speaking, democratic. On the other hand, Russia will probably avoid the many catastrophes that some have ascribed to its future—the disintegration of the state, civil war, successive revolutions, a military dictatorship, or even nuclear catastrophe. Instead, it will probably continue along a path of moderate, but ultimately decisive, transformation.

Notes

1. These advisors included Gennadii Burbulis, Mikhail Poltoranin, and later Sergei Shakhrai and Yegor Gaidar.

2. As one of the leading "democrats," Gavriil Popov, complained, "[T]he leadership of democrats in the ruling coalition is purely symbolic and formalistic. Behind this facade the real work of consolidating the power of the old nomenklatura is taking place." (*Nezavisimaia gazeta*, January 26, 1993.)

3. As a result, Russians began to refer to Yeltsin as "Demolition Man" and the "Terminator" of the Soviet Union.

4. It is important to appreciate, however, that Yeltsin and his allies often exaggerated the extent to which presidential decrees were being ignored at the local level, in an effort to explain their own weakness.

5. An ethnic Chechen, Ruslan Khasbulatov was never popular among Russians.

6. Alberto Fujimori declared martial law in Peru in April 1992.

7. The "directors' lobby" is made up mainly of managers of key industries and factories.

8. With jurisdiction over domestic organized crime, the MVD is comparable to the FBI in the United States. However, in Russia the security forces together are broadly referred to as "the military" by the media.

9. The fall-off in popular support for Yeltsin was evident in opinion polls conducted during the summer of 1992, when for the first time the percentage of those opposing Yeltsin's policies surpassed those supporting them. In one poll, 33% of the respondents stated they opposed the government's policies, while only 24% supported them and another 33% indicated only partial support. The same poll found rising support for Rutskoi, one of Yeltsin's greatest challengers. Nineteen percent of respondents said they viewed the Vice President favorably, 28% unfavorably, and another 36% partially favorably. Among rural inhabitants, Rutskoi's popularity actually surpassed Yeltsin's. (See *Nezavisimaia gazeta*, June 12, 1992.)

10. The National Salvation Front offered Russian society two possibilities: a "peaceful" assumption of power, which would mean the summoning of an

extraordinary session of the Congress of People's Deputies, presumably in order to impeach the president and amend the Constitution; and a "revolutionary" option, organizing mass protests against Yeltsin, whose overthrow, in their eyes, was simply a matter of time.

11. "The constitutional fabric of our state is currently under attack," wrote Zorkin. "The confrontation of various political forces has reached the level of extremes, with the possibility of armies being dragged into the fray." The Court has the right, Zorkin argued, "to examine the question of whether the highest authorities in the country are fulfilling their constitutional obligations to defend the political structure from attack." (*Izvestiia*, June 27, 1992.)

12. It is worth remembering that the results of the referendum of March 1991 accelerated similar tendencies. The concerns expressed by some regional leaders with regard to Russia's referendum therefore had a basis in recent history.

13. "Standing directly before any continued relationship with the Federation's central authorities is a new process of mutual adaptation," wrote A. Krimdakh and R. Turovsky recently. "On one side stands the 'old guard' of the regional bureaucracy; on the other, the new, anti-Soviet elite in the center. Both must rebuild a system of vertical relations all over again." ("Political Development in the Russian Provinces," *Nezavisimaia gazeta*, June 11, 1993.)

14. Even the liberal Russian press commented, "Yeltsin's Saturday announce-ment only outwardly appeared to demonstrate that he had seized the initiative, when in fact he has thrust himself into a situation which heretofore had been occupied by the Congress, and by Khasbulatov in particular. To go back now would mean losing everything, both politically and personally. [So Yeltsin has chosen] to go forward, to bring the struggle with the legislative branch com-pletely into the open at the worst possible time, in the absence of either an economic base or a social one." (Vitalii Tretiakov, "The President Stakes Every-thing," *Nezavisimaia gazeta*, March 22, 1993.)

15. Particularly galling to the deputies was the fact that the compromise allowed them to continue receiving all the financial and political perks of their jobs until their terms expired in 1996. This, they felt, smacked of a bribe in return for expected docility.

16. "If one sums up the results of each question, the electorate seems to have voted nonetheless to keep the status quo. Yes for the president; yes for his policies. But no to any changes whatever, including early elections.... . No mandate for more radical or more revolutionary measures was received by the president." (*Moscow News*, May 2, 1993.)

17. The original draft constitution came under immediate fire not only from liberals, who saw in it the outlines of authoritarianism, but from conservatives, who saw its loose federalism as threatening the integrity of the Russian state. The former secretary of the Security Council commented that in 1990 "the Russian Federation was a federative structure in name only; in practice it was a unitary system. Now it has become federative in reality, but those at the top continue to manage it as though it were a unitary system. It is that particular contradiction that will shatter everything." (Yurii Skokov, "I Chose the 'Subjects of the Federa-tion,'" *Nezavisimaia gazeta*, June 10, 1993.)

18. The national-patriots and former communists boycotted the convention.

19. A special commission on corruption accused the Vice President of maintaining a private Swiss bank account drawn on public coffers, charged the country's chief law officer, Valentin Stepankov, with plotting to murder a commission member, and announced that the Ministries of Foreign Trade, of the Economy, and of Energy were under official criminal investigations. It was later revealed that practically every accusation against the Vice President had been trumped up. (See Steven Erlanger, "In Kremlin, Hints and Allegations," *New York Times*, August 25, 1993.)

20. Both were released from Lefortovo prison in March 1994, under terms of a general amnesty offered by the State Duma to "all participants in the events of September–October 1993" as well as to the participants in the failed coup of August 1991.

21. Yurii Burtin, "An Alien Power," *Nezavisimaia gazeta*, December 1, 1992.

22. G. Vishnevskaia, "The Restoration," *Nezavisimaia gazeta*, August 18, 1992. The State Committee for the State of Emergency (GKChP), under Soviet Vice President Gennadii Yanaev, announced that Gorbachev had retired "for health reasons" in August 1991, and proclaimed a state of emergency in an effort to halt the process of reform.

23. Quoted in *Nezavisimaia gazeta*, October 8, 1992.

24. Quoted in *Izvestiia*, April 25, 1992.

25. Ibid.

26. Lev Timofeev, "Fascism at the End of the Tunnel," *Izvestiia*, June 12, 1992.

27. Quoted in *Nezavisimaia gazeta*, June 11, 1992.

28. Jadwiga Staniszkis, *Continuity and Change in Post-Communist Europe* (The Hague: Netherlands Institute of International Relations, 1992), p. 14.

29. Ibid., p. 21.

30. Philippe Schmitter and Terry Karl, in Peter Volten, ed., *Bound to Change: Consolidating Democracy in East Central Europe* (New York: IEWS, 1992), pp. 64–65.

31. Ibid., p. 66.

2

The Russian Economy
Since Independence

Richard E. Ericson

The failed coup of August 1991 was the beginning of the end for the Soviet Union. By mid–1991 it was already clear to virtually everyone that the Soviet Union was in a severe, inexorably growing economic crisis. Real economic activity was shrinking at unprecedented rates, with the consumer sector being hit particularly hard.[1] For example, in 1991 oil output decreased by 11%, that of chemical goods by 10–15%, coal by 11%, and light industry and food industry by 11–12%. State purchases of meat fell by 18%, of milk by 14%, and the grain harvest fell by 24%. Of the 130 food and consumption items necessary for everyday life, fewer than 12 were available with any regularity, as state store shelves stood generally empty. The food situation was seen as particularly cata-strophic, with widespread fear of famine in the coming winter. Rationing systems for the distribution of goods and foodstuffs were widely intro-duced without any guarantees of supply availability.

Barter was becoming increasingly the norm in economic transactions in 1991 as political barriers to trade rose between union republics, regions, and even cities. The consequent collapse in economic activity and interaction was aggravated by the collapse of the ruble as a medium, or even marker, of exchange, driven in part by a greater than fivefold increase in the money supply, unrestrained credit emission in response to claimed enterprise needs, and a budget deficit of over 20% of GDP. This led to inflation of about 20% per month by the end of the year, despite massive price controls and other obstacles to monetized exchange. It was also reflected in the sharp drop of the ruble's value in the limited exchange auction, from 50 per dollar to over 200 per dollar. In 1991 the hard-currency debt of the Soviet Union grew to over $72 billion, while hard-currency reserves shrank to near zero, export revenues collapsed, and the Soviet Foreign Economic Bank *(Vneshekonombank)* closed down, depriving its depositors of their money. From every perspective, the economy had fallen into a deepening crisis.

Furthermore, all hope of real economic reform had faded by the time of the attempted coup. Gorbachev had squandered the four years since beginning economic perestroika on a futile search for a controllable socialist market economy. Pursuit of this mirage had led to increasingly incoherent policies and repeated rejection of proposals for radicalization and more consistent marketization.[2] The last such proposal was the so-called "500–day plan" of academician Stanislav Shatalin, which was rejected by early 1991 for a statist compromise that made no sense from either a central planning or a market perspective. The catastrophic consequences of this policy incoherence fueled the disintegration of the union, which was about to be papered over by Gorbachev's "inter-republic agreement" in August 1991. That agreement, and the rapidly deteriorating economic situation, precipitated the attempt to end Gorbachev's "reforms" and return the Soviet Union to political stability and the normalcy of economic planning. That attempt was defeated, in no small part due to Boris Yeltsin's decisiveness and charisma.

Yeltsin stood for the revitalization of Russia, outside of the Soviet Union, through a complete radicalization of economic reform. Building on the key ideas of the "500–day plan," he proposed a general program of microeconomic liberalization, macroeconomic stabilization, and mass privatization to "give back to the Russian people what had been taken from them in 70 years of Communist oppression." Although short on details, the program was to make Russia a strong, modern economic power, to restore it to "great power" status in the world.

There was, however, no real plan of action, no detailed program in December 1991. There were just vague ideas, objectives, and slogans, the poorly understood example of Poland in 1989, and a small group of enthusiastic, radical economists determined to do something in the face of impending disaster. Yeltsin placed the development of reform in the hands of these largely self-taught economists, led by Yegor Gaidar, who were forced by circumstances to act with only the vaguest idea how. Their price and trade liberalizations and budgetary policies, adopted in the beginning of 1992, inaugurated the period analyzed in this chapter. Although frequently referred to as "shock therapy," it was hardly that. From the very beginning it was more an ad hoc, albeit market-oriented, response to an ongoing crisis. Indeed, the program and its subsequent policy directions were not even outlined on paper until the June "Medium-Term Economic Program" prepared by the government and outside economic advisors for presentation to the IMF.[3] Thus Russia plunged, without relevant precedent, theory, or experience, into the uncharted territory of building a modern market economy on the still disintegrating ruins of the Soviet command economy. It was a plunge taken with optimism, in ignorance of the depth of the problems to be overcome and with hope that the situation could not get much worse than it already was at the end of 1991.

It has now been three years since the disappearance of the Union of Soviet Socialist Republics. Ten of the fifteen former Union republics are still, if increasingly loosely, united in the so-called Commonwealth of Independent States (CIS), although only five of them seemed to take it seriously by mid–1993.[4] At that point, Russian pressure to create a fully Russian-controlled "ruble zone," denying the others the possibility of autonomous monetary policy, led to accelerated introduction of national currencies and repeated delays in setting up an interstate settlements bank, rendering the CIS economically irrelevant. Thus in the second year of independence differences in economic policies grew among the states of the former Soviet Union (FSU). For all their differences, however, in almost all of these new states economic performance in the first two years of independence was dismal (Tables 2.1 and 2.2). It is clear from the published partial reports on economic performance in each of these countries that the general depression that began in 1989–1990 has continued and deepened, albeit in different ways and at differing paces. Each is suffering from a shrinking level of real economic activity and severe structural disproportions, which are only now beginning slowly to change. Aside from Estonia and Latvia, the only states to pursue truly consistent monetary reform and stabilization, each is also suffering from a chaotic financial and monetary situation.

The greatest collapse and chaos have been associated with civil war (Georgia, Kyrgyzstan, Moldova) and/or interstate war (Armenia-Azerbaijan). The severe decline in real economic activity in the Baltic states seems associated with the sharp and near complete break of their ties with the other Soviet successor states, especially Russia, and the ensuing renegotiation, which has required great structural changes in the domestic economies. This major cost has, however, borne fruit in increasingly stable and well-functioning monetary and financial systems. The greatest stability in economic performance in the first year (Belarus, Kazakhstan, and most of Central Asia) was associated with a lack of serious economic reform coupled with continued substantial subsidization by Russia. Such policies became increasingly untenable as Russia cut back on subsidization, particularly of energy use, and eliminated the ability to create ruble credits at Russian expense. Thus only Uzbekistan was able to avoid

TABLE 2.1 Post-Soviet Economic Performance, 1992

State	1991–1992 Percent Decline in Real			Inflation Minus Personal Income Growth Rate[a]
	NI	Ind. Output	Trade	
Azerbaijan	25.5	25.0	60.0	NA
Armenia	41.6	52.3	73.4	516
Belarus	14.5	13.0	32.0	335
Estonia[d]	NA	40.6	NA	NA
Kazakhstan	17.4	16.2	10.2	274
Kirgizia	24.8	24.2	65.9	613
Latvia[d]	NA	39.0	NA	NA
Lithuania[d]	NA	45.6	NA	NA
Moldova	24.1	26.3	51.1	489
Russia	20.0	18.8	39.2	459
Tajikistan	NA	22.0	70.0	336[c]
Turkmenistan	17.6	21.4	45.5	272
Uzbekistan	21.8	8.4	33.5	235
Ukraine[b]	16.0	9.7	21.0	155

[a] Ten Months.
[b] CIS Goskomstat estimate.
[c] Six Months.
[d] Eleven Months.

Source: CIS Goskomstat, *Ekonomika i zhizn'*, No. 52, 1992.

serious reform while maintaining national income in 1993, because of its hard-currency earnings as a major exporter of energy. The two largest states, Russia and Ukraine, are polar cases. In January 1992 Russia took the lead within CIS: it plunged into serious, if not fully consistent, economic reform/transformation, while Ukraine strove to avoid following Russian initiatives by resisting more radical changes and supporting old economic structures as long as they supported Ukrainian independence from Russia. As a consequence, during the first year of Ukraine's independence its real economy appeared to be more stable than Russia's, while over time its financial situation deteriorated more rapidly and significantly less structural change took place.

As 1993 began, both of these key economies were redirected by shifts in policy positions: Russian policy under Viktor Chernomyrdin first turned more conservative and more oriented toward preserving existing levels of activity in the real economy; Ukrainian policy under Leonid Kuchma appeared to shift toward greater fiscal restraint, real structural

TABLE 2.2 Post-Soviet Economic Performance, 1993

| | 1992–1993 Percent Change in Real | |
State	National Income[a]	Industrial Output[b]
Azerbaijan	NA	–10.0
Armenia	NA	–39.9
Belarus	–15.0	–14.6
Estonia	NA	–32.4
Kazakhstan	–12.0	–12.1
Kirgizia	–27.0	–27.0
Lithuania	NA	–48.0
Moldova	NA	+7.0
Russia	–12.0	–16.2
Tajikistan	NA	–25.5
Turkmenistan	+19.0	+18.8
Uzbekistan	+2.5	+2.5
Ukraine	–8.0	–8.0

[a] *Kommersant*, No. 26, 1993, estimates.
[b] CIS Goskomstat estimate, published in *Business Observer*, January 1994, p.1.

Source: CIS Goscomstat, *Ekonomika i zhizn'*, No. 6, 1994.

change, and systemic transformation. However, policy gridlock and the accumulated impact of a year of fiscal irresponsibility blocked any real change in Ukraine, leading to a decline of real economic activity, accelerating inflation, and a governmental crisis, with Kuchma eventually resigning in mid–1993 following the resignation of virtually all reformers in the Ukrainian government. The result by the end of 1993 was true hyperinflation (over 90% per month), a demonetization and spreading collapse of economic activity, growing economic and political unrest, and a sporadic return to Soviet command and control policies without any noticeable favorable impact on the economy.[5]

The 1992 Ukrainian example, coupled with vigorous opposition to more inflationary policies by the new Russian minister of finance, Boris Fedorov, pulled Russian policy back toward attempting macroeconomic stabilization, albeit with greater attention to the support of priority sectors. This led in the second half of 1993 to a certain stabilization in both the monetary and real spheres, coupled, however, with growing political tensions and reform policy gridlock. Results of this impasse included the confrontation of September–October 1993, parliamentary elections on 12 December, and dramatic changes in policy-makers and apparently policy in January 1994.[6] Clearly, both Russia and Ukraine are struggling with deepening economic problems that neither truly understands. Policy-making, as might have been expected, has become a groping forward into uncharted territory, driven by an inability to hold to a fixed blueprint in the face of growing political and economic crises.

In all parts of the FSU the economic forces, processes, and outcomes are similar, although they may appear quite different.[7] Although specific policies in different countries are frequently moving in different directions, they are all driven by a need for radical transformation, toward market institutions. But the transformation is proving far more difficult than had originally been hoped. With the exception of Estonia—never part of the CIS—Russia was the leader in radical economic transformation in both 1992 and 1993, and has also suffered one of the most severe depressions in the CIS. It remains in many respects a microcosm of the FSU, having inherited most of its structures, resources, territory, and problems. Russia is the heart and soul of the CIS (and FSU) and the key to the successful transformation of that part of the world. Thus the remainder of this chapter will focus exclusively on Russia as the paradigm of what is happening or is apt to happen elsewhere in the CIS, at least while those states remain dedicated to some form of marketizing transformation.

Russian Developments

In 1992 and 1993 we saw both positive and negative developments in the Russian economy, although news headlines largely conveyed only the negative. The evolving situation can be characterized in five parts:

- depression in the real economy;
- financial and monetary chaos;
- disintegration of the state and economy;
- beginnings of real structural transformation and change;
- deep structural and infrastructural roots blocking real transformation.

This chapter addresses each of these in turn, building to the theoretical conclusion that for the transformation to succeed and real recovery to begin, three (infra-) structural obstacles must be overcome: the absence of real ownership and property rights; the absence of a real money that allows complex, particularly intertemporal intermediation; and the existing structure of capital and economic activity that ties up resources (social wealth) in wasteful, often value-destroying, activity. These problems block both macroeconomic stabilization and effective microeconomic liberalization with its anticipated generation of economically rational behavioral responses. They in turn are aggravated by deep psychological, social, and political attitudes that stand in the way of effective policy responses. I believe that they also lie at the root of the more visible problems such as lack of investment, economic crime and corruption, capital flight, and crumbling infrastructure.

Dealing with these problems will require, first of all, political will and action, but the political environment as of early 1994 is at best inhospitable. In December 1991 the political elite seemed united in support of Yeltsin's radical economic policies; however, it soon split as those whose power and prerogatives were threatened by the changes began demanding modifications or retreats. The referendum of April 25, 1993 gave President Yeltsin moral support and the political initiative, but not a definitive victory in the political struggle. He used this advantage to convene a constitutional assembly in June 1993 whose purpose was to write a post-Soviet constitution clearly delineating the powers and responsibilities of the various branches of government, as well as the powers of the central (federation) government vis-à-vis the regions and republics. A July draft was, however, left in limbo when the eighty-nine republics and regions were unable to agree, leading to adjournment of the assembly. The growing political confrontation with parliament, involving an accelerating war of laws and decrees, parliamentary revocation of presidential powers, and intransigence on new elections and the constitution, led Yeltsin to dissolve parliament on September 21 and call new elections and a referendum on the constitution for December 12, 1993.

It was hoped that the vote would yield not only a constitution that would clarify political and legal authority, but also a legislature to support economic reform and market transition. This would allow the government to deal with the lack of effective public administration and embark on a more consistent implementation of necessary marketizing reforms. However, the new parliament has proved almost as hostile to reform as was its predecessor. And the Chernomyrdin government initially seemed to be backing off from the Yeltsin reforms of 1992, although very little change in economic policy has actually taken place.[8]

Economic policy in 1993 remained hostage to the political struggle. The executive and legislature repeatedly issued contradictory decrees and laws, with little apparent impact outside of Moscow. Local governments of regions, cities, and republics openly ignored legitimate directives from the central authorities and regularly interfered in locally based economic activities and interregional interaction.[9] There were movements in most regions for independence or full autonomy, driven in large part by a desire for control over internationally salable local resources; moreover, regions rushed to declare themselves autonomous republics, as these were to receive greater rights and powers under the new constitution. This disintegration of federal authority and usurpation of political and economic powers by local and regional entities was a growing problem in 1993. It was somewhat defused in mid–1993 as the center allowed the devolution of much authority and brought the regions into the constitution-writing process in June.[10] It became significantly more aggravated in the fall as the confrontation between the president and the parliament heated up and central authority increasingly deadlocked. Decisive presidential action in October seemed to make the regions and republics more compliant, although the fundamental problem remained unresolved in early 1994.[11]

In addition to the disintegration of state administrative capabilities, the transformation of the economic system is impeded by the rampant growth of corruption and the large role of criminal "mafias" in the wake of the collapse of the mechanisms of the command economy.[12] Both have flowered as a natural response to the vast value distortions in the economy and the experience and capabilities developed in the second economy of the Soviet era; the distortions have opened up phenomenal arbitrage opportunities, and the still large "gatekeeping" role of bureaucrats in embryonic markets generates vast opportunities for corruption.[13] They are a growing problem for economic reform as they echo and reinforce the deep structural obstacles to true systemic transformation. Further, those involved have the most to gain from the distortions and irrationalities of the current hybrid system of incomplete, arrested marketization. However, they can be expected to fade into the background when the deep structural problems mentioned above are adequately dealt with.[14]

All of these factors impede the introduction of new, stable "rules of the game" that would allow economic agents to transform the bases of their behavior and new economic institutions to arise, as must occur if a real market economy is to develop. At present, due to the results of the December 1993 election and its apparent impact on government policy, there seems little hope that the political issues will soon be sorted out. A clear change in the priorities and policies announced in early 1994 is necessary for Russia to return to creating an environment for productive economic change and marketizing transformation. Only such change would allow it to productively address the problems of regionalization, criminalization, and economic corruption. Despite this unfavorable political turn of events, we are still beginning to see some movement toward the amelioration of the three deep structural obstacles to real economic transformation. This movement must now struggle against the political tide—at least temporarily—rather than being carried with it.

Depression in the Real Economy

Throughout 1992–1993 real economic activity in Russia contracted at unprecedented rates.[15] Although GDP reached 162.3 trillion rubles by the end of 1993 (from 15 trillion in 1992)—an unprecedented high due exclusively to inflation—real National Income (NI) was down 32% and GDP fell 29% from 1991 levels. Industrial production was down 31.3% over the two years, with most of the drop in each year occurring during the summer. Indeed, prior to November 1993, seasonally adjusted output had been essentially constant. The best sectoral performance was in agriculture, where the drop in the total real value of output relative to 1991 was just under 12%. Grain output grew by some 20% in 1992, only to fall seven percent in 1993, while animal products dropped by 16–19% and vegetable products by 13%. The sector with the worst economic performance was construction, reflecting a serious collapse in state investment. In 1992 overall investment was down by 45%, while construction activity dropped over 42%. Only 3 of 393 critical state projects planned for completion were finished by the end of the third quarter, although 54 were fully and 25 partially operational by the end of the year. In 1993 the collapse continued at a slower pace, with investment activity down 14% and construction activity down only seven percent. Only 122 of 652 priority investment projects were fully completed, while the volume of incomplete construction grew by almost 25%. The drop in activity in the transportation sector, 43%, exceeded that of the overall economy: railroad transportation dropped 18% each year, truck transportation dropped 25% in 1992 and 40% in 1993, and river and air transport fell over 55% in two years.

Shrinking economic activity in 1992 was also reflected in a 39% drop in retail sales (in constant prices), a drop in export volume of 25%, and a drop in imports of 21%, despite an increase of 37% in grain imports over 1991 levels. In 1993, however, the total volume of real retail sales stabilized (−0.5 percent), and the overall volume of internal trade increased by two percent as about 40% of that volume moved into the nonstate sector. Exports also stabilized, increasing by 1.4%, while imports fell another 27%, leaving a positive balance of trade of $16 billion. In the critical energy sector, oil production was down 12% in 1993, on top of 14% in 1992; coal, 9% on top of 5%, and even natural gas production fell by 3.4%

over both years. However, hard-currency-earning oil exports rose dramatically, reflecting the collapse in domestic use and the shift of trade within the CIS to hard-currency terms.

The one area in which the 1992–1993 depression was not reflected was employment. By the end of 1993, less than 1% of the labor force was officially unemployed (receiving compensation); 5.1% were unemployed by international standards and a further 5.3% only partially employed or on unpaid leave.[16] Moreover, a growing portion of the work force was becoming increasingly underemployed as state enterprises shied away from layoffs, which they could do due to easy credit and lax banking— part and parcel of the general crisis in the monetary and financial sectors.

Monetary and Financial Chaos

Two key factors lay behind the rather chaotic monetary and financial situation in Russia in 1992 and 1993. The first was the increasingly erratic monetary and fiscal policy after the first quarter of 1992, driven to a large extent by the intensifying struggle between government reformers on one side and the legislature and Russian Central Bank (RCB) on the other. This created waves of money and credit emission followed by periods of fiscal restriction and payments cutoffs, jointly disruptive of productive economic activity. The second and deeper factor is the nature of liquidity and the structure of financial intermediation in the Russian economy, which aggravated and reinforced the first factor, erecting serious barriers to economically oriented and motivated interaction.

In the first quarter of 1992, despite substantial price liberalization and an ensuing fivefold increase in the price level, the government was able to hold the budget deficit (cash basis) to 1.5% of GDP. Although in part due to accounting tricks, this still represented a major achievement as a commitment to stabilization, since the deficit had been 21.2% of GDP in 1991. In the second and third quarters, however, the deficit grew to 5.4% and 6.7% of GDP respectively; the inflation of the fourth quarter, together with some creative accounting, brought it back to about 5%, a substantial improvement over the previous year.[17]

The situation deteriorated in the first quarter of 1993 as subsidies to incomes and agriculture in particular rose, increasing the deficit of the consolidated budget to over nine percent of GDP. Then there appeared to be a return to greater fiscal responsibility in the late spring of 1993. Faced with the specter of hyperinflation, the Ministry of Finance under Fedorov and the RCB under Gerashchenko agreed to strictly limit state subsidies and credit emission in order to bring down inflation to ten percent per month and to hold the deficit under ten percent of GDP by the end of 1993.[18] However, this restraint faded rapidly in the political struggles of midyear; the expected budget deficit rose to 22.4 trillion rubles, with new subsidies to agriculture and industry and the indexation of state incomes. The year ended under severe budgetary stringency as the Ministry of Finance cut back on payments even for already contracted deliveries and state sector wages. Thus, at the end of the year the deficit was only 10.5% of GDP (15 trillion rubles), although deferred payment of 8 trillion rubles for contractual obligations had shifted another five percent of GDP into the deficit for the first quarter of 1994.[19]

In the first half of 1992 the amount of money (cash and enterprise funds) in circulation doubled (from 0.7 to 1.4 trillion rubles), then tripled to over 4 trillion rubles by October, and tripled again to almost 11 trillion rubles by the end of the year. This was the result of hyperactivity of the printing presses and a massive increase in (largely short-term) state credit to (state) industry (9–10 trillion rubles), resulting in 5.2 trillion rubles in outstanding credits at the end of the year.[20] In the first quarter of 1993, the RCB continued massive emission of credit in the support of what it considered critical sectors, resulting in 9.4 trillion rubles of outstanding short-term credit at the end of March.[21] Following a period of restraint, the RCB again issued massive subsidized credits during the summer in an effort to slow the sharp drop in industrial output, then returned to relative restraint for the rest of the year. Thus the 7.4–fold increase in money supply in 1992 was followed by a further 4.8–fold increase in 1993, placing over thirty-five times the amount of money in circulation as there had been at the end of 1991.[22]

This was accompanied by an explosion of interenterprise "credit," representing massive nonpayment of bills by state industry. Thus interenterprise debt rose to 3.2 trillion rubles (almost 50% of GDP) by July 1, 1992, fell to 650 billion rubles by October 1 due to RCB imposed mutual cancellations of debt and significant new credits, but immediately grew back to 1 trillion rubles by November 1 and to over 5 trillion rubles (over 30% of GDP) by mid–January 1993.[23] It continued rising (although just slightly in real terms) to over 7 trillion rubles at the end of April, but then fell back to 1.8 trillion rubles due to the tightening of monetary policy, a growing threat of bankruptcy proceedings, and administrative measures by the RCB.[24] In the second half of 1993, interenterprise debt again rose, crossing 11 trillion rubles by the end of September and causing new restrictive measures to be implemented on October 19, 1993, to prevent its further growth. However, the debt in the energy sector alone was reported to be some 16 trillion rubles at the end of 1993, an increase of about 13 trillion rubles in the fourth quarter alone. In addition, the state owed over 22 trillion rubles to other industrial enterprises by early 1994, according to Sergei Dubinin, the acting minister of finance.[25] In other cases enterprises showed a growing willingness in the second half of

1993 to withhold shipments when payment was not forthcoming, indicating a growing effectiveness of market constraints.[26]

The resulting increase in "liquidity" led to dramatic increases in the rate of inflation, although these increases were restrained by administrative restrictions on the liquidity of the ruble and rigidities in the archaic banking and settlements mechanisms. Thus wholesale prices, paid in enterprise funds, rose over 17–fold by October 1992 and over 34–fold by the end of that year. Retail prices had risen 13–fold by October, and were growing by over 25% per month at the end of 1992, resulting in a 26–fold increase over twelve months. The rate of inflation rode on two waves in 1993, dropping from a 26% monthly rate in January to 17–18% in June, then accelerating again to 26% in August before beginning a steady decline to 13% in December. It is worth noting that in 1993 wholesale inflation followed pretty much the same path as retail, although at a slightly higher level. Hence, wholesale prices in December 1993 were ten times their December 1992 level, while retail prices increased 9.4–fold.[27] In the face of such inflation, real consumer income fell significantly in 1992 but rose slightly (9%) in 1993. In the first three quarters of 1992 wages rose only 6.6 times and personal income rose even less (5.7 times), so in December both wages and incomes were only 12.3 times what they had been a year earlier. The trend continued in the first quarter of 1993, when incomes rose 1.4 times while prices rose 1.93 times, according to the official statistical reports. However, the trend reversed itself thereafter, in part due to state wage and income supplement indexing. Thus, according to official statistics, at the end of December 1993 wages were 8.6 times and real take-home pay was almost 11 times the December 1992 levels.[28]

As important as the instability in monetary and fiscal policy were the deep structural problems of the monetary and financial systems. These are a direct legacy of the command economy, which had no need for real money, real banking, or any kind of financial intermediation.[29] Throughout 1992 there remained a dual monetary system, with numerous bank restrictions on the use of one's own money and a lack of automatic convertibility between the two monetary circuits. This was coupled with an archaic settlements structure—including restrictions on the establishment of correspondence accounts between banks—which facilitated centralized control over the flow of funds but obstructed decentralized payments and the clearing of accounts without central bank participation. This made it easy for interenterprise debt to accumulate, as well as for the central bank to arbitrarily cancel such debts.[30] But it also meant that no enterprise truly controlled its own money, making the earning of that money and its careful use for payments somewhat irrelevant. All that was truly important to the enterprise was to be able to make the wage bill in cash rubles, and there were always credits—at phenomenally negative interest rates—available for that purpose; only documentation that the wages were "earned" by some production activity—e.g., overdue receivables—was required, just as in the preceding Soviet economy.

Thus in 1992, in order to "maintain production" (pay wages), state enterprises could regularly borrow at a 20–80% annual rate, while inflation was running over 20–25% per month. The RCB, with the support of a majority in the parliament, maintained this policy despite the objections of the government, to support production and employment and thereby prevent a social explosion. Hence the structure of the monetary system was maintained as one consequence of the political struggle that led to Gaidar's replacement by Chernomyrdin. It was also a major contributing factor to the growing financial chaos in Russia, as it undercut the incentives to use the ruble as a medium of exchange and to treat it as real money. Finally, continued massive credits to other CIS states to support their demand for Russian products had a similar source. Thus, for over half a year, Russia looked the other way as other CIS states issued massive ruble credits, and thereafter itself granted some 650 billion (mid–1992) rubles in credit to them, 250 billion rubles to Ukraine alone. By January 1993 the total debt of other CIS states to Russia exceeded 1.2 trillion (1992) rubles, and it kept growing in early 1993, pushing Russia to demand total control over the monetary policy of all states within the ruble zone in late June 1993.[31]

The prospect of hyperinflation and financial chaos led to a May agreement between the Finance Ministry and the RCB to restrict monetary emission and subsidized credits. This has led to a steady rise in the RCB rediscount rate to 210% per year (17.5% per month) since October 15, 1993, driving the real interest rate—paid by those without connections giving access to subsidized credit—to nearly zero in the final months of the year. A true shock was introduced to the financial system on July 24, 1993, when the RCB, with the agreement of Chernomyrdin but not the Ministry of Finance, introduced a "currency reform" involving the invalidation of Soviet-era rubles and a limited exchange for new Russian rubles. This had the positive effect of reducing the drain on Russian resources from other CIS states, but at the cost of undermining confidence in the ruble as a store of value and medium of exchange.[32] It was perhaps the decisive push for the other states, except Tajikistan, to introduce their own currency in the second half of 1993 because it forcibly removed them from the ruble zone. This gave Russia the possibility— which it began to exploit near the end of 1993—of demanding political concessions from other CIS states in return for ruble credits and subsidized ruble prices.[33] It ensured that the future "ruble zone" would be a

Russian and not a CIS vehicle. It also led to a further drop in CIS trade and a growth in CIS member indebtedness to Russian enterprises, particularly in the energy sector. Indeed, by the last quarter of 1993, over one-third of the more than 3 trillion rubles owed to Russian energy enterprises was owed by other CIS states.

The Unravelling of the State and Economy

All of these factors both reflected and contributed to the disintegration of the state sector as a cohesive economic organism through most of 1992. Decrees and laws of the center were ignored, if not taken as challenges to local autonomy that demanded explicit refutation.[34] In particular, tax laws and collection procedures have been challenged, especially by the republics of Tatarstan and Sakha (Yakutia).[35] Also in 1992, state orders in the industrial sector came to an end—including the elimination of some 80% of military industrial orders—culminating in the demise in October of the Russian Ministry of Material Resources (successor to Gossnab). Although some state orders continued to be placed, particularly with regard to agricultural procurement, they were increasingly ignored or preempted by local government action. Indeed many regional and local governments took to extracting tribute in kind, purportedly in lieu of taxes, which could be collected only in increasingly less valuable rubles, in order to acquire products and resources for trade among themselves. In effect a three-way barter trade seemed to have arisen among localities producing industrial products versus agricultural products versus consumer goods, orchestrated by local leaderships left over from the Soviet Union. However, this trade was at the expense of integrated economic interaction and market development throughout Russia.

Management behavior at the firm and enterprise level also reflected and furthered the disintegration. In many firms, sale of inputs from inventory replaced their use in production, as indeed far more could be earned that way—indicating, in the light of price liberalization, the value-destroying nature of much production activity in the FSU. There was also a scramble to export products, usually natural resources, that had an international market value. Exports not only earned far more at current rates of exchange than did domestic sales, but they earned it in a hard currency that kept its value and could be hidden from the tax authorities.[36] In view of the Byzantine and continually changing taxation and licensing requirements, and the weak auditing and control at ports and borders in 1992, such practices contributed massively to the growth of corruption and the disruption of legal trade. Even internally, enterprises with a desirable product increasingly insisted on barter—real goods for real goods—or payment in hard currency, so at the end of 1992 the government decreed it illegal to use hard currency for internal payments.[37] Thus the lack of "moneyness" of the ruble fed on itself, making it even less of a real money in the course of 1992.[38]

Such enterprise and local government behaviors reflect two deeper disintegrative forces: the growth of regionalism and the continued thriving of corruption and mafia activity. Regionalism, reflected in the drive for broad political and economic autonomy, strengthened throughout 1992 and 1993 as a political phenomenon, while by the end of 1992 the striving for economic self-sufficiency abated somewhat from the levels of 1991 and early 1992, as interregional barter and trade increased. The process seemed largely driven by a distrust and fear of the center built on the Soviet legacy of exploitation of local resources and people in the pursuit of the central administration's goals. In the name of building socialism, resources were extracted without adequate or equivalent compensation, the environment was destroyed, and local social and economic infrastructure was ignored except where necessary to achieve the central planners' goals.[39]

This long history of abuse, coupled with an illusion of appropriable wealth in local capital and resources, plus strong feelings of nationalism, have fueled the local drives for political autonomy with close local control of economic activity. This is particularly true of regions that sit astride major mineral and energy deposits; there foreign marketability adds to the illusion of wealth ripe for the taking.[40] Similarly, regions that were major, sometimes sole, producers of important industrial or agricultural commodities saw opportunities to use their monopoly power on nascent markets and rushed to exploit them. Finally, the arbitrary, capricious, and frequently excessive taxation policies of the Russian state, and its inability to provide even the level of income support and social services that the Soviet state did, reinforced the perception that economic opportunities would be better if unhooked from Russia, as the federation provides little in the way of tangible benefits for what it takes. Thus the moves toward autonomy by virtually all major regions of the Russian Federation—from Kaliningrad, Novorossiisk, and Sverdlovsk oblasts, to Chechnia, Tatarstan, and Sakha (Yakutia), to the Maritime Provinces—accelerated the disintegration of central control and old channels of economic interaction.

The response of the weak and divided federal government in 1993 to these pressures only aggravated the problem. The struggle for power between the president and the parliament led to a "bidding war" of subsidies and concessions to the republics. As special deals were cut, other regions entered into the fray to gain the same rights of control over resources and tax revenues as the republics. Thus several oblasts in the Russian heartland proclaimed themselves the Central Russian Republic, and Sverdlovsk Oblast became the Urals Republic in July 1993.[41]

These new republics lasted as long as the president and parliament were locked in political struggle; they successfully played off both sides to lay claim to local control of economic and political activity. In the aftermath of Yeltsin's decisive victory in October, however, the center was able to reassert itself politically, revoking the republic status of Sverdlovsk and other regions, pushing through a new constitution, and calling for new legislative elections, both central and local. While the issue was still not fully resolved in early 1994, even Tatarstan seemed to have accepted the Russian Federation as a true federal state, signing Yeltsin's interstate treaty on February 15, 1994.[42] Thus the political structure, particularly with regard to the oversight and regulation of economic activity, remains as confused as ever, posing a major obstacle to new economic activity and foreign investment in particular.

While incapacitating old central structures does not damage the prospects for transformation of the economic system, this regionalism also attacked the capabilities of the center to fulfill functions essential to the development of a unified market. The center should be able to provide the "public goods" of market substructure: a legal environment that guarantees and enforces property rights and private economic agreements; a real and sufficiently stable money; minimum regulation for social health and safety; a stable political and social environment; and a stable, simple system of taxation sufficient to support these activities. The benefits of these public goods fall sharply with a restriction of the scope of the market, although it is clearly better that they be provided locally than not at all. In the latter case, they would at best provide for a limited market system without the gains to trade that come from a greater extension of the market.

Unfortunately, many of the regions in Russia—in particular, the republics—are attempting to maintain a monopoly in political and/or local elite control over economic activity, rather than allowing individual and organizational initiative and entrepreneurship to determine the use of local assets and resources. Local authorities thereby undercut the foundation of wealth creation for a market economy, as well as restrict the opportunities for mutually beneficial interaction with other regions, while attempting to maintain economically wasteful interactions inherited from the past. Where this occurs, the disintegration of old structures and interactions loses its potentially beneficial effect. However, where local governments pursue liberal private property and free market-oriented policies—as is to some extent occurring in Nizhnii-Novgorod—this disintegration can help speed the process of transformation by removing centralized structures, regulations, and interactions that impede the development of market relations. In 1992 and 1993 both types of approaches were pursued in different parts of the Russian Federation, adding to the corrosion of political unity as well as to confusion in the economic environment.

As noted above, another characteristic of the economic situation was the major and apparently growing role of corruption and mafias in new and nascent markets.[43] Both are in a sense inevitable consequences of the breakup of the command economy. Corruption is the natural consequence of the lack of a transparent, rule-based framework for private and other nonstate interaction, while mafias thrive because the command economy ensured that the only integrative nonstate economic structures at the beginning of liberalization were illegal ones. Bribery and corruption are almost essential ingredients to get anything done, owing to remaining bureaucratic restrictions, habits, and patterns of acting outside official structures, the absence of well-defined and protected property rights, arbitrary and often punitive taxation; and the fact that access to critical inputs is often blocked by existing state structures. Further, organized, experienced illegal structures (mafias) have a strong competitive edge—if not an absolute monopoly—on the emerging decentralized, liberalized markets. Indeed, without an actively protective state, they are important for the protection of contract and property rights essential to real trade. In the absence of a sufficient, complete civil law, a framework for private economic interaction, and a properly functioning legal system to enforce it, corruption becomes a necessary component of "destatization," an unavoidable lubricant of nonstate economic activity.[44]

Despite their "naturalness" in the early stages of marketizing a command economy—i.e., their reflection of and responsiveness to market forces—both corruption and mafias pose a major barrier to the entry, entrepreneurship, and new competition that are the driving forces behind marketization. Agents operating illegally develop a symbiotic relationship with existing state structures, living off the microeconomic irrationalities and opportunities for arbitrage that they present and maintaining them with corrupting payments. The carcass of the state economy provides vast opportunities for exploitation by mafia monopolies, who protect themselves and their property with appropriate inducements in money or kind as long as the state does not provide adequate, equal protection to all. This creates a large set of agents with a strong interest in arresting the reforms, fixing the structure of capital and activity, and tying up resources, thereby preserving the lucrative opportunities created by an incomplete transition.

The resulting chaotic, intermediate state is unsustainable, however; it fails to provide incentives for investment, and its economic activity is essentially parasitic, living off accumulated wealth. This was apparently the situation in 1993, where illegal and quasi-legal structures played a large role in high-return activities requiring little investment: arbitrage and financial intermediation, wholesaling and transportation services, alcohol production and trade, and narcotics. By the beginning of 1994, however, it seemed that the limits of effectiveness of such activities were being reached. The lack of new or even replacement investment has reduced the capital stock to a desperate state, with major physical breakdown increasingly likely.[45] Thus many opportunities for exploiting existing assets are fading, together with the transfer and arbitrage opportunities that they presented when relatively new and functional.

In addition, it must be noted that in the fluid situation of 1992–1993, the distinction between legal and illegal activities was often unclear due to Russian social attitudes, the lack of legal protection for legal activities, and general local bureaucratic interference in both spheres. On the positive side, this situation allowed the beginning of decentralized, self-interested interaction in the pursuit of wealth, even if in some areas only among competing mafias; this provides a starting point for a more thorough and consistent reform of the legal and economic mechanisms necessary for a transition to a true market economy. However, it can become a starting point only if the property rights and wealth so generated become real, generally recognized, and legally protected.

Beginnings of Real Structural Change

Although a general characterization of the Russian economy in 1992–1993 must remain rather negative, a number of positive developments raise some hope for the future, despite several disturbing political and policy changes at the start of 1994.[46] The first year of independence brought the first signs of real structural change, although the changes were quite limited. The rather thorough breakdown of central taxation, internal trade, and budgetary discipline that had characterized the final months of the Soviet Union was halted after some initial chaos during the first two months of full independence. The first quarter of 1992 saw a remarkable control over budgetary expenditures that would have yielded a surplus had tax revenues been close to what they should have been. The year, however, began without working mechanisms for the collection of the new value-added tax (VAT) and income taxes. In addition, new excises and tariffs were introduced and tax rates altered several times, so that much was lost to administrative confusion. Only in March did tax collections become regularized, yielding a steady and growing flow of revenues, if only at some 40% of the expected levels. These increasing revenues helped limit the damage of the fiscal irresponsibility of the second half of the year. The revenue situation kept improving in 1993; in the first quarter only 40% of anticipated revenue was lost to tax nonpayment. But the situation improved slowly, leaving a 30% shortfall in revenues for the year.[47] Among the continuing problems were politically motivated withholding by local governments; confusion due to frequent changes in the laws, procedures, and regulations; and tax avoidance, made possible by the lack of information on much quasi-legal private economic activity.

Another positive development was a steady reassertion of central control over borders both external and internal to the Russian Federation. Agreements were reached with the republics of Tatarstan and Sakha (Yakutia) with regard to tax revenue-sharing and the control and ownership of natural resources in those regions. These agreements and other measures enforcing central authority eliminated many internal barriers to trade (such as city and regional export controls and tariffs), as well as more clearly marking the extent of the Russian market and protecting state revenues by restricting smuggling. Such minimal central control over the territory of the Russian Federation is a prerequisite, although by itself clearly insufficient, for enforcing a legal environment congenial to and supportive of market interaction.

There was also movement from below, indicating a revival of real trade and intermediation, replacing the inertia that had predominated after the collapse of the old command mechanisms. There were indications that firms and farms were beginning to hunt for better prices and look for new customers—prices and effective monetized demand were beginning to mean something. Barter between local and regional governments also seemed to move onto a more market-oriented basis, responding to demand and opportunity costs, albeit sometimes with locally extorted products and resources. Indeed, major enterprises often acted as (or in close coordination with) local government authorities to acquire goods needed by their locality in exchange for what they were able to produce (or pull from inventory). Thus there developed barter-based market contract deals, with mutually advantageous, flexible, relative prices, between regions and large enterprises exercising near-feudal social and political control over their localities—a positive development over the commanded interaction without equivalence of exchange that had predominated earlier.

By mid–1993 industrial inventories had shrunk from their bloated Soviet levels, yet they were no longer a primary factor limiting production. Instead production had come to be constrained largely by lack of effective (ruble-or dollar-backed) demand, reversing a key characteristic of the command economy. The impact of monetized demand was reinforced by the relative stability of the ruble exchange rate against the dollar for most of the year.[48] Further, interenterprise debt between autonomous firms and dealers shrank in response to greater incentives to collect and to new bank regulations and penalties imposed beginning in the second half of 1992. What grew dramatically were debts of the government for ordered products and debts to the highly regulated energy sector (largely by favored industries, which the government would not force to bankruptcy) and other CIS states. Finally, the distinctions between first and second economies, between private and public, and between economic behavior in the state and nonstate sectors blurred and seemed to be fading away in 1993. Thus the structure of economic activity, apart from where the state was most heavily involved, moved toward a market-value orientation, indicating some success of the implemented reforms.

The biggest structural change was a relatively rapid growth of the legal nonstate, quasi-private, and private sectors.[49] There are many new forms of business activity in these sectors, including leasing of industrial operations, especially as spinoffs from state enterprises; producer cooperatives in the trade, services, and construction sectors; small business in manufacturing, trade, and services as allowed under the 1991 Soviet law; joint ventures and wholly owned foreign subsidiaries; family farms and true agricultural cooperatives; and joint-stock companies formed prior to the forced "corporatization" (management restructuring) of state enterprises in 1992. By the end of the third quarter of 1992 each of these categories had a significant and growing number of operations. There were over 120,000 new producer cooperatives, over 60,000 small businesses, over 1,200 wholly or partially foreign firms, over 135,000 family farms, and over 2,000 independent joint stock companies. In addition, some 24,000 state enterprises had been privatized pursuant to the government's reform program, although only five percent of these were federal enterprises while over 82% had been municipal, and some 80% were in retailing and consumer services rather than in manufacturing. This again reflected the strength of "reform from below" as local leaders, particularly in medium-sized Russian cities, took the initiative in structural reform and privatization.[50] In addition, almost 4,000 state industrial enterprises had been leased to their management, and most others were beginning the process of management restructuring as a preliminary step toward privatization.

By October 1992 about one-third of all enterprises in trade and services were private; over 50% of all construction operations were in leased, cooperative, or small business forms and hence outside the state sector; and one-half of all kolkhozes and sovkhozes had been reorganized as true cooperatives. This process accelerated in the fourth quarter as another 23,000 (mostly small) state enterprises were privatized; over

77% of all state and collective farms reorganized; the number of family farms reached 184,000; and the total number of businesses organized under new, nonstate forms grew to over 950,000. This represented substantial progress in altering the organizational structure of the Russian economy; over 25% of employment is in, and over 35% of output then came from, the nonstate, (quasi-)private sectors of the economy.

On October 1, 1992, a new phase of the privatization campaign began: each Russian citizen was issued 10,000–ruble vouchers that could be used to purchase shares of state enterprises in privatization auctions. The first 20 voucher auctions took place in December 1992. This opened the drive toward mass privatization of newly corporatized large-scale industry that began in earnest in 1993, with 90 voucher auctions in January, 200 in February, 250 in March, and almost 600 in April. By April 1, 1993, over 17,000 medium and large state enterprises were corporatizing, the first step toward full privatization. In January and February alone, over 11,000 enterprises were privatized; 12% were "large" federal enterprises, and 71% small municipal enterprises. Furthermore, the number of private family farms had grown to 230,000 by the end of the first quarter of 1993.[51]

The privatization drive continued, if at a somewhat slackening pace, in the politically turbulent second half of 1993; indeed, it was the only area of reform in which significant progress was then made. By December some 40% of employment was reported to be in the nonstate sector, producing a slightly greater proportion of GDP. Enterprises of all sizes in all sectors outside of the defense industry and some key resource industries, such as energy, were subject to privatization; an additional 39,000 enterprises were at least partially privatized through direct sale (69%), usually to the management and workers' collective or through auctions (31%) in which vouchers were accepted as a means of payment. In 1993 the first real impact of privatization hit the industrial and construction sectors, where some 15,000 enterprises were removed from the state sector. By December, 75% of all retail trade was outside the state sector, together with over 40% of all agricultural output. Also by December over 95% of state and collective farms had been re-registered, although more than one-third chose to keep the same organizational form. In addition, over 270,000 private commercial farms controlled about six percent of agricultural land. At the same time, a new phenomenon appeared: private economic failure (again, reflecting growing marketization). Over 14,000 private farms went out of business, over 120 commodity and stock exchanges closed (of 303 registered), and 8 industrial enterprises were subject to bankruptcy proceedings under the December 1992 law. Finally, financial markets seemed to achieve a critical mass; there were over 2,000 private commercial banks with over 4,000 branches, some 60,000 savings bank branches, and about 1,000 new insurance companies. For the first time, these institutions in 1993 began operating largely with deposits that they had received (75% of their assets), rather than credits from the state bank, and they made more than 80% of the loans to the economy. All these developments have created a rather large and rapidly growing nonstate sector. It is the beginning of, and provides a basis for, marketizing structural change toward a qualitatively new economic system.

The changes, although quite broad, are so far rather shallow and fragile, however. Truly new operations are only loosely anchored in the economy, without fixed and lasting structures. There is as yet very little net real investment in these operations; any significant real capital still mainly comes as a transfer from the state sector, although much working capital originates in the second economy. Significant private outlays seem to be largely for protection and bribes. Private operations are concentrated in areas in which no significant fixed capital is required and operations can be quickly moved or folded without large losses—retailing, brokering and other forms of intermediation, and light services. Thus, through 1992, growth of nonstate economic activity, although substantial, remained essentially extensive and parasitic, rather than intensive and self-sustaining.

In early 1993, a new class of nonstate, but not yet truly private, enterprises began to appear: the medium-and large-scale "corporatized" and "privatized" state enterprises. These have inherited vast amounts of land, labor, and capital, which are tied into a rigid network of interactions and coupled with massive social obligations to the enterprise work force and communities. These enterprises seem also still to carry the legacy of dependence on state support, placing social above economic concerns, and lacking initiative in dealing with economic problems in ways other than by pleading for continuing state support. Their pleas for support seemed to be answered in early 1994, as a new government of "industrial managers" replaced the "reformers" of 1992–1993, with the aim of softening the reform. For over a year they have been facing market conditions that require new responses and behaviors, which they were indeed learning, and in doing so were laying part of the foundation of a true market economy. That foundation is threatened by any policies that underestimate the importance of a stable monetary environment.

Structural and Infrastructural Roots
Blocking Transformation

Why does the overall economic situation clearly remain critical despite these positive structural developments? It should first be emphasized that the serious economic problems facing Russia should not be considered a consequence of "shock therapy"; despite the substantial price liberalization of January 2, 1992, no comprehensive shock therapy was seriously attempted. Neither stabilization nor liberalization policies were sufficiently thorough even if to some they appeared shocking. Macroeconomic stabilization in 1992 was undercut from the very beginning by excessive credit emission, interest rates substantially below inflation (80% per annum versus 2600–3400% inflation), and a lack of internal ruble-commodity convertibility, control over wages, or ruble-foreign exchange convertibility. Moreover, after the first quarter, government fiscal irresponsibility grew, driven by political pressures from parliament and the state industrial and defense lobbies.[52]

There were also inconsistencies and failures in the liberalization program. Until October 1992, 150 of the most basic ("structure forming") industrial and consumer commodities were formally subject to state orders and controls. Critical prices—particularly in the energy sector—were subject to strict control, and even "free" prices were regulated through trading and retailing markup limits of 25%, well below those in most market economies. Over 2,000 firms were placed on a "monopoly" list, resulting in strict (if not always enforceable) central price and production assortment controls. Although import restrictions were initially fully lifted, massive export licensing remained (albeit not fully effective, due to porous borders). Finally, the taxation of production and exchange remained confused and capricious, creating a major barrier to rational free trade, both internally and externally. Thus the policies pursued, while undoubtedly disruptive, did not amount to the kind of substantial reform that had begun in Poland two years earlier.[53] The Russian government repeatedly bowed to political constraints, implementing a politically feasible rather than an economically rational policy.

If anything, the reform policy became less coherent in 1993. Only voucher privatization was pursued consistently and vigorously, due to its perceived political popularity. As largely a give-away to "insiders," it had the support of most managers and workers, including those with the most to lose from other aspects of real economic reform.[54] While there was some further liberalization of consumer prices (for the most part locally initiated), "monopolies" found themselves subject to increasingly effective price regulation, and energy prices, despite regularly decreed increases, remained controlled well below market levels. Monetary and fiscal policy fluctuated wildly under the push and pull of the political struggle, but despite a rise in the RCB's rediscount rate to 210% per year, it never approached the level of responsible restraint needed for macroeconomic stability. Restraint was achieved in the last quarter at the expense of nonpayment for goods and services and the cutting of credit to new entrepreneurial activities, rather than through the rationalization

of government economic activity. Increasingly, credits were targeted by
the government and RCB to support enterprises and operations left from
the Soviet era, freezing existing structures of production.[55] Taxation to
support the budget became more effective in 1993, yet also more burden-
some and highly capricious, driving most new activity to tax-dodging
and opening vast new vistas for mafia extortion and control. Thus two of
the three pillars of Russian reform, stabilization and liberalization,
became both less consistent and less radical in the course of 1993, while
the third, privatization, became increasingly captured by those controlling the preexisting structures of the economy.

In short, the primary cause of the deteriorating economic situation
has been a failure to undertake sufficiently deep radical reform, rather
than an excessive shock therapy. In particular, the transformation
program of the Russian government—as indeed of those also suggested
by the IMF and most foreign advisors—concentrated on issues that
presume the absence of three deep structural problems already noted
above:

- an absence of real money and hence of an adequate object for macroeconomic stabilization;
- a lack of well-defined ownership and property and hence of an
  object to privatization;
- massive distortions in the structure of capital, employment, and
  production and hence the need for major, disruptive resource real-
  locations fraught with political dangers.[56]

The scope and depth of these problems as well as of the intellectual
and cultural legacy of Soviet socialism separate the problems of transition in the FSU from all precedents, rendering them uniquely difficult.
These problems act as a virulent cancer, distorting, undercutting, and
perverting standard reform policies that have worked elsewhere. They
are a primary legacy of the successful Bolshevik and Soviet policy of
destroying market relations and behavior and replacing them with
command relations subsequent to directive central planning.

The first deep problem arose as the ruble lacked the inherent property
of "moneyness" throughout 1992—a generalized command over goods
and services both necessary and sufficient to consummate a transaction.
This lack of moneyness arises from the myriad administrative restrictions on a holder's use of his money. The ruble still circulates in two
largely separate circuits—*nalichnye* (cash) and *beznalichnye* (enterprise
funds). Full convertibility at a one-to-one rate is not guaranteed,
although in 1993 commercial banks were increasingly able to carry out
such conversion, at least for their biggest and best clients, in the major

money centers of Moscow and St. Petersburg. In many cases, however, the use of monies in separate circuits is restricted and indeed is subject to manipulation by the holding bank, subsequent to RCB orders. The moneyness of the ruble was also undercut by the capricious control over settlements flows by the RCB and the resulting lengthy and uncertain delays in ultimate settlement. The situation was further aggravated in 1992 and 1993 by the virtually unlimited credit sporadically available for political reasons and the ensuing rapid depreciation of the ruble as a unit of account, store of value, and medium of exchange.

The consequences of this situation were natural and predictable. There was a general flight from the ruble in 1992; almost anything else was preferable as a means of exchange.[57] When transactions took place involving rubles, there was a certain inattention to collection; why bother when it is of such limited use and in any case credit is always available at a vastly negative interest rate?[58] Those with products to sell sought to use hard currency or to engage in barter, often developing closed (autarkic) support networks with others they trusted. This led to a breakdown and subsequent lack of complex transactions and multilateral interactions, particularly of the sort involving intertemporal exchange. Further, it provided strong support for inertia: it maintained familiar ties in an increasingly chaotic situation and provided an argument for the necessity of continued central funding and subsidies, if only for social and political reasons. One should note a perhaps positive consequence of the unreality of the ruble: it helped hold off hyperinflation, despite the fiscal and monetary irresponsibility of the government and RCB up to mid–1993, because credits and subsidies did not have the same high-powered impact on liquidity that they would have had if agents truly cared about acquiring and using money. The ruble was sufficiently unimportant to be treated carelessly, so the velocity of money did not accelerate as much as it would have were the money full-bodied.

There was some progress in solidifying the ruble as a real money in the second half of 1993, as the RCB's technical changes in handling settlements in late 1992 began to bear fruit and the commercial banks gained strength and experience. The agreement between the RCB and Ministry of Finance on restricting subsidies and credits, improved taxation mechanisms and fiscal restraint of the government under Fedorov's pressure, and the effective expulsion of other CIS states from the ruble zone added to the strengthening of the ruble, were all reflected in a sharp reduction of inflation by the end of 1993 and the appreciation of the ruble against the dollar outside of the brief periods of political shock (e.g., the October confrontation). The growing reality of the ruble could also be seen in the increasing bite of effective demand on production, although it was ameliorated by a continuing payments arrears crisis throughout 1993. All of these gains, however, seem to be threatened by the Chernomyrdin government's new policy direction in 1994, especially in "fighting inflation by... non-monetarist means."

The absence of real property rights is perhaps even more serious. The heart of the problem is that with the exception of simple appropriable objects, *no one fully owns anything*. Property rights to complex objects or activities are incompletely assigned, and even when the owner is clear, rights are generally not fully granted to that owner. As under Roman law, meaningful property rights must at a minimum include the rights to manage and use, to control the output and income generated by that use, and to dispose of the property when and as the owner sees fit. The last criterion—the right to alienate at will for full capital asset value—is either questionable or denied in Russia and the other states of the CIS. The problem was most evident in the restrictions and prohibitions on the use and resale of land in the Russian Federation. It can also be seen in the early limits on the use of privatized small business in Nizhnii-Novgorod and in the lack of ownership rights associated with the holding of "shares" *(aktsii)* in former state enterprises.[59] Such restrictions relate to line of business, profile of production, structure of employment, and the maintenance at firm expense of local social support and welfare systems.

Privatization without clear, well-defined, and full ownership means very little. Few of the positive effects associated with privatization can be expected in such an environment. As property is not truly owned, "owners" cannot be expected to make net investments or to restructure the property in order to enhance its value; the value of assets remains largely inappropriable by the owners, except by chance. In such an environment, "asset stripping" and "rent seeking" are economically rational: ignoring future implications, economic agents will exploit assets for their maximum current value and for the operations in which they are embedded. And they will cry for state support to maintain existing assets and prevent "catastrophic breakdown" and "de-industrialization," rather than sinking their earnings and wealth into something that is not clearly owned.

Thus, as we can readily see in the current Russian situation, truly private operations, unable to rely on state support or even impartiality, are largely "fly-by-night," involving as few fixed assets as possible, and, when fixed capital is unavoidable, working with borrowed, leased, or stolen assets. This clearly biases private operations toward brokering, intermediation, trade, and services, and against production and investment—as those nostalgic for the old order repeatedly claim.[60] However, the problem lies not with privatization but with the lack of true property rights subsequent to privatization. Further, a lack of clear, enforced legal protection for contract and property further attenuates the property

rights of even fully appropriable objects. Without confidence in (and precedents for) the protection of ownership, all of the ambiguities in present
property and privatization laws work against their stimulating the kind
of positive economic response sought by the reformers in Russia.[61] This
problem is particularly insidious because it is not fully recognized or
appreciated—even by the Western advisors of the Russian government—
as an important part of the explanation for what has gone wrong in the
transformation so far: Why has there not been the natural supply-side
response to liberalization and other policy measures?

These two deep infrastructural problems are seriously affected by the
third problem—the deeply distorted structure of capital, employment,
and production. This is the consequence of some fifty years of "building
socialism," of channeling massive resources into industry and elsewhere
without economic rhyme or reason, or attention to cost or value. The
resulting structure created massive, highly specialized facilities, which
produced many unneeded products at extraordinary economic cost and
with much waste. These were maintained by a rigid network that provided necessary inputs and guaranteed output disposal without any consideration of or need for value equivalence in exchange. Thus the
structure was devoid of economic rationality; when it collapsed, so did
the rationale for most existing configurations of economic activity. The
consequent tragedy for the transforming Russian economy lies in a
microstructure of production that cannot produce useful output at a cost
less than its value. Further, the production facilities are nonconvertible as
ongoing operations—the value of the whole is far less than that of the
parts and indeed is frequently negative.[62] The parts—buildings,
workers, equipment—are economically usable, but only in radically different configurations and in significantly smaller bundles.

The ongoing damage from this structure of production can be seen in
virtually any measure of microeconomic efficiency. Waste is evident in
materials use: in October 1992, GDP was 15 times more steel-intensive, 9
times more rubber-intensive, and 6 times more energy-intensive than
that of the United States, and 12 times more energy-intensive than Japan.
Shutting down all production and exporting all currently extracted
natural resources would have increased GDP from some 9 trillion (mid–
1992) rubles to 15–27 trillion (mid–1992) rubles, showing the value-
destroying nature of much production.[63] One recent study estimates that
eight percent of all industrial output is net value subtracting—i.e., value
destroying—even if the costs of both labor and capital are zero, while
over 35% is gross value subtracting.[64] This means that there were at least
25 million workers employed but not creating any economic value.
Indeed, on December 11, 1992, L. Paidiev, a deputy economic minister,
asserted that 70% of state industrial enterprises were technically bank-

rupt, implying that over 30 million workers were not supporting themselves with their economic activity. A similar figure (75%) was given by
the new deputy economic minister, Y. Urinson, in a February 1994 press
conference.[65]

Clearly, the current structure of production and configuration of economic activity are exceedingly wasteful and must be completely changed
for new, market-based economic activity to predominate. This is particularly so as the old, wasteful economic structures tie up almost all social
resources, preventing their use in new, economically productive sectors
and ways. The continued provision of credits to the state sector ratifies
and reinforces its control over these resources, freezing out the private
and other nonstate sectors. The limited moneyness of the ruble further
prevents other sectors from bidding resources from the dying but
destructive state sector, while the lack of real property rights prevents the
securing of nonstate control over assets and operations that would allow
the growth and strengthening of new forms of economic activity. All
three of these fundamental problems thus feed on one other, emasculat-
ing new laws and reform efforts and thus indirectly supporting the
decaying structures of the command economy.[66] The new policy direction
of the Russian government in early 1994 seemed likely to exacerbate
these problems if it were implemented.

Hope for the Future?

Despite these serious problems, it would perhaps be unwise to end on
too negative a note. The task is immeasurably greater than imagined by
the reformers and their Western advisors two years ago. Genuine
progress at the structural and substructural infrastructural level, where
the roots of the deepest problems lie, will require support from a marketizing and liberalizing reformist government that understands the
true problem. Unfortunately, Russia has yet to have a government that
sufficiently understands or is capable of consistently pursuing coherent
reforms.

There have been positive developments in each of the three key
problem areas discussed above, however, and they seemed to be accelerating before the end of 1993. With respect to money, the RCB issued new
regulations in late summer 1992, as a result of which some correspondence accounts could be used between banks, thus allowing a more
rational settlement of transactions. Russia is also moving to gain control
over the quantity of rubles in circulation by cleaning out the ruble zone
within the CIS. Ukraine was effectively expelled in November 1992 and
the others forced out after the "currency reform" of July 1993. A new CIS
"bank" (clearinghouse) has been formed with the RCB firmly in control.

Indeed, in June 1993 Russia demanded full control over monetary policy of any state remaining in the ruble zone; Tajikistan immediately agreed, and more recently Belarus and Georgia. In 1993 monetary policy began to slow the growth of emissions and move toward positive, real interest rates, and real financial markets began to develop, including the first auctions of state debt. More significantly, the distinction between *nalichnye* (cash) and *beznalichnye* (non-cash) money is fading away as commercial banks face increasing competitive pressure, explore their limits, and grasp what real banks do, while the RCB learns to relax its administrative controls in pursuit of a settlements mechanism adequate to market interaction. Indeed, the distinction has all but disappeared, at least for larger economic agents and holders of hard currencies in the major money centers of Moscow and St. Petersburg. Finally, new, more stringent capital requirements for commercial banks are being introduced in 1994.[67] The banks meeting the new requirements should be better able to manage their clients' money.

With respect to property, the positive effects of privatization on microeconomic behavior are beginning to appear. The claim to ownership is being tested and to some extent enforced in practice even without explicit state support. Short-term incentives for increased efficiency in current operations are clearly provided by the limited but growing property rights associated with privatization. State enterprises privatized by the nomenklatura or workers' collectives also seem to respond to medium-term incentives, showing some faith that the ownership rights they claim will become full. Further, "privatization" in large state enterprises is going as well as or better than expected and is having a positive impact on short-run behavior, increasing demand-oriented production if not general economic efficiency. The new constitutional right to own land and the liberalizing presidential decrees are also important steps forward. The ability to freely use and resell land for productive purposes is formally granted but still restricted; the restrictions must disappear if the new constitution is to be implemented.[68]

There is still, however, a crying need for a supportive legal system, for regular contract enforcement and for protection of explicitly private property rights, so that full property rights are created and maintained. The December 1992 law on bankruptcy, while again a step forward, illustrates the problem; for all its discussion of rescuing, reorganizing, or closing failing enterprises, nowhere does it explicitly address the issues of ownership and transfer of equity in an operation, the heart of any market-based bankruptcy procedure.[69] Finally, a fully transparent and procedurally legal crackdown on extortion, corruption, and theft by political decision is necessary to satisfy expectations of full, real property rights. The protection of property rights in a properly oriented civil (contract and tort) law would also go a long way toward reducing opportunities for corruption and mafias in the economy. Together with reform and stabilization of the monetary system, the elimination of remaining price controls, the rationalization of tax and subsidy structures, and the reduction of licensing and regulatory requirements, the use of police power to prevent extortion and to protect private property, enterprise, and initiative will greatly reduce the opportunity, means, and motive for corrupt and mafia activity. These measures would create an environment in which it is easier and more profitable for mafias to become legitimate businesses and more dangerous for them to pursue extortion and other illegal activities. Unfortunately, little of this seems likely in the immediate future, although some crackdown on extortion and corruption may be coming under the new government.[70]

Finally, it must be noted that there have been positive structural changes in the real economy as well. Enterprises are sloughing off excess capacity and labor. Truly useless production is being shut down, if slowly; industrial managers recognize the need to do so, even when they are unwilling or afraid to move very rapidly. Much more would be done if the government and RCB, fearful of real unemployment and its social and political consequences and spooked by the illusion of "de-industrialization," were not supporting inherited—and in many cases value destroying—Soviet operations. There are many examples of the successful conversion of shops and subdivisions of state enterprises—including some in military industry—to new lines of economic activity.[71] In addition, the nonstate and truly private sectors are growing rapidly, as indicated above; and with the serious and explicit protection of property rights, their growth will take off explosively.

There is also much room for new, highly productive economic activity in a shift of sectoral structure. In 1991, trade and services comprised only four to five percent of economic activity, whereas in a market economy they would comprise 30–40%. Indeed, Sachs and Lipton estimate that even if they grow to only 15% of 1991 GDP, trade and services could absorb over 40% of the estimated excess labor in hypertrophic post-Soviet industry. In 1992 we saw the beginnings of such a shift in structure—to 12% of a significantly shrunken GDP—without, however, a corresponding shift in measured employment; subsidies and credits to industry reduced the need to lose workers, while most of the growth came from new operations frequently using unregistered workers or those formally holding a job elsewhere. Finally, entirely new financial and insurance industries have arisen and have begun to play a major role in financing investment, even in still state-owned industry.[72]

Thus, there has been genuine progress in economic transformation, despite the inconsistencies and problems in reform policy implementation. But the early 1994 political situation bodes ill for the future of these positive developments and indeed for the future of the Russian transformation to a market economy: the market reformers have abdicated, policy is largely in the hands of "experienced" managers of ministries and large enterprises; the new, more legitimate legislature (Duma), deadlocked between communists and nationalists and reformers of various stripes, is strongly asserting its prerogatives against the president; and the regions and republics are still asserting autonomy and the supremacy of local laws (albeit within a federal system).

Russia stands at a policy crossroads in a historically unprecedented situation. A complete cycle of reform, focusing on destatization and liberalization, has come to an end with the cabinet changes in January 1994. The institutional backbone of the command economy has been broken, but many of those who made that system work are still in positions of power and decision-making. At the same time, the incomplete reforms of 1992–1993 have had a major impact on economic attitudes and behavior, on institutions and interactions, and have made a restitution of the command economy virtually impossible without resort to massive terror. Thousands of new organizations are operating, and many more are latent, giving millions of people a reason to resist a full reversal of the reforms. The regions of Russia would strongly resist the loss of their autonomy and prerogatives, but they are also coming to recognize that disintegration of the Russian Federation would be a disaster for all. Hence, virtually all political actors in Russia speak of the need for continuing reform. However, there is widespread dissatisfaction with many of the outcomes, and the dissatisfaction is crystallized in the new Duma and Federal Assembly.[73] The political siren call is for slower, more careful and caring reform that prevents people from being hurt by the changes.

The feasible policy directions thus seemed to be threefold in early 1994. First was a renewal and radicalization of the policies supporting market transformation, building systematically on what had already been accomplished. This would involve completing liberalization; ensuring full property rights against the depredations of both the state and "mafias"; solidifying the ruble as a money through significant banking and financial reforms and serious macroeconomic stabilization; and the elimination of Soviet, and reconstitution (introduction) of state, social support systems, thereby lifting that responsibility from enterprises. The key to economic success is twofold: to attack the deep infrastructural problems outlined above and to address social concerns, shifting state support from enterprises and old institutions to individuals. The latter requires getting business out of the social safety net while increasingly removing the state from business activity, thereby significantly improving the effectiveness and efficiency of each. This policy direction is rather unlikely in the near future, however, unless other policies soon produce an economic disaster.

Part of the reason is that the opinion seems to have formed, both in Western and Russian policy, that further radicalization is neither feasible nor desirable. The argument seems to be that the Russian economy, polity, and society cannot withstand the strain that that would impose. This conclusion seems to me to be based on a misreading of the current economic and political situations. The critics of radicalization overestimate the depth of the structural changes that have already taken place or are underway. They also exaggerate the economic content of the dissatisfaction displayed in the December 1993 vote; those candidates explicitly espousing a centrist, moderate reform program (e.g., Civic Union) were all but uniformly rejected. The shift to extremes seems more to reflect an inchoate protest against lawlessness, the collapse of civil order, and the loss of purpose and pride in being Russian. All these sources of dissatisfaction could, indeed must, be addressed in the context and process of a more coherent, thorough transformation toward a modern market economy. The political and social problem is far more a consequence of the failure to consistently address the deep structural and substructural problems inherited from the Soviet system; it is a consequence of too much political compromise in the vain pursuit of social and political stability. It is not too much, but rather insufficiently radical reform that lies at the root of the failures so far. To slow down the changes, to attempt to stabilize the current incoherent and corrupt system, with its inconsistencies and uneven, partial progress, is a recipe for economic deterioration and perhaps even disaster.

The most striking alternative is to step back from "Western-style" reform and look for a unique, Russian "third way" to a (peculiarly Russian?) type of market economy. This takes as given the need to slow down the institutional and structural changes brought about by the reforms, to bring the state back to a stronger guiding role over economic change and development, with significant influence over direct investment, and to provide direct support for productive activities threatened by change. It assumes that monetary and financial considerations can remain secondary to social, structural, and output stability and that direct "non-monetarist" controls can effectively control inflation without disabling the market functions of the price system. The most coherent presentation of this approach appeared in a position paper drawn up by some of Gorbachev's old Academy of Sciences advisors (Leonid Abalkin, Stanislav Shatalin, Nikolai Petrakov, and Yurii Yaremenko) and presented to the government and Duma in January 1994.[74] It was immediately criticized by the reformist press and representatives of the new government as involving too much government regulation and control, particularly of prices. Thus it is unlikely to be adopted as a whole in the near future. Although breathtaking in its misunderstanding of basic economics, this program at least provides a coherently articulated alternative to the further radicalization of economic reform.

The most likely policy path lies in the incoherent middle: muddling along at a slower pace, cushioning or blocking further structural change unless it is explicitly sought by the government, maintaining and even enhancing the existing mechanisms of social support, and resorting to direct controls to deal with uncertainty and undesired changes in the financial sphere. This is claimed to be merely an adjustment in the pace of continuing economic reform in order to reduce its social costs and bring the state back into economic affairs at a level deemed appropriate to the particular culture and circumstances of Russia. In effect, it claims that seasoned (ex-Soviet) managers, if given sufficient power, can ensure greater stability and predictability in the political/economic environment and provide a basis for the controlled renewal of economic growth.[75] The best-case scenario for this approach posits that Chernomyrdin and Gerashchenko are committed reformers who have a deeper practical knowledge of the Russian economy than the reformers who preceded them. They understand the negative effects of the implementation of the reforms and hence how to correct for them. By targeting properly, they can rationalize the structural transformation and reduce its costs, allowing a necessary market infrastructure to develop. Further, they can maintain budgetary and monetary stability at least as well as did the young reformers in 1992–1993. Is this plausible?

This approach is highly unlikely to succeed, although it would undoubtedly generate a temporary and superficial improvement in measured indices of production. This approach forces key decision-makers to operate blindly, uninformed of true economic valuations, opportunities, and opportunity costs. The very interactive mechanisms that generate information crucial to rational economic decision-making would thus be stifled: the current structures of production and social support would be largely frozen in place; price and financial controls would distort or destroy essential valuation information; targeted investment would necessarily be uninformed by considerations of relative value or opportunity costs; "non-monetarist methods" of fighting inflation would again render the ruble less of a true money. Thus this approach would slowly but surely undermine progress toward a market economy. It would shore up now teetering, irrational structures; freeze into place the arbitrage and corruption opportunities of those in power and the mafias who know how to use them; systematically undercut incentives for economically informed production and investment decisions; create a new dependence on vertical administrative structures; kill the key signals required for economically rational restructuring; and require a progressive stifling of initiative and autonomous economic activity, as that would undermine the capability of the state to manage the reform by preempting its resources. Therefore the policy of slow, planned restructuring based on experienced managers' "feel" for the situation must soon go astray as essential market signals are destroyed.

These policy makers honestly believe themselves committed to true economic reform, but they lack understanding of what needs to be done. There is no coherent vision of the end result of reform, no understanding of what a modern market economy looks like and how it functions. The most fundamental issues of money and property are not addressed at all by these policy makers, whose understanding of market infrastructure is purely physical and superficial—banks, computers, telecommunications, etc. They largely ignore the interactions, laws, behaviors, and attitudes that breathe life into those institutions and objects. They also have a naive view of the role of the state and large organizations in a market economy, as they do not understand the critical role of the market environment and other competitive constraints on these economic agents. Thus, as they create structures, laws, and regulations that stifle real market activity and innovations, they will undermine progress in each of the critical areas discussed above: the ruble will become less of a money; property rights will become more tenuous; industrial policy will further entrench the structural problems inherited from the Soviet Union.

The greatest error of those who support such dirigiste economic policies is economic ignorance. They view themselves as economic reformers. But just as Soviet planners thought they were creating economic wealth as they generated massive waste, so these reformers would destroy market reform in the name of saving it. The consequence would most likely be an accelerating (if temporarily hidden) deterioration of performance and a substantial, painful delay in developing a modern market economy.

The Chernomyrdin government has apparently recognized this danger (as of mid-1994) and is refraining from undermining marketization and structural transformation. With a renewed political commitment to reform and economic transformation and an understanding of the obstacles to transformation discussed here, the prospects for recovery in a qualitatively new economic system are good; indeed, recovery and new growth become inevitable. I believe that this economic ignorance, the greatest barrier to both reform and economic prosperity in Russia—and indeed in all the new states of the FSU—will eventually be overcome. Then Russia will be able to take advantage of its vast natural and human resources. With the exception of the Baltic states and for all its problems and political uncertainties, Russia is the most progressive of the former

Soviet states and the most likely to succeed in radical economic transformation.

Notes

1. A thorough survey of the situation can be found in the World Bank report, *The Russian Economy in 1992* (Washington, D.C.: World Bank, 1992).

2. For a discussion of Gorbachev's reforms, see R. Ericson, "Soviet Economic Reforms: The Motivation and Content of Perestroika," *Journal of International Affairs*, Vol. 42, No. 2, Spring 1989; and R. Ericson, *The Soviet Union: 1975–90* (San Francisco: ICS Press, 1990).

3. The program was reportedly written by Yasin and Vasiliev in conjunction with the government economists in April, although it was only published in June 1992.

4. The ten members are Russia, Ukraine, Belarus, Kazakhstan, Uzbekistan, Kyrgyzstan, Tajikistan, Turkmenistan, Armenia, and Azerbaijan (observer status). The five apparently interested in maintaining close economic ties are Russia, Belarus, Kazakhstan, Uzbekistan, and Armenia. On January 22, 1993, they, together with Kyrgyzstan and Tajikistan, agreed to the creation of a CIS bank for payment settlements in order to maintain a common ruble zone of economic activity. Despite a number of summits and many technical meetings, they have been unable to come to a working agreement to allow the bank to begin functioning. Russia issued an ultimatum in June 1993 giving strict conditions under which CIS states would be allowed to remain in the ruble zone. See *RFE/RL Daily Report*, June 16 and June 28, 1993. Six members signed a ruble zone agreement on September 7, indicating the intention to coordinate economic activity under Russian monetary control. Finally, on December 20, 1993, all ten CIS members joined the CIS Settlements Bank, essentially on terms dictated by Russia (see *RFE/RL Daily Report*, September 8 and December 21, 1993).

5. By late 1993, Ukraine had expanded the use of state orders and allocations, enhanced price controls, reimposed mandatory foreign exchange surrender at about one fifth the market rate, and issued credits and subsidies of over 50% of GDP. Ukrainian industrial production was estimated to be down 18% and GDP down 20.5% in 1993 (see *The Economist*, November 20, 1993, pp. 58–59).

6. In 1993, of course, many dramatic political confrontations arose between President Boris Yeltsin and the Soviet-era Congress of People's Deputies and Supreme Soviet (see Chapter 1). The confrontations contributed to policy immobility and confusion, as well as to the failure to deal with the deep structural problems standing in the way of successful reform and a transition to a market system.

7. Only Turkmenistan seems to have avoided economic turmoil, maintaining its Soviet structures and standard of living by exploiting its vast natural (especially energy) resources and by continuing a special relationship with Russia. It relies on Russia for security and most imports, while selling resources abroad at world market prices.

8. The resignations in January 1994 of Yegor Gaidar and Boris Fedorov, the architects and prime movers of Yeltsin's 1992 economic reforms, coupled with

Chernomyrdin's statements about the "end of the period of market romanticism" and intended use of "non-monetarist methods" to fight inflation, seemed at the time to herald the clear change in policy direction (see *RFE/RL Daily Report*, January 17, 21, 25, and 26, 1994).

9. For a journalistic discussion, see *The Economist*, January 30, 1993, p. 47. Paul Goble of the Carnegie Endowment reports that some 14,000 local regulations directly contradicted central legislation in early 1993.

10. This is evident from the tone of the weekly discussions in *Ekonomika i zhizn'*. Also see the report on Siberia in *The Economist*, June 19, 1993, and on the regions in *The Economist*, March 27, 1993.

11. The constitution still gives republics substantially greater rights than other regions, although minimal central prerogatives for a unitary central state are preserved. Yeltsin, however, still is giving republics such as Sakha and Tatarstan special treatment that is apt to aggravate tension with other regions. (See *RFE/RL Daily Report*, October 27, 1993, on the tax agreement with Yakutia-Sakha, and *RFE/RL Daily Report*, February 16 and 24, 1994, on the new interstate treaty between Russia and Tatarstan.)

12. There was a major report in *Izvestiia* on January 26, 1994, on the strength of the mafias and their relationship to existing power structures.

13. For example, a new business still requires myriad "permissions" rather than being automatically registered on the initiative of the entrepreneur. Without these "permissions," there is no protection from criminal elements or the rapacity of local and central officials.

14. Corruption and organized criminal activity are a marginal part of every market economy and indeed can continue to play a significant role, as evidenced by Italy and Japan. In general, the larger the role of the state, the greater the opportunity, and hence the greater the incidence of corruption in any democratic market economy.

15. The State Statistical Committee report on economic performance for 1992 was published in *Ekonomika i zhizn'*, No. 4, February 1993, pp. 13–15. The report on performance for 1993 was published in *Ekonomika i zhizn'*, No. 6, February 1994, pp. 7–9. Unless otherwise noted, all statistics cited come from these reports.

16. Of course, many in the last category are employed in the still very poorly measured private and quasi-private sectors, making it hard to interpret these figures. Furthermore, many of the employed and unemployed are holding other (sometimes temporary) jobs, "off the books."

17. The official statistical report cited above gives the deficit as over 5.1% of GDP. *The Economist*, May 1, 1993, gives four percent, based on authoritative Russian statements, while the International Business Academy in Moscow (V. Popov) calculates it at five percent. These figures ignore debt service expenditures while including foreign lending as revenues, add the pension fund to the revenue side, and ignore part of the ruble emission made to cover excess expenditures (see V. Popov et al., *The Russian Economy in 1993: Forecasts and Annual Survey of 1992* (Middlebury: Geonomics, 1993), pp. 13–15.

18. For a first report, see *New York Times*, April 11, 1993. More details are given in *RFE/RL Daily Report*, April 13 and 20, and May 24 and 26, 1993. For example,

the RCB agreed to reduce credit emission to 3 trillion rubles in the second quarter of 1993 from 11–13 trillion rubles in the first quarter.

19. Figures are from the RCB and Ministry of Finance 1994 budget statement. (See *RFE/RL Daily Report*, January 26 and March 3, 1994.)

20. "Enterprise funds" *(beznalichnye)* are accounting entries in the books of the banking system that are not generally convertible into cash and can only be used for specifically authorized purposes, e.g. energy purchases or intermediate input purchases. They are non-cash monetary circuit, whilr cash *(nalichnye)* forms the other circuit. The two circuits were strictly separate in the Soviet system.

21. These figures were compiled from the State Statistical Committee's short statistical reports, "Facts and Figures," in *Ekonomika i zhizn'*, Nos. 14, 16, April 1993.

22. This history is followed closely in the *RFE/RL Daily Report* and in *Kommersant*. For an interesting summary evaluation, see Y. Gaidar, "Novyi kurs," *Izvestiia*, February 10, 1994.

23. The last figure comes from *RFE/RL Daily Report*, January 28, 1993. For a detailed discussion of the problem of interenterprise debt, see B. Ickes and R. Ryterman, "The Interenterprise Arrears Crisis in Russia," *Post-Soviet Affairs*, Vol. 8, No. 4 (1992),pp. 331–61.

24. The figures come from statements by B. Fedorov on May 21 and June 7, as reported in the *RFE/RL Daily Report*, May 24 and June 8, 1993. A new bankruptcy law went into effect in March 1993, and the Ministry of Finance has been pressuring the RCB to enforce it on those who do not or cannot pay their debts.

25. *RFE/RL Daily Report*, February 22, 1994.

26. *RFE/RL Daily Report*, October 20, 1993. There is also an interesting discussion in each of the first four issues of *Kommersant* in 1994.

27. The rate of inflation during one week in January 1993 reportedly topped 55% at a monthly rate (*The Wall Street Journal*, January 21, 1993). This marked the peak in inflation through the first half of 1993. (See *RFE/RL Daily Report*, June 9 and 25, 1993. Also see the Goskomstat annual report for 1993.)

28. Even in 1992, if one excludes the initial jump in prices in the immediate wake of liberalization in January, consumer incomes seem on average to have increased faster than the price level. This was argued by Mario Blejer, a World Bank economist, in a UN seminar on May 25, 1993 and seems supported by recent research of independent Russian economists (e.g., see *Argumenty i fakty*, June 25, 1993).

29. For a full discussion of Soviet money, banking, and finance, see G. Garvy, *Money, Financial Flows, and Credit in the Soviet Union* (Cambridge: Ballinger, 1977). A discussion of its natural role in the command economy can be found in R. Ericson, "The Classical Soviet-Type Economy: Nature of the System and Implications for Reform," *Journal of Economic Perspectives*, Vol. 5, No. 4, Fall 1991, pp. 11–27, and in the references therein.

30. For more on the settlement structure and interenterprise debt, see J. Sachs, D. Lipton, "Remaining Steps to Achieve a Market-Based Monetary System," in *Changing the Economic System in Russia*, ed. A. Aslund and R. Layard (London: Pinter, 1993), pp. 127–62; and Ickes and Ryterman, "Interenterprise Arrears Crisis."

31. On CIS interstate debt, see *Kommersant*, No. 8, 1993; and A. Aslund, "Economic Developments in Russia," in *Russia, Ukraine, and the U.S. Response*, ed. D. Clark (Queenstowne: M. Aspin Institute, 1993), pp. 13–21.

32. This reform was extensively covered in the Western press. See, for example, *The Wall Street Journal* and *New York Times*, July 25–27, 1993.

33. On September 23, 1993, nine of the CIS states signed an economic union agreement; Georgia joined at the end of 1993, and Ukraine chose to become an associate of the union. Only Turkmenistan has chosen to avoid entanglement, relying on its natural wealth and special relationship with Russia (see *RFE/RL Daily Report*, September 24, 1993).

34. For example, in June 1993 Kaliningrad oblast suspended federation customs laws as violating the rights of the locally declared free-trade zone (*The Wall Street Journal*, June 25, 1993, p. A8).

35. By the end of August 1993, thirty regions and republics were withholding taxes (see *Nezavisimaia gazeta*, September 1, 1993). In late October, Yakutia cut a special tax deal, while new sanctions were placed on others for tax evasion by presidential decree (see *RFE/RL Daily Report*, October 27 and 28, 1993).

36. Such behavior was a frequent topic of economic roundtables in *Ekonomika i zhizn'* in 1992 and early 1993. In early 1992, barter covered over a third of the turnover of ferric metals and industrial machinery and equipment, a quarter of coal shipments, and almost a fifth of processed metals (see *Ekonomika i zhizn'*, No. 14, April 1993, p. 1). Estimates of the loss of foreign exchange range up to $15 billion in 1992 (see Deutsche Bank, *Focus on Eastern Europe*, 30 January 1993) and another $14–15 billion in 1993 (*Kommersant*, No. 1, 1994).

37. Blejer claimed that as much as 70% of intra-industry trade in Russia was on a dollar basis by mid-April 1993 (informal seminar at the United Nations Economic and Social Commission of the General Assembly, May 25, 1993).

38. Moneyness is that bundle of attributes that make a currency or form of payment a full money, including fungibility, durability, and general acceptability.

39. For more discussion, see R. Ericson, "Soviet Economic Structure and the National Question," in *The Post-Soviet Nations*, ed. A. Motyl (New York: Columbia University Press, 1992), pp. 240–271.

40. This illusion rests on the mistaken belief that wealth resides in the resources themselves (and hence can be seized), rather than in their best economic use by agents free to pursue the maximization of wealth—i.e., to explore and discover the best among alternative uses.

41. These events are reported in the July 17, 1993 issue of *The Economist*, pp. 47–48.

42. See *RFE/RL Daily Report*, February 16, 1994. The new Sverdlovsk legislature, however, seems to want to revive the Urals Republic; see *RFE/RL Daily Report*, March 2, 1994.

43. This has received particular attention in the aftermath of the December 1993 elections, in which right-wing electoral success was based in part on successfully tying reform to criminal activity. See the articles in *Izvestiia*, January 26, 1994, and *The Economist*, February 19, 1994, pp. 57–58.

44. "Destatization" is the reduction of the direct role of state agencies and organizations in controlling economic activity.

45. This is the theme of the survey article "Ekonomika nestiazhatel'stva," in *Kommersant*, No. 1, 1994, pp. 37–42.

46. For an early discussion, see J. Sachs and D. Lipton, "Prospects for Russia's Economic Reforms," *Brookings Papers on Economic Activity*, No. 2, 1992, pp. 213–265 (it actually appeared in spring 1993); and M. Boycko, A. Shleifer, and R.W. Vishny, "Privatizing Russia," *Brookings Papers on Economic Activity*, No. 2, 1993.

47. See *RFE/RL Daily Report*, April 1, 1993 and March 7, 1994.

48. After rapidly falling in value during the first four months of 1993, the ruble stabilized at around 1000 per dollar in May to September, when the disbanding of parliament precipitated a political crisis. It then jumped to over 1200/dollar, stabilized at that level through the elections, then jumped to 1500/dollar before falling back to the vicinity of 1400/dollar (see *Kommersant*, No. 2, 1994).

49. The numbers are from the official statistical sources cited above. An unknown but probably sizable portion of this growth was from the legitimization of already existing second-economy operations. In particular, a large number of trading cooperatives seem to be of this origin.

50. It is interesting to note that the areas with the least structural change were national regions in which the eponymous national group was asserting autonomy within or independence from the Russian Federation. Thus Chechnia-Ingushetia, Tatarstan, Komi, Marii-El, Kalmykia, and Yakutia were the slowest to carry out privatization of any sort and had done the least by mid–1992 (see "Survey of Russia," *The Economist*, December 5, 1992, p. 24).

51. The most recent information comes from the official statistical report on the first quarter of 1993, cited above, and a report by A.B. Chubais and M.D. Vishnevskaia on privatization in 1993 to the Conference on the Economic Transformation in Russia, Stockholm School of Economics, June 1993. For a definitive study of the Russian privatization program, its laws and decrees, and its implementation to September 1992, see R. Frydman, A. Rapaczynski, J.S. Earle, et al., *The Privatization Process in Russia, Ukraine and the Baltic States* (London: Central European University Press, 1993), pp. 1–82.

52. Whatever the political motivations, or fears of "de-industrialization," this behavior was clearly economically irresponsible; it only added to macroeconomic chaos and inflation without doing anything constructive about the problems of capital and industrial structure, which it presumably was intended to address. The Russian fear of destroying "the industrial base" lies in a profound misunderstanding of basic economics, which prevents them from taking the appropriate legal and microeconomic measures to deal with the underlying problem.

53. This point is also made in M. Ellman, "Shock Therapy in Russia: Failure or Partial Success," *RFE/RL Research Report*, Vol. 1, No. 34, pp. 48–61.

54. See the study of Russian privatization in Frydman, Rapaczynski, Earle, Chapter 2. Some more recent discussion is contained in Boycko, Shleifer, and Vishny.

55. The clearest example is in the military conversion program implementing a presidential decree of March 1992; it essentially provides open-ended subsidies to the producers in the military-industrial complex as they search (in principle) for anything marketable that they can produce.

56. The resources tied up in supporting military industry are a clear example but represent only the tip of the iceberg; most civil industry, construction, transportation, agriculture, etc. is similarly inefficient and wasteful, if in varying degrees, due to the irrational structure of factor use and economic interactions. That is the most direct and visible legacy of Soviet socialism.

57. This problem was aggravated by the artificial shortages of rubles and credit at various times in the different circuits shortages that disrupted even traditional transactions. Shortages resulted from an underestimation of the price increases that liberalization provoked in the environment of extreme structural distortion and absence of a real money.

58. As Ickes and Ryterman note, receivables were more valuable than payment in full, as the latter had to be used to cover debts while the former could be borrowed against to make wage payments. Ickes and Ryterman, "Interenterprise Arrears Crisis."

59. The right to full and free sale of land was decreed by Yeltsin in December 1993 and is also (more vaguely) guaranteed in the new constitution. But the mechanisms for the assertion, transfer, and protection of title are yet to be established and exercised. For the decree, see *Ekonomika i zhizn'*, December 1993.

60. Without legally protected property rights, private economic activity acquires many of the characteristics of illegal activity, needing protection and depending on the good will of bureaucrats and the politically powerful for its continued existence.

61. This problem both aggravates and is exacerbated by political uncertainty. Will the reform regime last? Are its changes permanent? Without real property rights, however, even the most stable reform regime will fail to achieve true market-based recovery and growth. The picture is even cloudier with a regime as uncertainly committed to marketizing reform as Chernomyrdin's in early 1994.

62. While it is hard to sort out financial data in the current severely distorted value environment of Russia, it is clear that many enterprises cannot survive at any near opportunity cost (in some cases, world market) prices and capital and land valuations, regardless of the apparent great need for their product. The problem is deeply structural, independent of current financial results. For evidence on the smaller but structurally identical problem in Eastern Europe, see P. Hare and G. Hughes, "Competitiveness and Industrial Restructuring in Czechoslovakia, Hungary and Poland," *CEPR Discussion Paper No. 543*, April 1991. For statistics and a discussion of value destruction in Russian industry, see C. Senik-Leygonie and G. Hughes, "Industrial Profitability and Trade among the Former Soviet Republics," *Economic Policy*, October 1992, pp. 354–386; and J. Thornton, "Structural Change and Integration of the Soviet Far East into the World Market: The Case of Negative Value Added," manuscript, Department of Economics, University of Washington, 1991.

63. This is of course partly a function of the serious undervaluing of the ruble in exchanges, in large part due to its lack of moneyness. It is also an overstatement, as such selling would depress world market prices for those resources—a significant part of world demand for those resources is after all from Russia.

64. Senik-Leygonie and Hughes, "Industrial Profitability." The point is also argued in Lipton and Sachs.

65. *RFE/RL Daily Report*, December 12, 1992, and *Financial Times*, February 10, 1994. Of course, as noted above, financial results mean little in the current environment, although the ubiquity of potential failure after full price liberalization indicates a deep and substantial problem.

66. These include illegal second economy and newer mafia economic activities and structures that use extralegal means to acquire and secure resources at the expense of new private activity that is wholly legal.

67. Reported in the Western press—e.g., *The Wall Street Journal*, March 4, 1994.

68. For the most recent presidential decrees and an economic commentary, see *Kommersant*, No. 3, 1994, pp. 53–54.

69. The law was published in *Ekonomika i zhizn'*, No. 1, 1993, pp. 18–20. For an excellent study of what any bankruptcy law must do, see P. Aghion, O. Hart and J. Moore, "The Economics of Bankruptcy Reform, *Journal of Law, Economics, and Organization*, Vol. 8, No. 3, pp. 523–46. The failure to deal adequately with ownership is part of the explanation for its slow and incomplete application through the first quarter of 1994.

70. Unfortunately, the state still does not see the protection of private business as a primary responsibility. As noted in *The Economist*, February 19, 1994, police feel that they should provide "no special protection for the rich" (p. 58).

71. For a number of examples, see "Russia Reborn," *The Economist*, December 5, 1992. *The Wall Street Journal* also regularly carries examples of (at least temporarily) successful conversions.

72. According to the report for 1993, about 80% of real investment credit came from financial intermediaries.

73. The composition of these bodies may reflect more the attitudes of the old Soviet elites who have remained politically active than those involved in creating new economic institutions. Still, it seems clear that they reflect a general, to some extent inchoate dissatisfaction with the overall socio-political-economic situation after two years of "reform."

74. Discussions appeared in *Izvestiia*, January 29, 1994, *Kommersant*, No. 4, February 1994, and *Financial Times*, January 31, 1994.

75. This is in effect a claim of the primacy of politics over economic fundamentals; where there is a will, competent leaders with sufficient power can always achieve the goal.

3

Nationalism, Regionalism, and Federalism: Center-Periphery Relations in Post-Communist Russia

Gail W. Lapidus and Edward W. Walker

The centrifugal forces set in motion by Gorbachev's reforms not only precipitated the breakup of the Soviet Union but now threaten—at least in the view of many Russian and Western observers—to bring about the disintegration of Russia itself. Nevertheless, the regionalist and nationalist challenges confronting Russia have a rather different character from those that confronted Gorbachev, and they have until now elicited a less confrontational response from the Yeltsin government. In this chapter, we will examine the factors impelling and constraining political mobilization by ethnic and regional groups in Russia. Rejecting an overly determinist view of Russia's political future, we will consider in particular Moscow's ability to manage the political challenges from Russia's provinces by devolving economic and political power downward to governments in the regions and republics.

The Soviet Legacy

Soviet strategy for managing a multinational state involved built-in tensions whose explosive potential became manifest as a result of the Gorbachev reforms. In particular, the design of the Soviet state as a feder-

The authors would like to thank Sergei Arutiunov, Leokadia Drobizheva, John Dunlop, Gregory Grossman, Gavin Helf, David Hooson, Andrei Melville, Blair Ruble, Lilia Shevtsova, Galina Starovoitova, and Carol Timko for their helpful comments on earlier drafts of this chapter.

ation of ethno-territorial "union republics" that were, symbolically if not in fact, national states, both reified nationality as a central aspect of individual identity and created a setting in which liberalization would catalyze ethno-national mobilization.[1]

The position of Russia within this federation, however, was an anomalous one. On the one hand, Russia was the imperial center, and Russians were the beneficiaries of this position.[2] At the same time, the conflation of Russia with the Union deprived Russia of both the institutional and the cultural attributes of national statehood.[3] The dissolution of the Soviet Union—initially at least a liberating event for most of the non-Russian successor states—was traumatic for Russia and led to a bitter debate over who was to blame for the loss of empire. It also confronted Russia's political elite with a need to construct a new post-imperial, Russian identity.

Two features of Gorbachev's reforms played a critical role in the emergence of nationalism as a powerful political force in the *perestroika* period: the de-legitimation of Communist Party elites as a consequence of *glasnost* and democratization, and the deliberate as well as unintended process of resource redistribution brought about by Gorbachev's economic reforms. *Glasnost* unleashed a far-reaching competition for power and a simultaneous effort at re-legitimation in which nationalist ideology played a major role. Democratization in turn impelled republic elites to seek increased economic autonomy, thereby placing property rights—collective as well as individual—at the center of contestation.

Indeed, the dynamics of these processes are by now familiar. *Glasnost* led to cognitive liberation, which in turn meant that Soviet policy was subjected to growing critical scrutiny as well as the development of alternative cultural, economic, and political agendas. As the boundaries of permitted sociopolitical activism were gradually broadened, new political movements emerged—with the People's Fronts of the Baltic republics in the lead—that gave expression to the demand for national revival as a central component of reform. At the same time, democratization and partially competitive elections at both local and national levels created new legislatures that no longer served as mere rubber stamps for the Communist Party. Insisting that Soviet federalism be reformulated, political elites in the fifteen union republics grew increasingly assertive in their demands for greater autonomy from Moscow and centralized Soviet power. In some cases, these elites were responding to popular pressures for national sovereignty; in others, they sought merely to increase their own power and prerogatives.

Gorbachev's failure to respond promptly and effectively to the rapidly evolving situation only further weakened the central government's authority. So too did the growing challenge from the Russian Federation under the leadership of Boris Yeltsin.

Ironically, the immediate intent of the leaders of the attempted coup of August 1991 was to put a decisive end to the wrangling between the central Soviet government and the union republics by preventing the planned signing of a new Union Treaty. While the defenders of the Treaty hoped that it would preserve the territorial integrity of the USSR, the coup leaders feared that the Treaty would so weaken the Soviet center that the federal government would be powerless. In fact, however, it was the failed coup itself that doomed the Union. It was followed by the peaceful dissolution of the USSR in December 1991 and the emergence of fifteen newly independent states, among which Russia occupied the dominant position.

It soon became clear, however, that the centrifugal forces that split the Soviet Union were not confined to the union republics. Rather they extended to the administrative units within the union republics as well. Political weakness and economic chaos were contributing to a snowballing process of state-formation by ever smaller ethnic groups and regions.

The task of building a new system of state power, both vertically and horizontally, was made even more difficult by two additional features of the Soviet system: the extreme degree of centralized political power at the federal center, and the control of all aspects of economic as well as political life (including control over the military and security establishments) by the Communist Party. The void created by the disintegration of the Party as a nation-wide institution led to a rapid and uncontrolled fragmentation of power and the de facto autonomy of local economic, political, and military actors.

Both the structure and the boundaries of the new Russian state soon became contested. A variety of political groups, including former Communists and extreme nationalists, refused to accept either the abolition of the Soviet Union or the internationally-recognized borders of the new Russian state. In other instances, they laid claim to territories and populations beyond those borders. At the same time, various ethnically-defined administrative areas within the Russian Federation, including Tatarstan, Yakutia, Tyva and Checheno-Ingushetia, among others, not only asserted their own sovereignty but in some cases threatened outright secession.

The Impact of the Soviet Collapse on the Russian Federation

The role of the RSFSR in accelerating the dissolution of the Soviet Union had far-reaching consequences for state building in postcommunist Russia. In early 1990, Boris Yeltsin—who was then attempting to build an independent political base in the RSFSR to challenge Gorbachev and the old center—declared his support not only for Russian sovereignty but for the renegotiation of relations between the RSFSR's central government and the governments of the ethnically-defined autonomous areas within Russia as well. Drawing on the views of leading figures in democratic circles at the time—including Andrei Sakharov, Galina Starovoitova, and Viktor Palme—he responded to demands for greater rights from local governments by championing a doctrine of sovereignty "from the ground up," in which "the lowest government unit, closest to the people in villages or towns, delegates power to the next highest level, then to the republic parliament, then to the national parliament."[4]

Yeltsin's radical challenge to the Gorbachev regime won him a seat in the new USSR Congress of People's Deputies in March 1989, the RSFSR parliament a year later, and the chairmanship of the RSFSR Supreme Soviet in June 1990. On June 12, 1990, the new RSFSR parliament, following the lead of the Baltic republics, issued its own Declaration of State Sovereignty, asserting that the RSFSR had "complete authority... in resolving all questions relating to state and public life with the exception of those which it voluntarily hands over to USSR jurisdiction." It also asserted the "primacy of the RSFSR Constitution and RSFSR laws throughout the territory of the RSFSR," and stipulated that the "Congress of People's Deputies confirms the need to broaden substantially the rights of autonomous republics, autonomous *oblasts*, and autonomous *okrugs*, along with RSFSR *krais* and *oblasts*."[5]

This declaration had a far-reaching significance for the fate of the Soviet Union, as well as for the future development of Russia itself. By clearly dissociating the Russian state from the Soviet Union, and by identifying Russia with the other 14 members of the Union as equals, it not only attempted to define a new non-imperial Russian identity but also helped legitimate the sovereignty aspirations of the other union republics.

In leading the struggle for Russian sovereignty, Yeltsin adopted a complex political strategy. To compensate for the weakness of the democratic reformers in the central institutions of Soviet power, he resorted to a "horizontal" strategy that promoted ties among the republics that would curtail the center's powers. Yeltsin's personal struggle for power against Gorbachev was thus entwined with a broader institutional conflict between republic-based and central institutions. As RSFSR deputy Galina Starovoitova put it:

> The conflict between Yeltsin and Gorbachev is not simply a dispute between two men who do not like each other. There is an objective historical basis for the conflict: a clash of two opposing tendencies—namely, the striving of Russia to find its sovereignty and the striving of an empire to

preserve its former might. The president of the USSR, who does not have his own territorial domain inside the huge country, is, with the loss of power in Russia, in effect losing his power. For this reason, he naturally seeks to obstruct the growing sovereignization of the republics. [6]

Yeltsin's position was highly controversial, however, even in reformist circles. Initially, the "national question" was largely ignored by both Russian reformers and Party elites. Reformers, however, began to support national movements because of their desire for a Union-wide reformist coalition. Deeply ambivalent about the concept of national rights, their ambivalence toward their new partners increased as it became clear that the goal of many national movements was independence rather than reform. Moreover, the strong statist sentiments expressed by non-Russian leaders contributed to anxiety that espousal of the right to national self-determination could be directed not only against the USSR but also Russia. If Russia is only one of the [union] republics, Aleksandr Tsipko warned in early 1991,

> then it in no way differs from Tatarstan, Bashkiriya, and Dagestan. As a result, the stronger the striving of the RSFSR to free itself from the center, the stronger will be the desire of the autonomous formations to free themselves from Yeltsin. And in their own way, they are right. The relationship of "Russia to the autonomies" is constructed on the same principle as that of "the Union to the RSFSR." The election of a president of the RSFSR will produce a "domino effect."[7]

Indeed, within months of the Russian republic's declaration of sovereignty, every one of the autonomous republics within the Russian Federation would follow suit.

From the summer of 1990 through the end of 1991, Yeltsin sought the backing of the autonomies for his intensifying struggle with Gorbachev and the Soviet center by repeatedly promising support for their sovereignty and autonomy. Most notably, during a three-week trip in August and September 1990 that took him to Tatarstan, Bashkiria, and the Komi Autonomous Republic, he told local elites to "take all the sovereignty you can swallow," although he added they would be better off sticking with the RSFSR government in opposition to Gorbachev and the old center.[8]

His position began to change, however, after he entered into serious negotiations with Gorbachev over a new USSR Union Treaty late in the spring of 1991. By then, a growing number of RSFSR autonomies were demanding the enhancement of their status (i.e., from autonomous republics to full union republics, and from autonomous *oblasts* and autonomous *okrugs* to autonomous republics). Tatarstan's leaders were particularly outspoken, demanding that Tatarstan be a signatory to the Union Treaty with equal status to the RSFSR.[9] Tatarstan, they argued, had been arbitrarily denied union republic status by Stalin because it lacked external borders.[10] Tatarstan, Checheno-Ingushetia, North Ossetia, and Tyva refused to attach a question on the creation of a Russian presidency to the March 1991 referendum on the preservation of the Union. Hoping to maintain a united front against the center, Yeltsin resisted these demands even as Gorbachev and Soviet conservatives encouraged the localities to intensify their challenges to the Russian government.

Eventually, however, a compromise was worked out at a May 12, 1991, meeting between Yeltsin, Gorbachev, and the heads of the Supreme Soviets of fourteen of the fifteen RSFSR autonomous republics. The sovereignty of the autonomous republics was reaffirmed, and it was agreed that they would sign the Union Treaty as members of the USSR and the RSFSR.[11] Nevertheless, Tatarstan's leadership refused to support voting in the RSFSR presidential elections in June, and as a result, turnout in Tatarstan was only 36.6%, less than half the 75% figure for the RSFSR as a whole.

Relations between the RSFSR government and the autonomies deteriorated further after the failed August coup, particularly in those areas where local leaders had sided with the putschists. Indeed, Moscow democrats were convinced that an alliance was forming between the local *nomenklatura* and Soviet conservatives. On August 26, 1991, Ruslan I. Khasbulatov, Yeltsin's replacement as RSFSR Supreme Soviet Chairman, warned that Moscow might dissolve the legislatures in those autonomies that had supported the coup, specifically citing the three republics that were the most assertive advocates of sovereignty and autonomy—Tatarstan, Checheno-Ingushetia, and North Ossetia. Although no action was taken, relations with the autonomies worsened.

As the failure of Gorbachev's effort to preserve the Union became clear, officials in the autonomies became increasingly convinced that the principal challenge to local autonomy came from Yeltsin and "democrats" in the Russian government, not from Gorbachev and the dying Soviet center. These concerns intensified in the fall, after Dzhokhar Dudaev came to power as leader of Checheno-Ingushetia. Yeltsin reacted by declaring a state of emergency and ordering the dispatch of troops to the rebellious autonomous republic to enforce the Russian Constitution. Although these decisions were quickly reversed, officials in the autonomies saw them as a challenge to their sovereignty.

As Russia approached independence at the end of 1991, it was already confronting serious challenges to central authority from numerous regions around the country. Moreover, the absence of a unifying national ethos for Russia in the moral vacuum left by communism, along with the ambiguity of Russian statehood rooted in the Tsarist and Soviet imperial past, was already leading to a widespread sense of angst among Russian intellectuals, including many putative democrats. As Andranik Migranian argued, Yeltsin's doctrine of "sovereignty from the ground up" threatened to undermine Russia's territorial integrity as much as the USSR's:

> Our attempts to create all state institutions from scratch on a contractual basis are attempts to put into effect yet another grandiose utopia. ... The bomb planted under the USSR by the declaration of Russian sovereignty is, it seems to me, facilitating not only the destruction of the USSR but also—to an even greater extent—the destruction of Russia itself. ... Where are the geographical boundaries of the republic that is supposed to represent ethnic Russians?"[12]

The widespread anxiety about Russia's future at the time was expressed by the title of an article by a leading Russian specialist on nationality issues—"Will Russia Repeat the Path of the Union?"[13]

Russia's Federation Structure at Independence

Russia's growing center-periphery problems at the time of independence were in significant degree a legacy of the federal structure inherited from the Soviet era. The 1918 Constitution of the Russian Soviet Federated Socialist Republic (RSFSR) had characterized the new state as a "free union of free nations, a federation of Soviet national republics."[14] However, Russia's "federalism" was essentially administrative and formal, with its constituent parts lacking constitutionally protected autonomous powers.[15] It also had some peculiar features. Although it was formally a federation, it lacked even the window dressing of a federation treaty, unlike the USSR. And in contrast with the other union republics, Russia also lacked its own separate Communist Party organization, Academy of Sciences, television and radio stations. And finally, unlike the USSR, Czechoslovakia, or Yugoslavia, its ethnically-defined units encompassed less than half the territory of the country, forming distinct ethnic "islands" within the Federation.

The formal structure of hierarchical relations within the RSFSR distinguished between five types of administrative-territorial units, each with somewhat different rights. These units included forty-nine non-ethnically defined *oblasts* (provinces), six *krais*, and thirty-one ethnically-defined "autonomous" areas; sixteen of the latter were autonomous republics, five were autonomous *oblasts*, and ten were autonomous *okrugs* (Map 3.1).[16] These thirty-one "autonomies" (*avtonomii*) were located in four broad regions—the North Caucasus, the central Volga-

Map 3.1: The Russian Federation, 1993

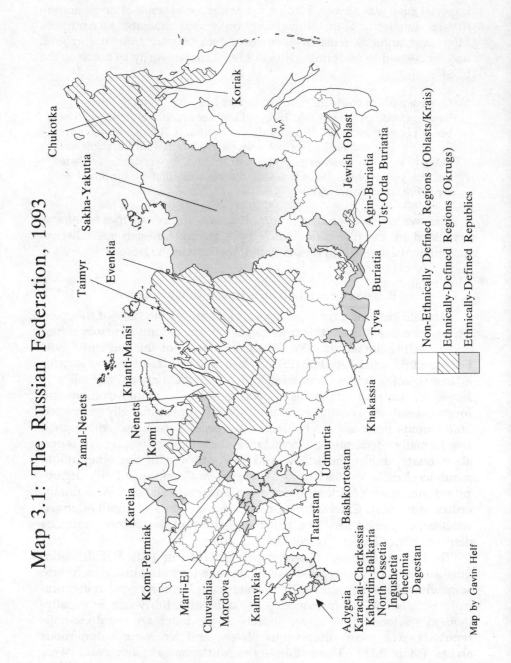

Non-Ethnically Defined Regions (Oblasts/Krais)

Ethnically-Defined Regions (Okrugs)

Ethnically-Defined Republics

Chukotka

Koriak

Sakha-Yakutia

Jewish Oblast

Agin-Buriatia

Ust-Orda Buriatia

Buriatia

Taimyr

Evenkia

Tyva

Khakassia

Khanti-Mansi

Yamal-Nenets

Nenets

Komi

Udmurtia

Karelia

Bashkortostan

Komi-Permiak

Tatarstan

Marii-El

Chuvashia

Mordova

Kalmykia

Adygeia

Karachai-Cherkessia

Kabardin-Balkaria

North Ossetia

Ingushetia

Chechnia

Dagestan

Map by Gavin Helf

Urals region, along the border with Mongolia, and, with one major interruption, along the northern rim of the country running from Karelia in the west to the Chukchi Autonomous Okrug in the east.

In 1991, an important modification was made to the RSFSR's administrative-territorial hierarchy, a change that would later be codified in the Federation Treaty of March 1992 and the constitution ratified in December 1993. The sixteen autonomous republics and four of the five autonomous *oblasts* were given the status of "republics," while the other sixty-six "subjects of the federation"—the forty-nine *oblasts*, seven *krais*, the "federal cities" of Moscow and St. Petersburg, the Jewish Autonomous Oblast, and ten autonomous *okrugs*—became known as "regions."[17] (See Table 3.1.)

A number of demographic factors make Russia less vulnerable to fragmentation along ethnic lines than were the former USSR, Yugoslavia, or Czechoslovakia. Despite Russia's complex federal structure, by world standards the country is ethnically rather homogeneous. Russians made up 81.5% of the total population of 147.4 million in 1989. Moreover, the ethnically defined republics are, with few exceptions, sparsely populated and contained only 15.7% of the federation's total population in 1989 (see Map 3.2).

In addition, not only is the total population of the republics relatively small, but the titular nationality is a majority in only five of the twenty-one (Chechnia, Chuvashia, North Ossetia, Tyva, and Ingushetia).[18] Russians, on the other hand, make up an absolute majority in nine (Adygeia, Buriatia, Altai, Karelia, Khakassia, Komi, Mordova, Sakha-Yakutia, and Udmurtia) and a plurality in another three (Bashkortostan, Karachai-Cherkessia, and Marii-El).

Moreover, the federation's minority peoples are extremely diverse. The largest minority, the Tatars, constituted only 3.8% of Russia's total population in 1989 (even though 5.5 million is nevertheless a comparatively large number for an ethnic group lacking a state); the second largest minority, the Ukrainians, made up only 3.0% of the total population (and lacked a separate "homeland" in the federation); and the third largest, the Chuvash, made up only 1.2%. No other minority constituted even one percent. (See Table 3.2.)

Finally, with the exception of the Tyvinians, and arguably the Tatars and some of the peoples of the North Caucasus, Russia's minorities lack a credible experience of independent statehood.

Challenges from the Republics

Despite its relative ethnic homogeneity, at the time of the Soviet collapse the Russian Federation faced many of the same fissiparous pres-

TABLE 3.1 Population of the Autonomous Areas of the RSFR (1989)

	Peoples	Total Population	Percent of Total	Percent Russian
Republics (21)[a]				
Adygeia	Adyge	432,046	22.1	68.0
Bashkiria	Bashkir	3,943,113	21.9	39.3
Buriatia	Buriat	1,038,252	24.0	70.0
Checheno/ Ingushetia	Chechen Ingush	1,270,429	57.8	23.1
Chuvashia	Chuvash	1,338,023	68.7	26.7
Dagestan	Avar	1,802,188	27.5	9.2
	Agul		0.8	
	Dargin		15.6	
	Kumyk		12.9	
	Lak		5.1	
	Lezgin		11.3	
	Nogai		1.6	
	Rutul		0.8	
	Tabasaran		4.3	
	Tsakhur		0.3	
Gorno-Altai	Altai	190,831	31.2	60.4
Kabardino- Balkaria	Kabard Balkar	753,531	48.2 9.4	32.0
Kalmykia	Kalmyk	322,579	45.4	37.7
Karachai- Cherkessia	Karachai Cherkass	414,970	31.2 9.7	42.4
Karelia	Karelian	790,150	10.0	73.6
Khakassia	Khakass	566,861	11.1	79.5
Komi	Komi	1,250,847	23.3	57.7
Marii	Marii	749,332	43.3	47.5
Mordova	Mordvinian	963,504	32.5	60.8
North Ossettia	Ossetian	632,428	53.0	29.9
Tatar	Tatar	3,641,742	48.5	43.3
Tuva	Tuvinian	308,557	64.3	32.0
Udmurtia	Udmurt	1,605,663	30.9	58.9
Yakutia	Yakut	1,094,065	33.4	50.3
TOTAL		23,109,111		

TABLE 3.1

	Peoples	Total Population	Percent of Total	Percent Russian
Autonomous Oblasts (1)				
Jewish	Jew	214,085	4.2	83.2
Autonomous Okrugs (10)				
Aga Buriatia	Buriat	77,188	54.9	40.8
Chukotka	Chukchi	163,934	7.3	66.1
Evenkia	Evenk	24,769	14.0	67.5
Komi-Permiakia	Komi Permiak	158,526	60.2	36.1
Koriakia	Koriak	39,940	16.5	62.0
Khanty-Mansi	Khant Mansi	1,282,396	0.9	66.3
Nenets	Nenets	53,912	11.9	65.8
Taimyr	Dolgan Nenets	55,803	8.9 4.8	67.1
Ust-Ordin Buriatia	Buriat	135,870	36.3	56.5
Yamal-Nenets	Nenets	494,844	4.2	59.2
TOTAL		2,487,182		
GRAND TOTAL		25,810,378		

[a] Many of the former autonomies have since renamed themselves. Russia's December 1993 Constitution lists the republics as follows: the Republic of Adygeia (Adygeia); the Republic of Altai; the Republic of Bashkortostan; the Republic of Buriatia; the Republic of Dagestan; the Ingush Republic; the Kabardino-Balkar Republic; the Republic of Kalmykia-Khalmg Tangch; the Karachai-Cherkess Republic; the Republic of Karelia, the Republic of Komi; the Republic of Marii El; the Republic of Mordvinia; the Republic of Sakha (Yakutia); the Republic of North Ossetia; the Republic of Tatarstan (Tatarstan); the Republic of Tuva; the Udmurt Republic; the Republic of Khakassia; the Chechen Republic; and the Chuvash Republic/Chavash Republic. (*Izvestiia*, November 10, 1993). However, in early November 1993, what had been Tuva adopted a constitution naming itself the Republic of Tyva, while on March 1994, Chechnia renamed itself the Republic of Chechnia-Ichkeria on the basis of a decree by General Dudaev (*Tuvinskaia pravda*, November 3, 1993, and *Radio Liberty Daily Reports*, No. 42, March 2, 1994).

Source: 1989 Census, in *Natsional'nyi sostav naseleniia SSSR*, Goskomstat, Moscow, 1991, and *Argumenty i fakty*, No. 13, March 1991, p. 1, translated in the *CDSP*, Vol. XLIII, No. 21, pp. 8–9.

Map 3.2: Population Density in Russia
1989 USSR Census

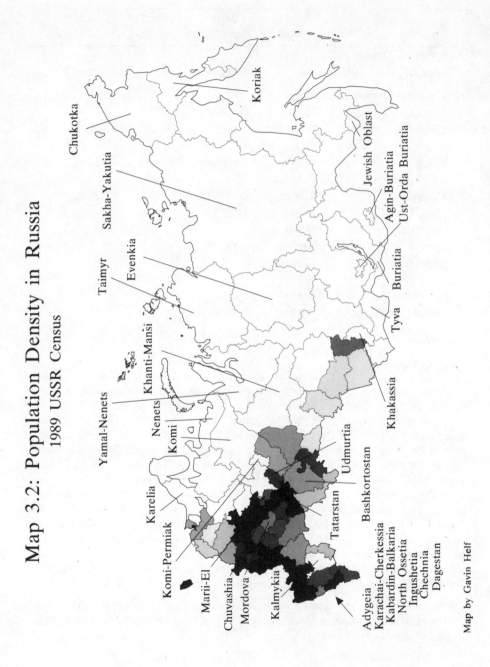

Chukotka

Koriak

Sakha-Yakutia

Jewish Oblast

Agin-Buriatia

Ust-Orda Buriatia

Taimyr

Evenkia

Buriatia

Tyva

Khanti-Mansi

Khakassia

Yamal-Nenets

Nenets

Komi

Udmurtia

Karelia

Bashkortostan

Komi-Permiak

Tatarstan

Marii-El

Chuvashia

Mordova

Kalmykia

Adygeia
Karachai-Cherkessia
Kabardin-Balkaria
North Ossetia
Ingushetia
Chechnia
Dagestan

Map by Gavin Helf

TABLE 3.2 Nationality Groups in the RSFR (1989)

Nationality Group	Population	Percentage of Total
Russian	119,865,946	81.5
Tatar	5,522,096	3.8
Ukrainian	4,362,872	3.0
Chuvash	1,773,645	1.2
Bashkir	1,345,273	*
Belorussian	1,206,222	*
Mordvinian	1,072,939	*
Chechen	898,999	*
German	842,295	*
Udmurt	714,833	*
Marii	643,698	*
Kazakh	635,865	*
Jew	536,848	*
Armenian	532,390	*
Buriat	417,425	*
Ossetian	402,275	*
Kabardinian	386,055	*
Yakut	380,242	*
Dargi	353,348	*
Komi	336,309	*
Azerbaijani	335,889	*
Kumyk	277,163	*
Lezgin	257,270	*
Ingush	215,068	*
Tuvinian	206,160	*
Peoples of the North[a]	181,517	*
Moldavian	172,671	*
Kalmyk	165,821	*
Gypsy	152,939	*
Karachai	150,332	*
Komi-Permiak	147,269	*
Georgian	130,688	*
Uzbek	126,899	*
Karelian	124,921	*
Adyge	122,908	*
Korean	107,051	*
Lak	106,245	*
Others	1,811,483	*
Total	147,021,869	

[a]Nenets, Evenk, Khant, Even, Chukchi, Nanai, Koriak, Mansi, Dolgan, Nivkh, Selkup, Ulch, Itelmen, Udege, Saami, Eskimo, Chuvan, Nganasan, Yukagir, Ket, Oroch, Tofalar, Aleut, Neigidal, Enets, Orok.

Source: 1989 Census, *Vestnik statistiki*, No. 7, 1990, pp. 72–75.

sures that had fragmented the USSR.[19] Demands for autonomy, sovereignty, and in some cases even secession, were gathering force in republics such as Tatarstan, Bashkortostan, Tyva, Checheno-Ingushetia, and North Ossetia. In other cases, republics and regions were involved in border disputes or seemed on the verge of disintegration.[20] Finally, broad regional coalitions were emerging in opposition to Moscow's authority, including the Confederation of Mountain Peoples in the North Caucasus (later the Confederation of the Peoples of the Caucasus); a Volga-Urals movement to unite Tatarstan and Bashkortostan; a Finno-Ugric movement seeking to unite Komi, Udmurtia, Marii-El, Mordova, Khanti-Mansi, and Karelia; a Central-Urals movement among various Russian *oblasts*; a movement to unite regions of the Russian Far East; and a broader alliance of republics and regions in the Siberian Agreement.

An intensifying debate over Russia's "federation structure" was a major obstacle to the drafting of a new constitution for the country. Not only the division of powers between the center and the territories but also the administrative borders themselves were in dispute. In particular, conflicts arose over whether the constitutive elements of the federation would be the existing or new administrative units; whether these constitutive units would be equal in local powers and representation at the center or whether distinctions should be made on the basis of size of population or ethnicity; and whether existing administrative units should be redrawn without regard to ethnic distinctiveness.

An even more fundamental problem of principle was whether to commit to a "national" or to a "treaty" constitution. At issue was whether the new constitution should be preceded by a treaty of federation voluntarily entered into by the constituent parts of the federation; whether those constituent parts would be given the right to ratify or reject such a treaty; whether "sovereignty" would rest with the center or the localities (e.g., would republic laws have precedence over federal laws, and would republic constitutions have to be compatible with the Russian Constitution); and finally, whether secession would be a matter for the voters in the constitutive units or would require approval by the federal parliament or a nationwide referendum.

Many Russian "democrats" at the time favored a non-ethnic federal structure modelled on the United States.[21] A country as large and ethnically diverse as Russia, they argued, could neither remain united nor sustain democracy if administrative divisions reinforced ethnic ones.[22] They also advocated a national constitution, arguing that a treaty would imply a right to refuse to enter the new federation or to secede from it unilaterally.

It soon became clear, however, that political realities made it impossible to carry out a redistricting that would abolish existing ethnic units.

Soviet propagandists had long insisted that "bourgeois" territorial federalism that ignored ethnic distinctiveness was less just than the "socialist" form of federalism that recognized the collective rights of ethnic communities. Minorities with their own administrative territories would resist changes that would deny them their particular privileges. Even the non-titular peoples living in the autonomies (including Russians, particularly where they constituted a majority) would have an interest in seeing that the autonomies were granted additional rights, particularly rights of ownership to local natural wealth. Finally, redistricting would have threatened the political influence and positions of powerful local elites.

As a result, by the beginning of 1992 consideration of major changes in Russia's internal administrative borders was for the most part abandoned. Instead, Yeltsin tried to convince local authorities to sign a federation treaty based on existing internal borders. Unlike Gorbachev's efforts to conclude a new Union Treaty for the USSR, Yeltsin's efforts were successful. On March 13, 1993, representatives of eighteen of the then twenty republics initialed a treaty of federation with Moscow.[23] A separate agreement was signed by representatives of the Federation's *oblasts* and *krais* that same week, followed by a third treaty signing with the autonomous *okrugs* and the Jewish Autonomous Oblast several days later. Then, on March 31, 1992, the three treaties (henceforth, "the Federation Treaty") were formally signed into law.[24]

The Federation Treaty ameliorated some of the tensions between Moscow and the republics and gave Yeltsin an important political victory. Nevertheless, it left many critical issues unresolved. What was meant by the republics' "ownership" of land and natural resources, for example, was left unclear. The distribution of profits from exports between the center and the provinces, relative tax burdens, and the extent and distribution of subsidization of local budgets from the federal treasury were left to future negotiation or enacting legislation. More importantly, the Treaty described the republics as "sovereign," which suggested, in view of Russian political discourse at the time, that the republics not only had a right to refuse to join the federation but could also secede at their own initiative. Nevertheless, the Treaty said nothing specific about a right of secession or secession procedures. Moreover, it stipulated that republic constitutions would have to be compatible with the federal constitution. Thus, while the Treaty further legitimized the notion of "sovereignty," it left unclear what specific rights it entailed.

Indeed, there were a number of indications at the time that the Federation Treaty would not resolve Russia's center-periphery problems. On March 21, 1992, an ambiguously-worded referendum was held in Tatarstan on sovereignty/independence similar to earlier referenda in the Baltic republics prior to the Soviet collapse. Contrary to expectations in

Moscow, and despite the fact that the referendum was declared illegal by the Constitutional Court, it was approved by 61.4% of those voting. This was followed by a decision by both Tatarstan and Chechnia not to sign the Federation Treaty.

The challenge to Russia's territorial integrity presented by Tatarstan was taken particularly seriously in Moscow and was seen by many Russians as a test of the center's willingness to defend its territorial integrity. Located in the middle of the Russian Federation along the lines of communication between Siberia and European Russia, the republic occupies more territory than the three Baltic states combined, while its population was larger in 1989 than those of four of the union republics—Estonia, Latvia, Turkmenistan, and Armenia. Tatarstan also lacks external borders and has been part of Russia since the conquest of Kazan by Ivan the Terrible in the sixteenth century. Finally, Russians made up 43.3% of the population of the republic in 1989, only slightly less than the Tatar population's 48.5%.

Nevertheless, Kazan continued to demand the same sorts of autonomous powers and protection that the union republics, including Russia, had demanded from the Soviet government in the late Gorbachev era. The only reason Tatarstan had been denied the status of a union republic in the USSR, Kazan argued, was an arbitrary decision by Stalin not to give union republic status to areas lacking external borders. Moreover, Tatar nationalists cited figures about Tatarstan's size and population to support their argument that they deserved special treatment.

Kazan followed up its refusal to sign the Federation Treaty by adopting a new constitution on November 6, 1992. The constitution asserted that Tatarstan is a sovereign state and a subject of international law that may be "associated" with the Russian Federation through a bilateral treaty.[25] The Russian Constitutional Court, however, promptly ruled that these provisions violated the federal constitution.

Just what Tatarstan's leaders intended, however, was unclear. Unlike Chechnia (see below), Tatarstan did not declare independence. Rather its president, Mintimir Shaimiev, insisted that Tatarstan be allowed to enter the Russian Federation through a bilateral treaty with Moscow, not as one of many constituent members of the Federation. He also argued that the republic had the right not to join the federation and would retain an independent right of secession not subject to approval either by a referendum in the rest of the Federation or by the Federation parliament. Moreover, despite the relative moderation of the Tatar leaders, a small group of radical Tatar nationalists continued to call for full independence and the formation of a new state uniting the Muslim peoples of the Volga region.[26]

An even graver challenge to Russia's future was posed by the first outbreak of large-scale ethnic violence on its territory. In fall 1992, clashes between Ingush and Ossetians in North Ossetia's Prigorodnyi *oblast* left some 150 people dead and up to 60,000 Ingush refugees pouring into Ingushetia. Yeltsin responded by declaring a state of emergency, and 10,000 federal troops moved in to end the fighting. The state-of-emergency remains in force, and negotiations between Ingushetia and North Ossetia over the return of Ingush refugees to their homes in Prigorodnyi *oblast* have led nowhere.

Sharp ethnic tensions emerged in other areas of the North Caucasus as well. In Kabardino-Balkaria, the arrest of the leader of the Confederation of the Peoples of the Caucasus by federal officials in September 1992 for inciting ethnic discord led to weeks of demonstrations and violence in the republic's capital, which subsided only after the Confederation leader mysteriously "escaped" from a Rostov prison. In Karachai-Cherkessia, separatists were agitating for the establishment of distinct Karachai, Cherkess, Abazza, and Cossack republics. Likewise there was pressure to create separate Kabardin and Balkar republics. In Dagestan, territorial disputes were intensifying between the Kumyks, the Chechen-Akkins, the Avars, the Laks, and local Cossacks, while the Lezgins pressed for unification with their ethnic kin across the border in Azerbaijan. These tensions were greatly aggravated by the ongoing turmoil across Russia's border in Georgia, and particularly by the involvement of a curious alliance of fighters from the Confederation of the Peoples of the Caucasus and Cossack irregulars on the side of the separatists in Abkhazia.[27]

These mounting center-periphery and ethnic problems were aggravated over the course of 1992 by the intensifying legislative-executive conflict in Moscow. In need of their political support, both Yeltsin and his Moscow opponents began to outbid each other in currying the favor of local authorities. Russian nationalists in the Supreme Soviet, who might otherwise have advocated an "iron-fisted" approach to the republics, cooperated with conservative deputies from the republics who shared their anti-market, anti-liberal, and anti-Western views. At the same time, Yeltsin aggressively courted local leaders as allies in his struggle with parliament, not only making significant economic concessions to win their support but also granting the republics and regions considerable economic autonomy in the belief that economic decentralization would prevent conservatives from reversing marketization and privatization should they come to power in Moscow.[28]

As a result, neither Yeltsin nor most of his opponents in the parliament openly advocated a hard line toward the republics, backing away from a military confrontation with Chechnia and entering into negotiations with Tatarstan over its relationship to the federation. As Yeltsin advisor Gennadii Burbulis suggested at the time, the government was willing to consider an "asymmetrical federation" in which different republics would enjoy different rights.

Yeltsin's efforts brought him the needed support. Most significantly, the Council of the Heads of the Republics, which Yeltsin had created in October so he could deal directly with republic leaders, agreed to allow the April 25, 1993 referendum (see below) to take place on the territories of the republics. They did so, however, only after Yeltsin promised that Russia's new constitution would not only incorporate the Federation Treaty but would grant both republics and regions additional rights. Nevertheless, republic elites realized that the political impasse in Moscow enhanced their autonomy, and they therefore denied both Yeltsin and parliament the unqualified support either would have needed to resolve the stand-off.

Challenges from the Regions

To many Russians, the system of "ethnic federalism" inherited from the Soviet past seemed profoundly unfair. Why should the inhabitants of Karelia, where Karelians make up only ten percent of the population and Russians almost seventy-five percent, enjoy special economic privileges simply because they live in a region arbitrarily designated an autonomous area? Similarly, why should the people living in Sakha-Yakutia be given ownership of the enormous natural wealth of the republic while Russians in resource-rich Tiumen are not granted that right? And why should the Republics of Altai, Ingushetia, or Tyva, with their tiny electorates of 126,000, 144,000, and 172,000, be granted greater representation in a federal parliament than the city of Moscow with its almost 7 million registered voters or St. Petersburg with its almost 4 million? Indeed, while many Russians might agree that the ethnic republics should enjoy particular cultural and symbolic rights such as non-Russian language schools, citizenship, and a state flag, they view economic and political privileges for the republics as legalized discrimination against Russians.

These sentiments were expressed with growing frequency during 1992 and early 1993 as officials in the Russian-dominated *oblasts* and *krais* began demanding the same economic and political rights as the ethnic republics. Slighted by what they perceived as Yeltsin's pandering to the republics, they began to withhold tax revenues from the center, embargoed the export of consumer goods and agricultural products, asserted ownership rights over land and natural resources, and entered into bilateral trade agreements with other regions and with foreign ventures in violation of Russia's federal laws.

Meanwhile, tensions between legislative and executive authorities in the regions and republics sometimes mirrored those at the center.[29] Local executives, including many republic presidents, tended to side with Yeltsin, while local legislatures tended to side with the federal parliament. Local soviets, like the federal parliament, had been elected in March 1990 under less than fully competitive conditions, and they remained an institutional stronghold of the traditional elite. The fear of these local deputies, then, was that if Yeltsin were to disband the federal parliament, he would disband the local soviets shortly thereafter.

Despite tensions between local executive and legislative authorities, the two branches nonetheless shared a common stake in defending the particular interests of their region or republic against the center. The result was an extremely complicated political game in which republics competed with regions, republics competed with republics, and regions competed with regions for privileges and handouts from the center, while central authorities outbid each other in seeking the support of the localities.

Yeltsin's strategy for resolving the intensifying crisis of Russian statehood was to adopt a new constitution that would create a more coherent and stable institutional order. To do this legally, however, he had to convince the Congress of People's Deputies, which had the formal right to amend the existing constitution, to ratify a new constitution. The Congress, however, proved unwilling to adopt any constitution that would bring about its own pre-term dissolution.

Yeltsin's attempt to resolve this impasse through a popular referendum on his draft constitution was therefore consistently thwarted by parliament. When in late 1992 he finally persuaded parliament to allow him to hold a referendum, it did not directly address the constitutional issue. The referendum took place on April 25, 1993, and Yeltsin won on all four questions: 58.7% supported the president; 53.1% supported his social-economic policies; a slim majority voted against pre-term elections for the president; and 67.2% voted for pre-term elections for parliament.[30]

While the referendum gave Yeltsin a considerable political boost, support for Yeltsin in a number of republics was very low. In ten of twenty-one, a majority voted against the president, with Yeltsin receiving support from only 2.3% of the voters in Ingushetia and 14.2% in Dagestan.[31] Chechnia refused to hold the referendum, while in Tatarstan almost 80% of the electorate refused to vote, rendering the referendum invalid. Thus Yeltsin received majority support in only nine republics.

Among the regions, Yeltsin did best in the Urals (Sverdlovsk, Perm, and Cheliabinsk *oblasts*), the Far East, the cities of Moscow and St. Petersburg, the Central Region (Moscow, Vladimir, Ivanovo and Yaroslavl *oblasts*), the Northwest (Murmansk and Arkhangelsk), and in parts of Eastern and Western Siberia. By contrast, he did poorly in predominantly agricultural regions such as the western border *oblasts* (Briansk, Orel, and Smolensk), the Volga region, and particularly in the conservative "Black Earth" *oblasts* of Belgorod, Voronezh, Kursk, and Tambov.[32] Nevertheless, overall Yeltsin failed to receive majority support in only sixteen of the sixty-eight regions.[33]

In four cases, including the city of St. Petersburg and the powerful Vologda and Sverdlovsk *oblasts*, an additional question was attached to the April referendum asking if the region should be elevated to republic status. In each case, the question was approved by substantial majorities. Indeed, the regions began to engage in their own "parade of sovereignties." In the following months, Astrakhan, Amur, Cheliabinsk, Chita, Kalinin, Perm, Orenburg, Kurgan, Sverdlovsk, and Vologda *oblasts*, as well as the city of St. Petersburg and Primorskii *krai*, either declared sovereignty or republic status, or announced their intention to do so in the future.[34] Moreover, the trend toward the formation of regional coalitions was given a boost by the declaration of a Central Russian Republic of eleven *oblasts*, including Moscow *oblast*, as well as by the establishment of a "Urals Republic" by Sverdlovsk *oblast* that threatened to include a number of its neighboring *oblasts* as well.

Other regions began to adopt their own "regional charters," while the number of those refusing to meet their obligations to the federal treasury grew to over thirty. Defending their actions, local officials claimed that the Ministry of Finance was not living up to its obligations to provide funds for local expenses, including grain purchases, teachers' salaries, and the salaries of officials in the Interior and Defense Ministries.[35] As a result, federal revenues fell well short of expectations.[36]

Nevertheless, Yeltsin interpreted the referendum as a popular endorsement of the need for a new constitution. He therefore followed it up by convening a "Constitutional Convention" in early June to work out a draft constitution. Because the Convention lacked legal authority to adopt a new constitution itself, the hope was that its draft would then be ratified by the Congress of Peoples's Deputies, an elected Constitutional Assembly, a newly elected parliament, or the "Federation Council" (see below). If these proved politically impossible, it might also be legitimated by popular referendum. However, despite the fact that the Convention was made up largely of Yeltsin's supporters, his draft ran into considerable opposition and was significantly modified.[37] The key sticking point was the "federation structure," with the republics predictably insisting that they be described as "sovereign states" and that the Federation Treaty be included in the constitution's text, while the regions demanded the same political and economic rights as the republics.

In general, the republics found few allies at the Convention; in four of its five working groups, a majority opposed describing them as "sovereign states." The sole exception was the group chaired by Yeltsin's advisor Sergei Shakhrai, which included representatives from the republics. Nevertheless, with Yeltsin's support a compromise was worked out that gave the republics most of what they wanted.

The compromise draft was approved by the Convention on July 12 and was promptly sent out to territorial executive and legislative authorities for comments. Again, Yeltsin and his allies hoped that the draft would be approved by a significant majority of the republics and regions. And again their hopes proved unrealistic as it quickly became clear that many local legislatures and executives would either reject the draft or attach unacceptable amendments.

At this point Yeltsin made one last effort to win the backing of the republics and regions. In a meeting in early August in the Karelian city of Petrozavodsk, he followed up a warning to the localities on the dangers of separatism with a call for the creation of a Federation Council consisting of a representative from the legislative and executive branches of each of the eighty-nine subjects of the federation. Apparently Yeltsin hoped that the Federation Council would insist on new parliamentary elections, ratify a new constitution, and act as an interim legislature until new elections were held. He also suggested that the Council might serve as the upper body of the new legislature until the term of office of the soviets expired in the summer of 1995.[38]

Nevertheless, by the beginning of September it had again become clear that Yeltsin had overestimated his powers of persuasion and patronage. His proposal to create a Federation Council received only qualified support from the local leaders, who had no reason to expect that he or any future government would preserve the Federation Council as the upper house of a new legislature for very long. Moreover, regional and republic leaders seem to have resented the fact that Yeltsin was trying to buy them off at the expense of their constituencies.

Having reached a dead end after counting so heavily on support from republic and regional authorities, Yeltsin finally abandoned the effort to find a legal solution to the crisis of power and launched his "democratic coup," dissolving parliament by decree on September 21 and announcing new parliamentary elections for December 11–12, 1993.

The October Crisis, the December Elections, and the New Constitution

In the short run, the dramatic storming of the parliament by the Russian military on October 4, 1993 significantly strengthened the hand of the central government. Yeltsin moved quickly in its aftermath to reassert the authority of the federal government, decreeing that elections be held for a new federal parliament on December 12, 1993 and that the draft constitution be put to a national referendum that same day. He also called for the dissolution of local legislatures that had sided with his opponents after his September 21 decree; ordered new elections for all *oblast* and *krai* soviets by March 1994; fired several heads of administration for having opposed him during the crisis; and decreed that, for the time being at least, all heads of administration would be appointed by the president; limited the influence of the territories at the Constitutional Convention (which continued to meet to make last-minute amendments to the draft constitution); and decreed that the constitution would be ratified by a simple majority vote on December 12.

At first, the regions and republics seemed to accept these tough measures; only Chechnia announced that it would refuse to allow voting to take place on its territory on December 12. The acquiescence of the republics was put at risk, however, by a series of measures announced by Yeltsin in the following weeks that decisively challenged their status. First, the language describing the republics as "sovereign states" was removed from the draft constitution. So too was the text of the Federation Treaty, as well as provisions for dual citizenship allowing the republics the right to their own citizenship laws. Second, Yeltsin and his advisors moved decisively to equalize the rights of the republics and the regions. Finally, Yeltsin made clear that those regions and republics in arrears to the federal treasury would have to pay up or face economic reprisals, including reductions in their share of export earnings, access to imports, and subsidies from the center.

In effect, Yeltsin was throwing down the political gauntlet to the republics. Now that the political crisis in Moscow had been resolved, he implied, the center would no longer tolerate violations of its laws or engage in an endless process of bilateral negotiation with each of the eighty-nine subjects of the federation over export earnings, tax revenue, subsidies, and property.

Nevertheless, the draft constitution was finally approved in the December 12, 1993 referendum.[39] Official returns indicated 58.4% of those voting had supported it, although turnout was only barely over the 50% needed for a quorum—according to official statistics, only 54.8% of the electorate voted in the referendum.[40] Moreover, opposition to the constitution was stronger in the republics than in the regions.[41] Overall, 32.3% of the electorate voted for the constitution in the regions, with only 23.6% supporting it in the republics. Among all those voting in the republics, only 47.9% voted for the constitution, compared with 60.0% in the regions. Only nine republics (Buriatia, Altai, Ingushetia, Kabardino-Balkaria, Kalmykia, Karelia, Marii-El, Sakha, and North Ossetia) registered over 50% turnout and majority support for the constitution. Polling did not take place in Chechnia, while in Tatarstan, where nationalist parties had urged people not to vote, turnout was under 15%. Turnout was also below 50% in three other republics—Udmurtia, Khakassia, and Komi—while for the 21 republics as a whole, turnout was 49.2%. In the sixteen republics where turnout exceeded 50%, a majority rejected the constitution in seven (Adygeia, Bashkortostan, Dagestan, Karachai-Cherkessia, Mordova, Tyva, and Chuvashia).

Despite this demonstrated opposition, the new constitution was by no means a complete victory for proponents of a strong central government or a purely territorial federation. The Constitution does not reconfigure Russia's existing administrative borders in order to eliminate ethnically defined administrative units. Moreover, republics and regions are given considerable rights and responsibilities. The federal government has jurisdiction over federal organs of power; over its own social, economic, cultural, and ecological policies; over foreign policy; and over questions of war and peace (Article 71). Other powers are assigned to joint jurisdiction and require mutual agreement between the federal government and the federation subjects (Article 72). These include protection of human rights and the rights of ethnic minorities; ownership of land, minerals, and other natural resources; environmental protection within the territory of the subjects of the federation; general principles of taxation and subsidies; and coordination of foreign economic relations. Importantly, Article 73 specifies that all powers not specifically assigned to the federal government or to joint jurisdiction rest with the regions and republics. And finally, the republics and regions are awarded powers of independent legislation (Article 76) and taxation.[42]

There are other provisions that benefit Russia's ethnic minorities and republics as well. Among these are extensive individual rights, including equality before the law regardless of race, nationality, or language (Article 19). In addition, the constitution specifies that republics can establish their own state languages (Article 68); that all peoples have the right to use their native language and to create the conditions for its study and development (Article 26, Article 68); and that the rights of "small indigenous peoples" will be respected in accordance with the norms and principles of international law (Article 69).

The new constitution leaves many details to be resolved by future negotiation and enacting legislation. Many provisions are vague or ambiguous, while others are contradictory. If the constitution remains in effect, Russia's Constitutional Court will therefore play an extremely important role in interpreting its provisions and in adjudicating conflicts between central and local authorities. Most importantly, flexibility is built into the new constitution in Article 78, which allows executive organs of the federal government, by mutual agreement, to delegate some of their powers to the regions and republics, and likewise executive organs of the regions and republics can delegate some of their powers to the federal government. This leaves open the possibility of bilateral agreements between Moscow and the subjects and the further development of an "asymmetrical federation."[43] In short, the constitution is a milestone, not an endpoint, in Russia's troubled path to a new federal system.

The Roots of Moscow's Conflict with the Provinces

In attempting to explain Russia's ethnic and center-periphery problems, it is useful to distinguish three types of challenges. The first involves interethnic "horizontal" conflict between particular ethnic groups, as in the North Caucasus. The second involves ethnically driven, "vertical" challenges to Moscow (as with Tyva, to a certain extent with Tatarstan, and with much of the North Caucasus). Finally, the third involves non-ethnically driven political and economic opposition to central authority (as in the case of many regions).

Horizontal interethnic conflicts, like those in the North Caucasus, usually result from longstanding territorial disputes and traditional hostilities as well as from more immediate political and economic factors. The North Caucasus, and indeed the Caucasus generally, is a region of enormous ethnic and religious diversity and deep commitments to traditional territorial homelands. In many cases, the ethnic groups of the region also have histories of mutual enmity, and many, including the Cossacks, have warrior traditions. Under the best of circumstances, then, it would be difficult to preserve ethnic harmony in the area. When regime transitions bring about a collapse of central authority, previous institutional arrangements, including borders and property rights (particularly in Soviet-type systems, where internal borders were of marginal political importance and property was collectively owned), are contested. As a result, elites often find they can best preserve their privileged position by "playing the ethnic card." Under these circumstances, ethnic conflict in ethnically heterogenous areas seems almost inevitable.

Vertical ethnic mobilization in opposition to the center likewise has multiple causes. It is not irrelevant that Tatars and Tyvinians, for example, often feel that Russians are disdainful of their traditions and culture. Moreover, Tyvinians have a memory of recent statehood—until 1944, when it was forcibly incorporated by Stalin into the USSR, Tyva (then called Tannu-Tuva) was an independent state. The republic is also ethnically relatively homogeneous (64% were ethnic Tyvinians in 1989, the highest number for any titular nationality in Russia's autonomous republics other than Checheno-Ingushetia, and higher than in the former union republics of Kazakhstan, Kyrgyzia, Latvia, Moldova, and Tajikistan). On the other hand, Tyva lacks natural wealth and has been heavily subsidized over the years by Moscow, as Tyva's leaders are well aware. Indeed, Tyva decided not to hold a referendum on independence because, as members of parliament pointed out, 90% of the Tyvinian government's budget is paid out of subsidies from the center.[44] Nevertheless, Tyva has been very assertive in demanding greater autonomy and sovereignty. In November 1993, Tyva adopted a radical constitution that declared sovereignty and claimed not only the right to leave the Federation on the basis of a referendum held in Tyva alone but also the "the right to its own territory and natural wealth, and to determine its own state structure and foreign and domestic policy."[45] Thus Tyva's interest in preserving the government-to-government subsidies it receives from Moscow has not stopped it from presenting central authorities with a serious political challenge.

Clearly, then, those who argue that separatist sentiments and ethnic tensions in the former Soviet Union and Eastern Europe are rooted solely in economic self-interest are over-simplifying the problem. Nevertheless, while the ethnic factor has been important in some cases, in others it has been insignificant or absent. In these instances, separatist and regional challenges to Moscow result primarily from economic and political factors. Economic disputes between the federal government and local authorities include disputes over the share of tax revenue to be turned over to the federal treasury by local governments; over the amount of subsidies to local governments from Moscow; over subsidies for local industry and agriculture; over prices for goods such as fuel, electricity, and wheat; over the share of hard currency export earnings to be retained by local governments; over relief for particular enterprises or collective, state, and private farms on interest rates from state banks; and finally, over ownership, including use, profit, and alienation rights, of natural resources and land, as well as of physical assets such as electric power stations, railroads, roads, electric transmission systems, and telecommunication systems.

In other cases, conflict between the federal and local government is over who makes policy and controls particular organs of state power. For example, control over the privatization process and local privatization boards has often been sharply disputed, with both federal and local authorities wanting the proceeds of sales of state assets. Moreover, local elites have a strong interest, often opposed by reformers at the center, in protecting access to rent-seeking opportunities, including control of export licensing, licensing and taxing of foreign investment, and control over privileged positions. In these cases, at issue is not only revenue and power for local elites, but also opportunities for illegal income through bribes, kick-backs, and so on.

Clearly, then, Russia's center-periphery problems are not reducible to demands for "self-determination" or political independence by ethnic minorities or to border disputes between ethnically defined territories. Indeed, the complexity of Russia's center-periphery problems is suggested by the fact that no single indicator (e.g., support for Yeltsin in the April 1993 referendum) is available for assessing the seriousness of the challenge to the center from a particular area. For example, there has certainly been opposition to economic reform from local authorities in certain cases, as has been widely reported in the media. But opposition to economic reform, or to Yeltsin himself, is not the same as support for separatism or opposition to a strong central government. The anti-Yeltsin sentiments in Russia's "Black-Earth" region, for example, come from an overwhelmingly Russian area that opposes marketization because financial stabilization requires cuts in the federal government's massive subsidies for agriculture. In Nizhnii Novgorod, on the other hand, support for economic reform has not meant strong political support either for Yeltsin or for the federal government in its struggle with the federation subjects.[46] Neither do other sources of tension with Moscow—declarations of autonomy or sovereignty, unilateral assertions of ownership rights, refusal to meet obligations to the central treasury, refusal to enforce federal laws, efforts to control local privatization boards, efforts to control local taxation agencies, and local restraints on trade across regional borders—necessarily mean support for separatism or anti-Russian feelings. For example, Sverdlovsk *oblast's* declaration of sovereignty, where the population was 89% Russian in 1989, hardly suggests a vote against Russians.

The most contentious economic conflict between center and periphery has been over the relative share of taxes paid to the federal treasury by the federation's subjects—whether ethnic republics or regions—along with the revenue they receive to help finance local budgets. The fact that certain territories are net contributors to the federal treasury while others are net subtractors has led to accusations that certain areas are being "exploited." Moreover, of the fifteen subjects of the federation that receive more from the federal treasury than they put in, fourteen are republics.[47] This fiscal redistribution, it is pointed out, has very little to do with economic justice—Tatarstan, for example, is one of the richest subjects of the federation, but nevertheless receives more per capita in net subsidies than any other republic except Tyva, North Ossetia, and Komi.

As was the case in the old Soviet Union, however, determining which subjects of the federation are "exploited" and which are "subsidized" is virtually impossible. Those who complain about fiscal redistribution ignore a host of factors other than relative tax burdens and government-to-government subsidies, including direct subsidies to local industries, pricing policy for wheat and other products purchased by the state, low-interest loans to farms and industrial enterprises, and assignment of property rights to natural resources and other assets. Nor can one predict the effects of market liberalization on local economies.

Nevertheless, some generalizations about the different interests of agricultural, industrial, and extraction areas are possible. Agricultural regions, particularly the more prosperous ones, have good reason to resist marketization. Traditionally conservative, they also have been highly subsidized by the state; according to recent estimates, agricultural subsidies make up some 12–13% of GDP.[48] These subsidies take a number of forms, including state purchases of wheat and other farm commodities at favorable prices; discounts on fuel, machinery, and other inputs for farms that sell their products to the state; interest rates of 28%, well below the commercial rate of 180% (itself negative in real terms) to these same farms; and debt relief. Indeed, agricultural subsidies are central to the struggle over the federal budget deficit, and efforts to reduce these subsidies, as well as the fact that traditional *nomenklatura* elites have been able to maintain their positions in executive and legislative organs in rural areas more easily than in the cities, help explain why many agricultural regions have voted against Yeltsin and his economic policies.

In contrast to the relatively uniform resistance of rural areas to Yeltsin's economic reform program, the economic interests and political positions of industrial regions are more varied. In areas concentrating in the production of military hardware, local authorities have an interest in resisting financial stabilization through cutbacks in defense spending. However, they also have an interest in attracting foreign investment and finding foreign customers, which tends to make them less parochial and conservative than their rural counterparts. Much the same can be said of any industrial region that has a chance to market its goods abroad and survive in a competitive market. For those that do not, resistance to market reforms initiated in Moscow will likely be significant. A final complicating factor is that even where industrial regions support Yeltsin, as in Sverdlovsk *oblast*, there may be strong resistance to the demands of the republics for political and economic privileges.[49]

Regions with a high concentration of natural wealth have the greatest interest in declaring "economic sovereignty" and asserting ownership over their resource endowments, even as they tend to be relatively open to market reforms and generally supportive of Yeltsin.[50] This is not always the case, however. In some instances, natural wealth makes the political elite even more reluctant to lose control of the economy and turn assets over to the private sector. Moreover, a high concentration of natural wealth in ethnic republics like Tatarstan makes separatism both more attractive and more possible. Indeed, economists in Tatarstan point out that the value of petroleum reserves and other resources in their territory is considerably greater than the admittedly substantial government-to-government subsidies they now receive from the center. The same is true for resource-rich regions in Siberia like Tiumen *oblast* and Krasnoiarsk *krai*—indeed, the vision of some members of the Siberian Agreement association is of a multitude of underpopulated Siberian "Kuwaits." For the Russian Far East, finally, there is the added attraction of developing trade links with, and attracting foreign investment from, Japan, China, the U.S., and the Newly Industrializing Countries (NICs) on the Pacific littoral.

Finally, the poorer regions of Russia that lack developed agricultural, industrial, or extractive economies and have limited natural resources fear the loss of subsidies from the center as a result of fiscal stabilization. Hence, they tend to oppose marketization and to be less inclined to pursue economic or political sovereignty.

Conclusion

Under the best of circumstances, the consolidation of Russian statehood will be problematic for many years. In the short run, leaders in the republics may refuse to consider Russia's new constitution binding. Indeed, the constitutions of many republics assert the priority of local laws over federal laws, thereby violating the new Federation constitution. As for the regions, evidence suggests a relatively strong and growing identification of Russians with their regions and regional leaders rather than with the nation as a whole or central leaders in Moscow.[51] It is also very unlikely that the "war of the budgets," or disagreements between Moscow and the provinces over ownership of natural resources and other assets, will soon abate.

Particularly problematic will be the situation in the North Caucasus. Despite recent talks between Moscow officials and various Chechen politicians, Chechnia will likely continue to insist on independence, at least as long as Dudaev remains its leader. Even if some kind of agreement is reached, however, the extent of Chechen involvement in organized crime, and the resultant hostility of Russians toward Chechens, and indeed toward the peoples of the North Caucasus in general, will persist. Most importantly, the enmity among the many peoples of the North Caucasus, and particularly between the Ingush and North Ossetia over the Prigorodnyi district, will create acute problems for Moscow for years to come.

A reduction of tensions with Tatarstan, on the other hand, seems likely. Unexpectedly, Moscow and Kazan signed a bilateral treaty on February 15, 1994 that at least temporarily defused the conflict. The treaty states that Tatarstan is united with Russia on the basis of the treaty as well as the constitutions of the two states, despite the contradictions in the two documents.[52] It also affirms Tatarstan's right to its own "international and economic relations" with foreign states and asserts that the Tatar government "decides questions of the ownership, use and distribution of the land, mineral wealth, forests, and other natural resources, as well as the state enterprises, organizations and other movements and immovable state assets located on the territory of Tatarstan."

The Treaty has provoked opposition from Tatarstan's radical nationalists—although it recognizes Tatarstan's "sovereignty," it does so only insofar as that sovereignty does not violate the Russian Constitution. The Treaty likewise has provoked opposition from Russian nationalists, who oppose the special status afforded Tatarstan on the grounds that it weakens the Russian state and sets a precedent for other republics. But despite these difficulties, the Treaty signifies the willingness of the Yeltsin government to remain flexible in its relations with the provinces and to accept an evolving, and asymmetrical, federation based on negotiation and compromise, not force. Moreover, the Treaty may serve as a useful model for ameliorating tensions elsewhere in the former Soviet Union— for example, between Ukraine and Crimea.

Nevertheless, in the long run Russia will continue to face ethnic and center-periphery problems under the best of circumstances. Many of its ethnic minorities lack administrative recognition for purely arbitrary reasons, and will likely demand it. The ethnically defined *okrugs* will probably demand republic status. Titular peoples in the republics will insist on affirmative action policies or quotas reserving positions in republic governments and local businesses. Likewise they will demand the right to study and use non-Russian languages in schools, and possibly in business and government affairs as well, and they may also press for particular privileges for "indigenous" businesses. In general, their very plausible argument will be that institutional protection and group rights are necessary to protect their cultures against Russification. With equal plausibility, Russians will respond that these group rights discriminate against Russians, particularly the many Russians living in the republics.

Despite these difficulties, it is unlikely that ten years from now we will see a significantly smaller Russia. Least unlikely is the secession of Tyva. It is also possible, should Moscow decide it is unable or unwilling to remain involved in the area, that some parts of the North Caucasus might secede (although ethnic turmoil in the North Caucasus, and indeed in the Trans-Caucasus in general, is even more likely to invite Russian military intervention to restore civic peace). An even more remote possibility is the successful secession of Tatarstan, Bashkortostan, or the other republics of the Volga-Urals region—any government in Moscow, whether democratic or not, would find it very difficult to accept the independence of such a large and strategically important part of Russia. Least probable of all is the secession of republics such as Sakha-Yakutia where population density is low, Russians form a substantial majority of the republic's inhabitants, and nation-state consciousness is weak.

Indeed, it is important not to underestimate Moscow's strengths in its struggle with the provinces. The federal government has many economic, political, and coercive levers at its disposal to defend the country's territorial integrity. If, for example, Tatarstan insists on separate citizenship, Russia could deny Tatar citizens federation citizenship and insist that Tatar citizens obtain visas before entering Russian territory. Likewise Moscow could respond to Sakha's claims to ownership of its vast mineral wealth by charging exorbitant taxes for goods transported through its territory or airspace. Nor is it likely that the independence of any of the republics would be recognized readily by the international community. Moreover, the difficulties the Soviet successor states are experiencing, as well as the ethnic warfare in the former Yugoslavia, have made clear that secession is no panacea. Both the leaders and the citizens of Russia's republics and regions will therefore think twice before pushing for full independence. Finally, Russian national identity, however ambiguous, is very deeply rooted—and while nationalism, it should be remembered, is in some cases a solvent, in others it serves as a powerful binding agent.

In the final analysis, the best way for Russia to preserve its territorial integrity would be to concentrate its energies on consolidating democracy, building a structured party system at the federal level, establishing a sound currency, and creating a common economic space. On the other hand, if Russia's economy continues to deteriorate, if its new political institutions fail to consolidate, or if the Russian state is unable to establish order and combat crime, then Russia will face two grave dangers. The first is that economic chaos, and particularly the debilitating effects of hyperinflation, will loosen the integumen binding the country together to the point that it fragments. Much more likely, however, and ultimately more catastrophic, is a fascist-like reaction that seeks to unify the country by mobilizing Russians against some imagined internal or external enemy—indeed, Russian expansionism, not fragmentation, is the greater threat to international order and Russian prosperity. The result would almost certainly be ethnic violence and inter-state war.

Notes

1. For a more extensive discussion, see the chapters by Ronald Suny, Gail W. Lapidus and Victor Zaslavsky in *From Union to Commonwealth: Nationalism and Separatism in the Soviet Union*, eds. Gail W. Lapidus, Victor Zaslavsky and Philip Goldman (Cambridge: Cambridge University Press, 1992); and Victor Zaslavsky, "Nationalism and Democratic Transition in Post-Communist Societies," *Daedalus*, Spring 1992.

2. For example, not only did Russians occupy a dominant position in the central political, administrative, and military elites, but the fact that Russian was the *lingua franca* of the Union conferred significant advantages on native Russian speakers. Not surprisingly, the growing assertiveness of national movements in the non-Russian republics was first manifested in highly controversial efforts to alter language policy in favor of the titular nationalities.

3. In addition to certain institutional factors, constraints on the expression of Russian nationalism and lack of distance from the Soviet imperial center contributed to the weak development of Russian identity among Russians (see Leokadiia Drobizheva et al., *Russkie: Etno-sotsiologicheskie ocherki*, Moscow: Nauka, 1992).

4. *New York Times*, May 31, 1990. Certain democratic critics of Soviet federalism were calling at the time for "sovereignty" for the union republics as well as for the equalization of all ethnic units in the Soviet federal administrative hierarchy. This would have meant linking the restructuring of the Soviet federal system with a restructuring of federal relations within Russia as well. See, for example, Andrei Sakharov's draft constitution prepared shortly before his death, which asserted the basic right of not only the republics but "each nation" within the USSR to self-determination, while giving republics (which included all ethnically defined federal units) a right of secession from the union (*New Times*, No. 52, 1989, pp. 26–28).

5. Charles Furtado and Andrea Chandler, eds., *Perestroika in the Soviet Republics: Documents on the National Question* (Boulder: Westview Press, 1992), pp. 325–326. The vagueness of the language status of the autonomies had been controversial for some time, as this rather vague wording suggests (see, for example, *Izvestiia*, June 12, 1990, translated in *CDSP*, Vol. XLII, No. 23, p. 14).

6. *Komsomol'skoe znamia*, June 7, 1991, as cited in John Dunlop, *The Rise of Russia and the Fall of the Soviet Empire* (Princeton: Princeton University Press, 1993), p. 24.

7. Cited in John Dunlop, *The Rise of Russia and the Fall of the Soviet Empire* (Princeton: Princeton University Press, 1993), p. 64.

8. *New York Times*, September 2, 1990. Yeltsin also suggested at the time that he was willing to give the autonomies ownership of the natural resources in their territories (Bill Keller, *The New York Times Sunday Magazine*, September 23, 1990).

9. The Volga Tatars, along with their Bashkir neighbors, are Turkic-speaking and traditionally Muslim.

10. This argument was not new—it had been raised on numerous occasions by Tatarstan's leaders in the pre-Gorbachev era as well, particularly during the debate over the 1977 USSR Constitution. What was different was that the local leaders could make their demands openly and had increasing leverage over the center as a result of popular mobilization.

11. *Izvestiia*, May 13, 1991, translated in *CDSP*, Vol. XLIII, No. 19, p. 1. The agreement made it more difficult for Yeltsin to resist the sovereignty and autonomy demands of the republics after the USSR's collapse.

12. "An Indissoluble Union," *Izvestiia*, September 20, 1990, translated in *CDSP*, Vol. XLII, No. 39, p. 2. See also Aleksandr Tsipko, "Crisis of Russia's Statehood," *Rossiia*, July 6–12, 1991, translated in *CDSP*, Vol. XLIII, No. 28, p. 7; Alexander Tsipko, "The Drama of Russia's Choice," *Izvestiia*, October 1, 1991, translated in *CDSP*, Vol. XLIII, No. 39, pp. 1–4; Andranik Migranian, "Can Yeltsin's Russia Survive?," *Moscow News*, No. 40, p. 8; and an interview with Tsipko, "If the Nation Doesn't Recognize the Value of the State, It Is Dangerously Ill," *Komsomol'skaia pravda*, January 14, 1992, translated in *CDSP*, Vol. XLIV, No. 6, pp. 12–14. It should be noted, however, that many of the advocates of "sovereignty from the ground up" saw their goal as reforming the USSR federation, not destroying it.

13. Leokadiia Drobizheva, "Povtorit li Rossiia put' Soiuza," in Lilia Shevtsova, ed., *Rossiia segodnia: Trudnye poiski svobody* (Moscow: Institut mezhdunarodnykh ekonomicheskykh i politicheskyzh issledovanii, 1993).

14. "Constitution (Fundamental Law) of the Russian Socialist Federated Soviet Republic," in Aryeh L. Unger, *Constitutional Development in the USSR: A Guide to the Soviet Constitution* (New York: Pica Press, 1981), pp. 25–26.

15. In 1918, the dominant position of the Bolshevik center was ensured by the principle of "democratic centralism" generally, as well as by particular provisions giving the All-Russian Congress of Soviets and the Central Executive Committee jurisdiction not only over admission into the federation, secession, and internal are administrative borders, but over "all matters of general state importance" as well (Article 49).

16. While *krais*, like *oblasts*, are predominantly Russian, they are distinguished from *oblasts* in that they contain a small minority population within them and administratively subordinate to the *krai*.

17. The twenty republics increased by one in mid–1992 when Moscow recognized the division of Checheno-Ingushetia into the separate Chechen and Ingush Republics. Also, while formally the *oblasts* and *krais* have a different status from the Jewish autonomous *oblast* and the 10 autonomous *okrugs* (hence their separate treaty with the center in March 1992), in practice their rights are very similar. Thus they are referred to collectively in Russian political discourse as the "regions."

18. No data is available on Ingushetia, which separated from Chechnia after the 1989 census was taken. It is likely, however, that the Ingush constitute a significant majority in their new republic, especially after the inflow of Ingush refugees in the wake of the ethnic violence in North Ossetia.

19. For an overview, see *Moscow News*, No. 14, 1992, p. 8.

20. Border disputes included Ingush claims on the Prigorodnyi district of North Ossetia; the desire of North and South Ossetia to unite; Kalmyk claims on Astrakhan and part of Dagestan; Tyvinian claims on Krasnoiarsk *krai* and

Mongolia; and finally, Tatar claims on Astrakhan, parts of Kazakhstan, and indeed all of what was once the Kazan khanate. In many cases, these disputes were complicated by territorial claims by minority peoples deported during the Stalin era, including the Volga Germans, the Ingush, the Kalmyks, the Balkars, the Chechen-Akkin, the Avars, and the Ossets.

21. Valerii Tishkov, Director of the Institute of Anthropology and Ethnology of the Russian Academy of Sciences and head of the State Committee on Nationality Affairs from March 1992 to October 1992, was an important advocate of this approach. See also the interview with Oleg Rumiantsev, Chair of the Working Group of the Constitutional Commission of the Russian Parliament, in *Moscow News*, No. 10, 1991, p. 5, and the interview with Moscow Mayor Gavriil Popov in *Izvestiia*, October 3, 1991.

22. At one point, plans were drawn up for a new federal structure based on two types of constitutive units, "republics" and "lands." The twenty ethnically defined republics were to be balanced by an approximately equal number of non-ethnically based lands. This would have entailed a considerable consolidation of existing *oblasts, krais*, and autonomous *okrugs* (see "Poiasnitel'naia zapiska k proektu konstitutsii rossiiskoi federatsii," *Rossiiskaia gazeta*, October 11, 1991).

23. The text of the Federation Treaty can be found in reprints of the Russian Federation Constitution between April 1992 and December 1993.

24. Most surprising was the willingness of Bashkortostan's leaders to sign. The reason was a last-minute agreement on the republic's right of ownership to the natural resources on its territory, freedom to engage directly in foreign economic transactions, and right to an independent system of taxation. Earlier, the Bashkortostan parliament had voted to suspend the jurisdiction of the Russian Federation's new Constitutional Court on its territory (*Moscow News*, No. 16, p. 5).

25. *Izvestiia Tatarstana*, December 12, 1992.

26. The Bashkirs, however, have been wary of being dominated by the more numerous Tatars (see Ann Sheehy, "Tatarstan and Bashkiria: Obstacles to Confederation," *RFE/RL Research Report*, Vol. 1, No. 22, May 29, 1992).

27. Formally, the Russian military remained neutral in the conflict, although there were frequent reports of a Russian "tilt" toward the Abkhaz through weapons sales and "safe zones" identified by the Russian military as out-of-bounds for conflict but that in fact served the interests of the Abkhaz. The extent of this support, and whether it came as a result of orders from either military or civilian authorities in Moscow, is unclear.

28. For example, late in the summer of 1992 Yeltsin dispatched Prime Minister Yegor Gaidar to Sakha, where he signed an agreement setting up a joint stock company to exploit Sakha's diamonds and confirmed a major Sakha-De Beers deal that Moscow conservatives had attacked as disadvantageous to the Federation. Gaidar also indicated that Yeltsin's government would support the right of local governments to control the disposition of their natural resources and gather their own tax revenues, meeting their obligations to the center through transfers of revenue.

29. The best-known example occurred in Mordova, where a pro-reform and popularly elected President was thrown out of office by a conservative legislature.

Yeltsin decreed that in doing so, the Mordovan parliament had violated the Russian Constitution's provisions on a unified structure of executive power and the separation of powers, but he was overruled by the Constitutional Court (for background, see Wendy Slater, "Head of Russian Constitutional Court under Fire," *RFE/RL Research Report*, Vol. 2, No. 26, June 1993).

30. Details of the returns can be found in *Rossiiskaia gazeta*, May 19, 1993, p. 2. See also Aleksandr A. Sobianin, Eduard B. Gelman, and Oleg N. Kaiunov, "Politicheskii klimat v Rossii v 1991–1993 gg," *Mirovaia ekonomika i mezhdunarodnye otnosheniia*, No. 9, 1993; and Ralph S. Clem and Peter R. Craumer, "The Geography of the April 25 Referendum," *Post-Soviet Geography*, Vol. 35, No. 5, pp. 323–325.

31. Yeltsin had become very unpopular in the North Caucasus (with the exception of North Ossetia) because of his failure to support the Ingush in their conflict with the Ossetians or to support the Abkhaz secessionists in Georgia.

32. In the Black Earth *oblasts* of Belgorod, and in Voronezh, Kursk, and Tambov *oblasts*, Yeltsin received the approval of only 39.6, 49.7, 42.1, and 44.0% of the voters respectively, well below the 58.7% approval from the country as a whole (*Rossiiskaia gazeta*, May 19, 1993, p. 2). Moreover, his support in these *oblasts* fell from the 50.8, 57.4, 54.2, and 44.6% who voted for him in the June 1991 presidential elections.

33. The others were Altai *krai*, Arkhangelsk, Briansk, Lipetsk, Orel, Penza, Pskov, Riazan, Smolensk, Ulianovsk and Chita *oblasts*, as well as the Ust-Ordynsky Buriat autonomous okrug (*Rossiiskaia gazeta*, May 19, 1993, p. 2).

34. Rumors in Moscow suggested that Yeltsin's advisor Gennadii Burbulis had encouraged Sverdlovsk *oblast* to declare sovereignty as a counterweight to the demands of the republics for sovereignty and greater autonomy. Apparently the expectation was that if leaders in the regions began demanding equal treatment, the republics would temper their demands for greater powers.

35. See Radik Batyrshin, "Nalogovaia voina tsentra i regionov," *Nezavisimaia gazeta*, September 1, 1993, p. 3.

36. Estimates of the total shortfall ranged from 15% to 40%, although much of this was due to the failure of businesses and private individuals to pay taxes (see *RFE/RL Daily Report*, July 30, 1993).

37. See Vera Tolz, "Drafting the New Russian Constitution," *RFE/RL Research Report*, Vol. 2, No. 29, July 16, 1993, pp. 1–12.

38. Thus, rather than facing a complete loss of office, local leaders would be guaranteed a post and even an apartment in Moscow. As a final demonstration of his willingness to use material rewards to garner political support, Yeltsin also signed a decree authorizing a 50% increase in salaries for executives and guaranteeing them full salaries for one year after leaving office.

39. The text of the new constitution, which came into force on December 24, 1993, is in *Izvestiia*, November 10, 1993. The referendum returns are in *RFE/RL Daily Report*, No. 246, December 27, 1993.

40. For this and the following information on election returns, see *Biulleten' Tsentral'noi izbiratel'noi komissii Rossiiskoi Federatsii*, Vol. 1, No. 12, Moscow, 1994. See also the map published in *Segodnia*, December 21, 1993, p. 2. The 54.8% figure is the percentage of the electorate actually given ballots on the day of the election,

not the percentage who correctly filled in those ballots. The second figure gives a result of 53.1%.

41. On the other hand, opposition parties (the Liberal Democratic Party, the Communist Party of the Russian Federation, and the Agrarians), apparently won a majority of votes in only six of the republics (Marii-El, Chuvashia, Dagestan, Ingushetia, North Ossetia, and Karachai-Cherkessia).

42. This latter power can be inferred from Articles 73 and 76, as well as from the fact that Article 71 gives the Federal government jurisdiction over *federal* taxes and fees only.

43. A similar provision in the Spanish constitution has allowed for asymmetrical federal-state relations in Spain. See Manuel Garcia Alvarez, "'Ob asimmetrii' v territorial'nom ustroistve ispanskogo gosudarstva i rossiiskoi federatsii," *Konstitutsionnoe soveshchanie*, No. 3, December 1993, pp. 49–54.

44. See Vera Tolz, "Regionalism in Russia: The Case of Siberia," *RFE/RL Research Report*, Vol. 2, No. 6, February 26, 1993, p. 8; and Zoya V. Anaiban, "The Inter-Ethnic Situation in Tyva," unpublished paper presented at the University of California at Berkeley, November 16, 1993.

45. *Tuvinskaia pravda*, November 3, 1993.

46. See Mary Cline, "Nizhnii Novgorod: A Regional View of the Russian Elections," *RFE/RL Research Report*, Vol. 3, No. 4, January 28, 1994, pp. 48–54.

47. See Leonid Smirniagin, "Politicheskii federalizm protiv ekonomicheskogo," *Segodnia*, June 25, 1993; and Leonid Smirniagin, "Federatsiia: protsessy, idushchie snizu," *Rossiiskie vesti*, No. 121, 1993, p. 2.

48. *RFE/RL Daily Report*, October 24, 1993.

49. For example, after his *oblast* declared itself the "Ural Republic" on July 1, 1993, the head of administration in Sverdlovsk and one-time Yeltsin ally, Eduard Rossel, made clear that the reason was opposition to the privileges afforded the republics in both the Federation Treaty and Yeltsin's draft constitution (see *Rossiiskie vesti*, July 3, 1993, p. 1, translated in the *CDSP*, Vol. XLV, No. 27, p. 1).

50. Indeed, these are also the areas where support for Yeltsin increased the most between the 1991 Presidential elections and the April 25 referendum (see Dmitrii Oreshkin, "Regional'nyi pasians nakanune Dnia Konstitutsii," *Segodnia*, June 8, 1993).

51. See Andrei Melville, "Public Attitudes and the December Elections in Russia," paper to be presented at the XVI World Congress of the International Political Science Association, Berlin, August 21–25, 1994; Sergei P. Pavlenko, "Tsentr-Regiony: Kto Kogo?," *Mezhdunarodnaia zhizn'*, April 1993, pp. 89–95; and Mary Cline, "Nizhnii Novgorod."

52. See the compilation of documents on Moscow-Tatarstan relations put out by the Committee for Federation Affairs and Regional Policy of the State Duma, dated February 23, 1994. The treaty is also in *Rossiiskaia gazeta*, February 17, 1994.

4

From Redistribution to Marketization: Social and Attitudinal Change in Post-Soviet Russia

Victor Zaslavsky

An enormous social transformation is underway in post-Soviet Russia. Yet the contours of a new Russian society, arising from the wreckage of the Soviet empire, remain undefined. The noted Russian historian Mikhail Gefter, in his article, "Stalin Died Yesterday," has argued that one of the most salient characteristics of Stalinism was the liquidation of developmental alternatives.[1] The singularity of totalitarianism meant not only that the ruling Communist Party attempted to maintain power at any cost to society, but strove (paraphrasing Stalin) to "impose its own social system as far as its army could reach."[2] We are now witnessing the creation of a new type of relationship between state and society under conditions of freedom and democracy unknown throughout the long history of Russia. Under such unprecedented conditions, a variety of policy options is available to the political elite, and the first alternative models of social development are finally being tried. This chapter explores several interconnected issues. First, it analyzes the underlying principles of social stratification and the resulting social structure of the late Soviet society. Second, it discusses the phenomenon of state-dependency and the social type of worker it created. Third, it examines some major trends of the current social and cultural changes in Russia. Finally,

The author is grateful to Professor Yurii Levada and Dr. Lev Gudkov for their substantial advice and criticism and to the Social Sciences and Humanities Research Council of Canada for financial support.

it discusses the attitudes toward Russia's transformation prevailing among major social groups and categories of Russian society.

The Soviet Social Structure and the Principles of State-Engineered Stratification

During the formative years of Soviet society in the 1930s, coercion became the major organizing principle of the emerging social system. Striving for rapid industrialization, Stalin used terror to compensate for a lack of necessary investment capital. Violence became the means both to suppress all enemies of the one-party regime as well as to mobilize an enormous underpaid workforce. The three basic interdependent characteristics of this new social system, the Soviet-type society, that came into existence and took root during the Stalinist era included a one-party dictatorship, a centrally-planned economy, and a powerful and growing military-industrial complex.[3] Although these basic traits were preserved and even strengthened following the death of Stalin, the Soviet-type society as a whole underwent significant political, economic, and social changes during the ensuing period. The most noteworthy trend in its socioeconomic evolution was the gradual shift from coercion to material incentives, while its political evolution moved in the direction of the "corrupt routinization" of a Leninist regime.[4] As a result, the mobilizational society gave way to one whose stable functioning was achieved largely by means of a social compromise—an organized "consensus" based on passive docility and obedience, extracted from the population less through terror than by a slow, but definite growth in living standards.[5] The main goal of a Soviet-type economy was a constant growth in the state-controlled surplus, while the centrally planned redistribution of this surplus became the major mode of economic coordination. The central government gradually became a vast mechanism for the redistribution of wealth, allocating it in such a manner as to support the extensive growth of heavy industry—particularly the military sector— and buttress the stability of the one-party regime. In effect, the state succeeded in creating a "dictatorship over needs," reallocating the economic surplus directly to those groups considered critical for maintaining the regime's internal stability.[6]

In Soviet-type societies the party-state apparatus became the primary structural agent of society after the nationalization of all private property. The redistributive state was responsible for the entire social structure of society. It determined the size and composition of different social groups, and the relationships between them. The Soviet state controlled all the hierarchical distinctions in the division of labor by establishing levels of remuneration and strict rules of social mobility. The state created boundaries and administrative barriers between social groups; introduced regulations and informal procedures governing intergroup transfer; even created administrative ties between individuals and the positions they occupied in the division of labor. The state's priorities were enshrined in a complex system of social and territorial hierarchies. The position of a particular group depended on its importance, either real or presumed, to the smooth functioning of the system as a whole. In a society where the state redistributive apparatus, rather than market exchange, determined the ranking of the various social groups, the divisions in society came to resemble castes far more than classes.[7] The Soviet social structure acted as a state-enforced mechanism for determining the appropriate levels of consumption. As one Russian scholar commented, in its simplest form the structure functioned like a ration-card system in the years during and after the Second World War. "There were ration cards for laborers and their dependents, cards for children and the elderly, cards for military and civilian industrial workers. There were also groups which did not have state-guaranteed access to supplies, such as collective farmers. And other groups—labor camp inmates—whose rights to supplies had been formally denied."[8]

For this reason, even today an analysis of the structure of Soviet-type societies presents significant theoretical and practical difficulties. The pattern of social stratification created by the Soviet redistributive state has been inadequately studied precisely because central control over mass media and scientific inquiry within the USSR, supported by the powerful apparatus of state censorship and official disinformation, did not permit empirical research. The Soviet state and its ideological apparatus spared no effort to inculcate the idea that the USSR was rapidly approaching a state of social uniformity. As a known Russian sociologist wrote, "even the faintest allusions to the existence of stratification in Soviet society were suppressed."[9] In practice, those researchers who attempted to paint more realistic pictures of society were compelled to rely exclusively on private research, participant observations, and anecdotal evidence.[10] Only during the era of *perestroika* were Russian sociologists finally allowed to embark on empirically grounded research. Tatiana Zaslavskaia and Rozalina Ryvkina were among the first to seriously attempt a description of the real social structure of society.[11] They came up with a preliminary hierarchy of vertically organized social groups delineated on the basis of industrial sector and worker qualifications, and identified 78 different social groupings in society. As the authors themselves stressed, the absence of reliable statistics and previous empirical research made it impossible to determine the size of each category. The first studies on the actual size of the principal social groupings began to appear in the late 1980s. For example, according to the cal-

TABLE 4.1   Main Professional or Social Groupings (by percent of the total workforce)

Nomenklatura	0.7%
Administrators and Managers	3.5%
Literary and Artistic Intelligentsia—"creative intelligentsia"	1.8%
Technical Specialists	18.8%
Low-Skilled Clerical/Technical Workers	5.0%
Industrial—"blue-collar labor"	41.3%
Service Workers	13.0%
Peasants and Agricultural Workers	15.0%

Source: Aleksei Kochetov, "Istoki 'novoi' sotsial'noi struktury," Svobodnaia mysl', 9, 1993, p. 68.

culations of Aleksei Kochetov, the structure of Soviet society during the mid–1980s can be describes as in Table 4.1.

As Kochetov observed, however, uncovering further contours of stratification was impossible "because all the indicators of social differentiation—power, income, prestige, education, lifestyle, consumption, etc.—could be correlated only within the ruling administrative and managerial elite. For society at large, educational and labor qualifications were often inversely correlated to official income, which furthermore did not reflect real earning power."[12] These results suggest that analysts still need to precisely identify the role the redistributive state played in the stratification of society.

A detailed study of the Soviet social structure remains an urgent task for future research. It requires an in-depth examination of archival materials and statistics that for decades have been inaccessible to scholars. A wide use of oral history methods is also imperative. The testimony of various party-state functionaries who supervised and directed the activities of the Soviet redistributive state will reveal a great deal about the precise pattern of state-engineered stratification. For our purpose, however, it is sufficient to recognize that stratification in Soviet society was organized through several interrelated subsystems of political, economic, territorial, and ethnic stratification, controlled by the state, combined with a system of economic stratification originated within the market economy over which the redistributive state had only partial control. The present "great transformation" underway in Russia involves the dismantling of the established social structure of the late Soviet society. A brief overview of its major components is, therefore, necessary for understanding the direction and the magnitude of the current social change.

The most powerful and privileged groups at the top of the Soviet social pyramid realized direct control over the state and its redistributive system. These groups included members of the Communist Party nomenklatura, who often occupied parallel positions within the state apparatus. Next to the nomenklatura, the economic managers of key state industries, including the corps of the various ministries, the enterprise managers and other lesser-ranked managers should be mentioned. They were followed by a large group of service workers, assistants, salespeople and others directly employed in trade and services. Despite the different weight these various groups held in the hierarchy of political power, they were united by their common responsibility for the smooth functioning of the redistributive machinery of state, in return for which they extracted substantial economic advantages. In the heyday of Soviet-type society, central planning successfully relegated market relations to a secondary place. During the final decades of the Soviet Union, however, the importance of various black and "grey" markets was constantly growing in proportion to the Soviet economic decline and the increasingly routinized corruption of the one-party regime.[13] The phenomenon of a "second economy" sprang up. To some extent this second economy was a source of goods and services produced and sold outside of state control, although it functioned predominantly as a continuation of the state redistributive network and should be properly viewed as its illegal or semi-legal extension.[14] As the second economy and the official redistributive machinery steadily merged, the principal operators of both groups became increasingly linked. Making use of the state's monopoly of political and economic power, the members of both groups came to represent the Soviet "elite."[15] According to Russian estimates, the incomes in these groups could have been hundreds of times higher than the country's average wages.[16]

To a significant extent, the creation of a Soviet middle class was similarly the product of the activities of the redistributive state. Whether because of the perceived importance of their positions in the division of labor or because of their connections to those economic and military sectors considered most vital to the state, several territorial, ethnic, and occupational groups were routinely favored with preferential treatment. Wages, housing, and related services were allocated by the state in accordance with the priority of heavy industry over consumer-good production. The vast wage differences between these two sectors led to an exodus of manpower to heavy industry at the expense of less privileged sectors. In addition, under conditions of a semi-free labor market, enterprises were compelled to compete with one another in order to attract labor, creating additional privileges in the form of available housing and increased availability of consumer goods. In this competition heavy industry, backed by ample state investment, was able to offer the most favorable terms to its employees.

The highest priority treatment was always reserved for the military sector of the economy, for which an entire system of so-called "closed" enterprises was created. These enterprises formed the backbone of the entire military-industrial complex and reinforced its central position in the Soviet economy. Commanding top priority in the supply of raw materials and manpower, military factories were able to attract the latest technology and the most qualified workers. The military-industrial complex was able to pay the highest wages, establish the best retirement conditions, provide better-quality housing, medical care, and durable consumer goods to its workforce. The closed enterprises greatly facilitated the exercise of political and economic control over the population and reinforced the tendency toward social stability.[17] This comparatively numerous and upwardly mobile group of highly skilled, well-paid industrial workers, engineers, and scientists employed in military, nuclear, and space industries came to represent the bulk of the state-dependent middle class. For the post-Stalin generations, they became symbols of success and social accomplishment that other, less privileged strata aspired to replicate.

A complex set of measures initially adopted by the Soviet regime to control internal migration and labor supply developed eventually into an elaborate system of territorial stratification. A hierarchy of territorial settlements was established. The administrative status accorded to a city by the Party leadership determined both the level of capital investment it received from the state and the development of the city's industrial and civil infrastructure. On this, in turn, depended the quality and availability of consumer goods and housing, the level of services and socio-cultural institutions, even the salaries of state employees and white-collar professionals, such as doctors and teachers.

Having introduced the top-priority category of "closed cities," the redistributive state had taken a decisive step in the organization and administration of this territorial-based system of social stratification.[18] Closed cities were considered the most important settlements in the country, with rights to permanent residence conferred only by birth or by special permission of the city administration. The hierarchy of population settlements in the redistributive state led to the establishment of a stable hierarchy of status and to the emergence of new social groups and categories whose members had different life chances and enjoyed very different levels of consumption. The closed cities also played an increasingly important role in structuring access to higher education and promoting the growth of the group of Soviet specialists traditionally known as the intelligentsia. Indeed, the major universities of the country were all located within these closed cities, as were the majority of specialists with a higher education. The proliferation of elite schools and specialized services such as private tutoring in closed cities gave their residents a decisive advantage in access to prestigious universities and other institutions of higher education. Membership in the Soviet elite and educated middle classes, thus, took on an increasingly hereditary character. The redistributive state solved the inherent problem of population stagnation in closed cities by creating a special category of "guest laborers" hired by the closed city enterprises and given a temporary residence permit—the so-called *limitchiki*. This new social category bore a strong resemblance to the Gastarbeiter in Germany or Switzerland, and like them, occupied a niche at the very bottom of the social structure. For the party leadership and economic managers, the *limitchiki* represented a convenient group, whose passive compliance and labor discipline were virtually guaranteed. This fact explains the growing presence of *limitchiki* in the Soviet social structure. Thus, between 1960 and 1980, an inflow of *limitchiki* to Moscow was maintained at the level of nearly 100,000 workers per year. Most remained in the city as temporary residents, while the fortunate managed to acquire permanent residency status. As a result, the actual or former *limitchiki* comprised around 15% of the total labor force in Moscow, Leningrad, and other closed cities.[19]

These and analogous policies of creating special "top priority" enterprises and entire industrial sectors, privileged geographic regions and settlements, and an accompanying system of most-and least-favored social and ethnic groups exemplify the enormous role the Soviet redistributive state played in creating and maintaining a hierarchical social structure. Using its position both as the sole employer for the entire labor force and as the primary agency of redistribution, the state established a political-administrative ascription for membership in major social groups and categories. Treating certain strata as strategically crucial to the maintenance of internal stability, the state skewed the economic surplus highly in their favor. By erecting and controlling the administrative barriers between different groups, the state became the principal regulator of intergroup mobility.

The Redistributive State and the State-Dependent Worker

The legacy of the Soviet-type society is not limited to its peculiar social structure and particular system of entrenched social stratification. Ironically, the notion that the Soviet-type society represented a specific civilization which had created its own unique cultural "genetic code" deeply imprinted in the population and revealed by a host of uniquely "Soviet" values, motivations, attitudes, and behavior patterns, was first invented and then widely disseminated by Soviet propaganda.[20] Yet during the past decade, the idea that the populations of Soviet-type societies reveal certain deep-seated attitudes and behavioral characteristics after decades of communist-style modernization has found confirmation in a number of studies conducted both before and after the fall of the Soviet Union.[21] Indeed, Piotr Sztompka justifiably concludes that the sources of remarkably similar thinking and cultural patterns across widely differing former socialist countries "lie in their common socialist structures, rather than in their idiosyncratic histories."[22] The Soviet-type societies generated a specific psychological and social type—the "state-dependent worker"—characterized by particular attitudes toward work and toward the redistributive state.[23] These attitudes were displayed in acts of work avoidance rather than self-discipline and productivity, a general disdain for work in all state-managed economic sectors, and a specific disinclination to risk personal initiatives. The state-dependent worker values security over achievement. The state-dependent workers were intimately connected with the entire system of state-engineered stratification and the attendant redistribution of goods and rewards. In the complete absence of democratic controls in a vast country endowed with enormous resources, post-Stalinist social policies were at once paternalistic and simultaneously highly inequitable. The redistributive state guaranteed job security to all, yet it bestowed privileges on a few select social groups according to a preconceived design. As a result, productivity and rewards became disconnected, and incentives for innovation and greater productivity were destroyed. The redistributive state achieved a peculiar trade-off between stability and productivity. While worker needs and expectations were often quite low, an omnipotent state guaranteed cradle-to-grave benefits, including complete job security and low prices for staples and housing, however substandard. As Yegor Ligachev, once Gorbachev's rival for Communist Party leadership, has put it, "the most valuable aspect of Soviet life was always people's confidence and security with regard to the future."[24] Such paternalistic policies were the principal preconditions for a stable, consensual relationship between the rulers and the ruled. They determined the fundamental norms, attitudes, and expectations of the Soviet population, and in turn, contributed decisively to the generation and proliferation of the state-dependent personality.

But whatever the state's initial success in maintaining this social pact, it eventually came to naught through the regime's wastefulness and ineffectiveness, which was the result of the combination of central planning, one-party dictatorship, and militarization of the economy. The economic stagnation aggravated by increased expenditures by a military-industrial complex locked in open competition with the West, together with the needs of a growing population whose consumption patterns were changing as a result of newly accessible information about Western consumer society, left fewer and fewer resources available for redistribution.[25] Already in 1971, Mikhail Gefter noted that the Soviet system's dual ambition of asserting complete control over every aspect of human existence and providing a "multifaceted cradle-to-grave security" was increasingly strained. "With every day the system's failure to deliver on its promise is becoming ever more glaring."[26]

Soviet Collapse and the Ongoing Transformation of Russia's Social Structure

The dramatic collapse of the global communist system modeled on the Soviet Union has entailed the colossal transformation of the countries' social, political, and economic structures. This process began later in Russia than it did in the majority of East European countries, but once underway, the social change has been gaining in momentum. The progressive dismantling of the redistributive state and rapid transformations in power and property relations are leading to a rapid overhaul of the social structure that Russia inherited from the Soviet Union. Basic trends and the first results of social change may be discerned even within the brief space of a few years. Among the main social phenomena accompanying the collapse of the old system that deserve particular attention are: the birth of a new property-owning class, the transformation of the middle class, and the changes in status of various social categories, including the young, the elderly, women, and certain territorial-based populations.

Today, Russian society is in flux. The system of privileges and advantages once enjoyed by the beneficiaries of state redistribution is disappearing. After the dissolution of the USSR the policies of preferential treatment of "indigenous" nationalities in the country's administrative and managerial structures lost their rationale. The system of territorial stratification is similarly coming to an end, with its administrative heart—the permanent residence permit system, the *propiska*—declared officially unconstitutional. Although *propiska* still exists in large cities, its role in the allocation of housing and permanent employment is diminishing rapidly. Indeed, the process of disintegration has already acquired such momentum that one can correctly speak of the state redistributive system only in terms of its remnants and the inertia they exert on reforms.

The late 1980s and early 1990s witnessed the process of primary capital accumulation and the emergence of a new "post-Soviet" class of property owners. What is the role of the old nomenklatura ruling elite in these ongoing processes? After the Soviet disintegration the nomenklatura as a social group lost its monopoly on political power and control over society. The careers of many individual members of the nomenklatura have been destroyed. The "losers" have been substantially more numerous than could have been predicted for two reasons. First, due to the exceptional cadre stability of the Brezhnev period, the nomenklatura turned into a ruling "gerontocracy." For many members of the group there simply was no time to adapt to the changing circumstances.

Second, a significant portion of the nomenklatura that controlled the activities of the lower strata of the apparat, central planning, ideology, and cultural production have lost their functions and simply exited the political stage altogether. Nevertheless, the nomenklatura as a whole has been remarkably successful in making use of its enormous "head start" in the process of privatization. Already during the Gorbachev period, those who were charged with administering the redistributive machinery of state had begun to commercialize it. During 1987–1991, laws were enacted which nullified the state's monopoly over foreign trade, allowed the creation of small-scale businesses, and even permitted joint ventures with foreign partners. The strict control over foreign-currency transactions was weakened and foreign-currency ownership was decriminalized. These laws opened previously unforeseen possibilities for legal profit-making operations within state enterprises. Many, particularly younger members of the nomenklatura moved into the organs of state administration and seized the opportunity to legally exploit state enterprises. Striking deals with newly created private firms, they often became co-owners, underwriting operations with their investment. Making extensive use of personal contacts, they began to market information, services, and official licensing. Playing the role of essential middlemen, they began to capitalize on an extremely ill-developed and lopsided market characterized by a near total absence of freely accessible information and business "networking" contacts between wholesalers and retailers.

In other words, Russia is witnessing the birth of a process already dubbed "political capitalism" in Eastern Europe.[27] Those who occupied key positions in the political bureaucracy still control the budgetary allocation of state subsidies and have become the primary beneficiaries of privatization. This segment presently forms the backbone of the rapidly growing class of property owners. Through a network of financial organizations acting as intermediaries, the nomenklatura is selling, often at "dumping" prices, raw materials, oil, and competitive Russian manufactured products on the Western market. They have deposited part of the proceeds from these sales in Western bank accounts but have spent most of their profits on Western-made goods, which they subsequently resell at a profit in Russia. Thus, the process of state property privatization initially took the form of a privatization of foreign trade.

The social groups connected with the second economy play an active part in this process. The state redistributive nomenklatura, especially those supervising the service sector, and the organizers of the second economy had already begun to converge in the Brezhnev period. Under the new circumstances of post-Soviet Russia, this "fusion" process has been accelerating. Former operatives of the shadow economy quickly launder their accumulated capital and reinvest it, making use of the new financial structures designed for this purpose. In the words of Lilia Beliaeva, a process of "mafia-nomenklatura privatization" is taking place through stock markets created from previously existing state monopolies.[28] According to analysts, Russia's legal entrepreneurs consist mainly of two basic types: the "nomenklatura entrepreneurs" who are making good use of their past personal and professional connections and access to the state redistribution system, and those previously connected with the Soviet second economy, "more often than not with a criminal past." These businessmen operating in the present semi-criminal environment "make up the majority of the nouveaux riches called the 'new Russians.' In Moscow, according to commonly accepted estimates, their number approaches 300,000, in St. Petersburg, nearly 150,000, and throughout Russia as a whole, they number anywhere from 1.5 to 2 million."[29] Many representatives of the old nomenklatura have thus accumulated considerable wealth to compensate for their lost monopoly over political power.

The further development of "bottom-up" as well as "top-down" privatization has recently created a new stage in the transition to a market system. As the hierarchical system of central planning and political power disintegrates, a barter economy is coming into being, replacing the old "command-administrative economy." State property is being privatized, with enterprise directors and young, highly skilled technical specialists at the forefront of this new phenomenon. Under these circumstances of economic reorganization, the upper echelons of enterprise management, together with the managers of newly organized banks and financial intermediary organizations, have become the co-owners of former state enterprises. Naturally, high-level managers seek to become the private owners of a considerable amount of property, but more than anything they are interested in continuing with their managerial functions. They are not coming up against serious opposition, for, as Vitalii Naishul' has noted, Russia has been a stranger to social democratic models of worker participation in management.[30] In reality, very few groupings in the labor force are laying any claim to worker participation, favoring income guarantees instead.

The implementation of Anatolii Chubais' privatization program, in existence now for more than two years, has been strongly influenced by this lack of interest and experience on the part of industrial workers in taking responsibility for their enterprises under privatization. In theory, privatization of state property must proceed in accordance with the "real" value of the holdings in question; but with a weak market system and a widespread absence of investment capital and individual savings, there are no effective procedures for establishing these "real" market values. On top of this, a volatile political situation aggravated by a continuing economic crisis has compelled the reformers to accelerate privatization to make it irreversible. The result has meant a colossal gain in property holdings for the high-level enterprise management.

The 1994 privatization experience of the "Zil" automobile factory, which once manufactured limousines for the Soviet elite, is perhaps typical. According to an employee's account, although the firm's net worth was putatively around one trillion rubles, its management estimated the cost of the factory to be slightly more than three billion and issued the corresponding stock to be sold to the enterprise's employees. The vast majority of the stock was bought by the director, the assistant director, and other members of the management at bargain prices, and they became instant multimillionaires in the process. The entire scheme never encountered any workers' opposition, not only because the workers, "largely former *limitchiki*, were afraid to lose their jobs," but mainly because the workers themselves were deriving considerable advantages from the privatization process.[31] In a word, privatization is responsible for the renewal of Russia's economic elite, which now includes a growing portion of the high-level management, as well as administrative and managerial specialists. It is also responsible for the birth of an increasing population of small-scale proprietors. Regardless of the specific criticism of the way it has been carried out, privatization is now the primary agent of social differentiation in Russia's turbulent transition period.

The composition of the Soviet middle class, which social scientists have identified on the basis of education and occupational skills, consumption levels, urban lifestyle, and interests, is highly amorphous.[32] According to Blair Ruble, it includes "urban-based, professional, paraprofessional and highly skilled socio-occupational groups from the working middle class, highly skilled manual workers and workers-technicians to university-educated specialists, and the Soviet intelligentsia, particularly young professionals."[33] During the years of the disintegration of the redistributive state, this group has experienced perhaps the greatest transformation of all. The decline of the Soviet intelligentsia has been particularly noticeable. The intelligentsia has traditionally played the dual role of providing intellectual support and legitimation to the Communist regime while simultaneously acting as the source of opposition. The nature of their work made them lean toward a liberal reorganization of a one-party state, sometimes to the point of outright dissent. Russian researchers particularly stress the intelligentsia's ambivalent position in the aging Soviet regime: it was ensuring the smooth functioning of the system and simultaneously "fulfilling its traditional historical role as an opposition force acting as partial ideological saboteurs."[34] Yet being a group both politically and economically dependent on the state, the intelligentsia rarely went beyond advocating a liberalized, "reformed" Soviet system. Basically supporting the regime, the intelligentsia managed to preserve its unique position in society between the powers-that-were, which they hoped to reform, and the people, whom they hoped to civilize and enlighten. Yet it was precisely that shield of state dependency created by the Soviet system for the intelligentsia which both freed it from having to compete in the market and made it an ineffective and unproductive social category, especially during the transition to a new economy. The institutions which supported and employed the intelligentsia, such as government-financed literary journals, the various "creative unions" of writers, artists, film-makers and other cultural producers, and the vast centers of the Academies of Sciences, are presently being disbanded and losing not only their state subsidies but their very purpose in the new society. Members of society are now increasingly focusing on private problems of everyday existence and survival. The composition of society and the very orientation and criteria for personal conduct are becoming more complex. Western mass culture is penetrating Russian society, gaining popular acceptance. In these new conditions "the intelligentsia as a social stratum and the ideological culture and a specific type of world outlook it was disseminating" are becoming obsolete and unnecessary.[35]

As a result, the Russian intelligentsia is rapidly differentiating into a group of professionals and intellectuals, in composition and function similar to their Western counterparts, and a large mass of "intellectual workers" with university degrees. Many of the latter, in the opinion of sociologist Lev Gudkov, "are often poorly prepared, passive, de-skilled, not ready for painful retraining, and thus remain doomed to degradation and impoverishment, since they stand no chance to adapt to the new conditions."[36] Accordingly, as sociological evidence indicates, "the level of anxiety, expectation of all kinds of catastrophes and calamities among those with higher education (particularly those living in large cities and regional capitals) exceeds the corresponding indicators of other groups by a factor of two or three."[37] It is the Soviet intelligentsia that produces the avalanche of catastrophic writings in the mass media concerning the coming ruin of Russia and Russian civilization. These predictions are provoked by a far from novel social phenomenon, which occurs when a group leaving the historical scene confuses its own exit with a general demise of society and culture.

The collapse of the redistributive state has taken a huge toll on another group which has occupied a central place in the Soviet middle class—that of technical specialists, engineers, and skilled workers employed by the elite enterprises of the military, particularly the atomic and space industries. Indeed, the price society at large paid to maintain this hypertrophied military-industrial complex was enormous. Aside from being the major cause of the tremendous waste of resources and of the technological backwardness of the civilian sector of the economy, the military-industrial complex has played a preeminent role in maintaining the status quo and opposing reform. The lion's share of the educated and skilled labor force, which might have constituted a crucial element in the reform movement, was instead thoroughly integrated in the Soviet system thanks to an extensive system of privileges the redistributive state granted to the military sector.[38] This arrangement ensured that the social base for reform during the critical early stages of the economic crisis would be quite narrow, and that the chances for an authentic reformist leader to get to the top would be minimal. The Party bureaucracy and the military-industrial complex became preoccupied with fundamental reform only after the systemic crisis had reached the point of no return.

The military-industrial complex is now paying the piper. Already during *perestroika*, economic crisis had become severe enough that the central authorities had to reduce financing the military-industrial complex. The economic reforms of post-Soviet Russia, launched by the Gaidar administration in January 1992, have deliberately and dramatically slashed resource allocation and capital investment to the defense sector.[39] Correspondingly, this sector has lost its priority status in the state budget, and its unified administrative management was broken up. The more conservative government of Prime Minister Chernomyrdin has promised to improve state investment in this sector, but to little effect. In the cutthroat competition for state subsidies, the military-industrial complex has been compelled to wage a desperate rear-guard battle against the needs of the energy and agricultural business sectors. Today, the position of the military-industrial complex is far from auspicious.[40] The sharp decline in state support has deepened the sense of inertia associated with state dependency that is particularly visible in this sector. As Erik Whitlock has aptly noted, "defense industry managers have shown themselves incapable of dealing adequately with the new economic environment and the opportunities presented them. They have waited too long to move more aggressively into the manufacturing of new product lines in the expectation that the state would intervene and provide financial support. They have demonstrated an almost equal lack of skill in the areas of product marketing, prices, and so on."[41]

The process of adaptation to the market has nonetheless begun even in the military-industrial complex. As a result of internal differentiation, certain enterprises have shown reasonable levels of professional managerial competence, technological prowess, and potential for export. Their chances for successful adaptation to internal and global markets appear good.[42] However, a significant portion of this sector stands no chance for market success without an expensive multi-faceted conversion, which the state simply cannot afford. In fact, the Russian government is gradually instituting a policy advocated years ago by the emigre economist Igor' Birman and long considered paradoxical or even comical: to stop production without shutting down the factories which make unwanted goods. Such measures at the very least save fuel and natural resources and thus leave more for the market, eventually increasing social wealth.[43] Employees work shortened hours, take leaves of absence, but continue to receive their salaries, although erratically and sometimes without corresponding inflationary adjustments. Under such conditions, those who can find new jobs do so, often in the private sector. The "company towns," however, which made up an important part of Soviet military-industrial complex, find themselves in a particularly difficult situation, since opportunities for new employment are very limited. The Russian press frequently details the protests and strike threats of employees of nuclear development centers or plants for the production of atomic submarines, who were once an elite group with living standards among the highest in the country.

Examining the transformation of the Russian middle class, it would nonetheless be misleading to focus exclusively on the more noticeable and spectacular processes associated with the decline of groups like the intelligentsia and the military-industrial complex employees. The most important and promising changes underway have to do with its transformation from a class defined by the redistributive state activities to a middle class more characteristic of an economy in which market relations predominate. Many skilled workers in state enterprises have made the adaptation to working in a market system, as have an even larger part of workers in the private sector. The formation of a genuine middle class which relies on a market system will be a protracted process. A significant percentage of entrepreneurs as well as hired workers still remain wary of breaking their ties with their old workplaces and often continue to work in state enterprises, but "are simultaneously making preparations to move to the private sector altogether."[44] Keeping their old positions and their guaranteed state salaries thus acts as a buffer against the possible failure of one's business or against a wholesale reversal of pro-market government policy.

Among the workforce employed in the Russian economy today, sociologists have identified two categories, which, thanks to their acceptance of innovation and their positive attitudes toward the ongoing changes, have become a social-psychological base for the emergence of a new middle class. Primarily, these groups consist of workers who are more concerned about the size of their incomes than about guarantees of continued employment. Many of them believe, not without justification, that their chances for success in a market system are high. Their general state of mind is positive and their adaptability to new conditions is above average. This general attitude, according to the estimates of public-opinion surveys, is held by approximately one-quarter of the entire adult population.[45] A second category consists of new entrepreneurs who are actively engaged in creating their own businesses in the private sector. In surveys conducted by the Russian Center for Public Opinion Research, up to 10–15% of respondents, chiefly younger people under 30, can be so categorized.[46] Naturally, the size and fluctuation of the membership of this group depends, first and foremost, on the course of reform in the country as a whole, and on the success and general prestige of the entre-preneurial group in society. Yet for the past three years, the percentage of those having their own business has increased rapidly, from four percent in 1991 to eight percent in 1993.[47] As Tatiana Zaslavskaia has noted, one of the larger sociological consequences of continued reforms has been the "growth of the middle layers of society, consisting of the most skilled, active and enterprising citizens."[48]

As to the population at large, sociological research shows that although economic reforms have disrupted the reproduction of state-dependent workers, most of the employed population still fits into this category. Longitudinal studies on attitudes toward social differentiation and inequality revealed that more than half of the respondents remain firmly in agreement with state policies providing "small but guaranteed income."[49] Inevitably, this attitude prevails far more in the public sector than in the private. Obviously, the system of state dependence and bureaucratic redistribution that minimized individual risk, guaranteed job security, price stability, and a generally egalitarian income policy regardless of labor productivity, is mainly responsible for the continued resilience of such widespread attitudes in Russian society. In a survey conducted during the autumn of 1992, up to one-half of respondents agreed with the statement that "it would be better if *perestroika* never happened."[50] Doubtless, the overwhelming majority of these were state-dependent workers.

Sociological analysis has demonstrated extremely varied reactions to the collapse of the Soviet system depending on a person's gender, age, occupation, area of residence, and whether they are "winners" or "losers" in the new system. Today, the greatest division in Russian society is due to age. Surveys reveal that among the age cohort of 25 and younger, 74% prefer a market system to a centrally planned one, while among those 40 and older, only 36% express such a preference.[51] A positive stance on the part of younger people toward the social transformations underway can be taken for granted precisely because the young constitute a growing majority of the upwardly mobile members of society. More than any other group, young people supported the demilitarization of the state, including the Soviet withdrawal from Afghanistan, the reduction in the size and influence of the armed forces, and the decentralization of the Soviet Union. The younger generation enthusiastically supported the growing openness toward the West, which they saw as a guarantor against return to the status quo ante. Interest in the West, specifically the United States, Germany, Japan, and other developed countries, among young Russians remains extremely high. While there are certainly young right-wing extremists, such as those who supported Vladimir Zhirinovsky in the December 1993 elections to the Federal Assembly,[52] the preponderant majority "react happily to events which open doors to both private life and personal initiative."[53] Characteristically, this group judges the social transformation in pragmatic fashion, in terms of the increased availability of quality imported goods, personal housing, and trips abroad. From the late 1980s, young people have increasingly marked the "opportunity to earn a good living" as the chief indicator of positive change. Analogies between post-Soviet Russia and Weimar Germany can now frequently be found in the mass media.[54] Yet it is precisely the cardinal difference in the attitudes of younger people in the two societies that negates their outward similarity. Unlike their Weimar counterparts, young people in Russia are generally satisfied with the overall direction in which society is headed, for they have been the primary beneficiaries of the collapse of the authoritarian gerontocracy of the old regime.[55]

At the opposite end of the age spectrum are, unsurprisingly, the groups who make up the principal "losers" from the collapse of the old system. It has already been observed that in Soviet-type societies mental habits, adaptive behavior, and defense mechanisms which evolved as a direct result of prolonged indoctrination and as a way of coping with socialist conditions "outlive their times, become petrified in social structures, cultural patterns and popular consciousness, and remain fully operative in post-communist societies."[56] This best characterizes the older generation. The economic situation of this group after the ruin of the redistributive system is particularly dramatic and precarious, as many have watched their life savings disappear as a consequence of price liberalization and hyperinflation. Because the Soviet state used pensions to battle unemployment, setting the retirement age at 55 for women and at 60 for men, the number of those receiving retirement pensions is particularly large, approaching one-quarter of the total population and nearly 40% of those able to work. While the precise financing of the social retirement fund remains unclear, there is every reason to suspect that this fund—always controlled by the state and never by the recipients of the pensions—lacks adequate resources to meet the growing needs of this age bracket.

Indeed, one of the most bitter legacies of Soviet society is that the surplus value created by the labor of today's pensioners was long ago frittered away by the state. As a result, the current working population must contribute an ever larger portion of its output to subsidize a huge and continuously increasing number of retirees who have no other resources at their disposal. The structural position of this group reveals that their principal, if not sole interest, remains the preservation and strengthening of the central state as the single agent capable of preserving the social safety net. Opinion surveys invariably demonstrate that the majority of retirees prefer a planned economy to a market one. In democratic elections, no single political party will be able to achieve much without the support of these people, who are known for their regular voting habits. Generational change, next to economic stabilization, thus becomes a crucial precondition to Russia's successful transition to democracy.

Women make up the second category of the population which, at least in the short run, has suffered more than it gained from the collapse of the redistributive state. Growing discrimination against women was a significant feature of Soviet society.[57] The double burden of work outside and in the home led to continuous inequalities in professional life, aggravated by the prejudices held by the male political elite against "successful" women. Women have always taken on the bulk of the lowest-paid occupations in society. Besides, the combination of early retirement and significantly longer average life span results in women far outnumbering men among pensioners. The first stage of the market transition inevitably strengthens discrimination against women. Economists from the Russian Academy of Sciences argue that "the basis of this discrimination lies in the lack of competitiveness of women in the labor market, due to their maternal functions. The strengthening of 'protective' laws, requiring enterprises to provide benefits to women only, complicates the position of women."[58] As a result, many women, especially those with children, are forced out of their jobs. Women now comprise approximately 70% of those unemployed. The pay differential between men and women is growing and women now make up no more than 25% of the better paid private sector work force.[59] Russia's democrats made a serious mistake in the last elections by overlooking the particular issues which face women in the course of reform. By failing to come up with a special program to defend women's interests, the democrats allowed the "Women of Russia," a group close to the communists, to fill this void and receive a noticeable percentage of the vote.

Age and qualifications, despite their importance, are insufficient to define the full range of economic, social, and political preferences of industrial workers. The difficulties encountered by specific factories and branches of industry in the process of transition play an enormous role in shaping the attitudes of their workers. Leonid Gordon, using these factors, singled out four groups of workers, identifying them on the basis of social characteristics and political outlook.[60] Skilled workers in industries making a smooth entrance to the market, in all likelihood, possess a democratic trade-union perspective and fully support democratic changes and the transition to the market economy. Less-educated, low-skilled workers in the same industries are often quite indifferent to democracy and favor the transition to a market economy under conditions of authoritarian rule. In the branches of industry and enterprise whose market entrance is highly problematic, skilled workers have a tendency to support utopian-democratic, anti-capitalistic ideals. In favor of democratic transition, they are simultaneously interested in preserving the Soviet redistributive system. Less qualified workers in these branches of industry simply long for the restoration of the political and economic system of the Soviet era. This schematization, linking the social condition of different groups of workers with their possible social and political attitudes and viewpoints, has proven useful in investigating the alternative visions of the miners' movement and the myriad unions and other organizations representing the interests of industrial workers in post-Soviet Russia.[61] It helps us to understand empirical data on the attitudes of workers in the military-industrial complex or workers from industries of the Far North, which are experiencing significant difficulty in the transition to a market economy.

Russia's Socio-Psychological Climate and Prospects for the Future

The rapid stratification of the population and the rapid growth of economic inequality, combined with the articulation of group interests, would lead us to expect opposition to market reforms to continually grow and perhaps become overwhelming. The redistributive state still

remains an ideal for a significant part of the population. Victor Yaroshenko justly noted that "the idea of cradle-to-grave social justice exercised
by a 'paternalistic government' that defends, educates, and punishes its
subjects is lodged deeply in the popular consciousness."[62] The progressive decline of the redistributive state has adversely affected huge strata
of the population. Undoubtedly, many people "might welcome the stability of the Brezhnev years over the chaos of the post-Soviet transition."[63] The social base of various nostalgic anti-reform programs is
much narrower, however, than the numbers of people negatively affected
by the change. To grasp the reasons for this we should investigate several
over-arching attitudinal trends characterizing the social atmosphere of
today's polarized Russian society: the mass acceptance of the irreversibility of reform, the growing de-politicization of society and the adaption to
crisis, borrowing de Certeau's phrase, through "the practice of everyday
life."[64]

A new socio-psychological climate is now taking shape in the country.
The first characteristic of this climate is above all the acceptance of the
irreversibility of change. The deep transformation in the mentality of the
population crystallized simultaneously with the liberalization of prices
and other Gaidar reforms in 1992–1993. The economist Nikolai Shmelev
was one of the first to note that there passed a moment when "the entire
population, from the man on the street, to directors of enterprises, to
bureaucrats, realized that there was no way back."[65] The entire course of
perestroika prepared the way for this mentality shift. It happened as an
"inevitable result of the increase in society's openness and official recognition of the idea that the civilized world is unified by universal
values."[66] Another important factor was the elimination of censorship
and the flood of information about the backwardness and colossal wastefulness of the Soviet system, and the ecological damage which the
system visited upon the world and the Soviet population. Undoubtedly,
the overwhelming majority of Soviet citizens knew from personal experience at work and in the process of day-to-day life about the ineffectiveness and disorganization of the Soviet economy. The burst of information
in the mass media generalized this personal experience and helped convince the population that the country simply lacked the resources to
support a new redistributive state. Characteristically, in 1988 surveys,
only six percent of the respondents gave a negative overall evaluation of
the Soviet experience. In 1989, this figure rose to 34% and in 1990 it
reached 50% of the respondents.[67] The current mood is also characterized
by the widespread belief in the unpredictability of the immediate future
and the growth of a general anxiety and lack of certainty. This is reflected
in changes in the ranking of problems considered most urgent, which
serves as an important indicator of social change.[68] Until 1992, the popu-

lation was primarily worried about food shortages and the lack of consumer goods. This was a logical reaction to the rule of the redistributive state, which still sought to maintain low prices for basic products but was not in a position even remotely to satisfy the demand. The liberalization of prices and the decriminalization of the possession of hard currency radically changed the situation. Since 1992, high prices have been Russia's most serious problem. The unregulated growth of prices rather than empty shelves came to the fore as a problem for most of the population.

Unemployment is also increasingly becoming an issue. In 1991, surveys conducted by the Russian Center for Public Opinion Research showed that only seven percent of respondents worried about unemployment, ranked by the majority among the least important social problems.[69] Within a year, the problem of unemployment became one of the greatest issues of concern, even if the number of officially registered unemployed in the early 1994 was hardly more than one percent and the bankruptcy law had not yet been implemented.[70] The growing fear of unemployment arises from a recognition that market reforms are irreversible and the widespread awareness that the economy is suffering from an enormous redundancy of labor.

Finally, one of the more notable characteristics of the socio-psychological situation in the country is the growing de-politicization of the population. The period of *perestroika* was the last period of mass political mobilization. Then, a significant part of the population still thought that the question of power and the choice of a concrete program were critical for an immediate increase in the standard of living. Now, the acceptance of the inevitability and irreversibility of reform has combined with a growing understanding that the possibility of quick and easy exit from the crisis simply does not exist. As a result, the illusion of the government's omnipotence is disappearing, while interest and participation in politics are rapidly decreasing. The country is witnessing an exhaustion with politics, so that the current political struggle in Russia is carried on by weak political groups and parties lacking significant popular support.

The basic problems of daily life, adaptation to the ongoing crisis and family survival worry the population more than political or ideological issues. The very character of daily life has fundamentally changed. In the words of Andrei Illarionov, "life in and of itself has become more complicated and dynamic and has ceased to be stable, predictable, and guaranteed. It demands ever-increasing efforts simply to maintain, let alone to increase, one's standard of living."[71] According to the leading Russian sociologist Yurii Levada, "numerous surveys and studies show that people are now increasingly focussing on daily human interests and demands of the family, health, children, and basic standard of existence."[72] A relatively autonomous sphere of economic interests, which could not exist in the Soviet redistributive state, is intensively forming. The influence of the free market is strongly felt in people's daily lives. Recent statistics demonstrate a growth in the production of certain durable consumer goods, a significant shift in the import policy toward a greater share of consumer products, and a fundamental change in the structure of the GNP. The share of the GNP allocated to consumption has grown from 35.9% in 1992, to 40.5% in 1993.[73] "The tactics of consumption," as Michel de Certeau observed, "thus lend a political dimension to everyday practices."[74]

Even more important, a large part of society received some kind of property: many citizens became owners of their apartments, many workers received shares of their enterprises, and many got private plots of land. As the economic observer for the *Moscow Times* noted, the free market solved the problem of empty shelves, while the private plots parceled out by the Gorbachev and Yeltsin governments over the past five years averted the theoretical threat of starvation. The population relies on the government neither for potatoes nor vegetables, 80% and 65% of which are grown on private plots. The production of meat and milk on these plots is also growing.[75] Most sociologists agree that while the radical liberalization of prices and galloping inflation have seriously hurt most of the population, the idea of the centrally planned economy has not made a comeback. As a whole, we are witnessing a slow but noticeable growth in the acceptance of private economic initiative—especially in farming and consumer goods and services.[76]

It is still too early to conclude that the Russian economic crisis has hit bottom. The structural transformation of the economy is a long-term project. In order to complete this process, a large number of people must change their habits, ways of thinking, and professions. This ultimately requires a generational change. However, despite all of the social dislocation, inflation, and growth of economic inequality, daily life in Russian society preserves a certain regularity, which creates the basis for the future economic and political stabilization of society. For the first time after decades of the command economy and the redistributive state, the Russian population now lives under conditions of increasing market relations. People are beginning to feel, in the words of Fernand Braudel, the "enormous creative powers of the market, of the lower story of exchange, of the self-employed artisan or even of individual resourcefulness—creative powers which provide the economy not only with a rich foundation but with something to fall back on in times of crisis, war or serious economic collapse requiring structural change."[77]

Given the general economic chaos resulting from the destruction of the Soviet Union and its redistributive state, the nomenklatura-mafia privatization, the slow structural transformation of the economy, the enormous social inertia and opposition to reform from state-dependent workers, it is difficult to be optimistic about the short-term prospects for a general economic recovery in Russia. Many observers of the reform process in Russia have come to the conclusion that the traditional Soviet elite still preserves its power in the provinces, that economic rationalization has not begun yet, and that the drop in production and standard of living remains the only tangible result of the ongoing changes.[78] Typically, Michael Burawoy and Pavel Krotov discuss Russia's development in terms of the growth of merchant capitalism. According to their conclusions, "the relations of exchange and distribution have changed dramatically, marked by the liberalization of prices, the rise of barter, the development of cooperatives and the advent of consumer culture," but "the old relations of production persist."[79] Merchant capital seeks profit from trade and tends to leave intact indigenous systems of production. Under these conditions, workers assume even greater control of the shop floor than they had during Brezhnev's organized consensus. Old production monopolies keep controlling resources, credit, and distribution and do not turn into competing enterprises. As a result, merchant capital actively inhibits the independent development of modern capitalism. Burawoy and Krotov conclude that the Russian transition to modern capitalism is essentially a failure and Russia is doomed to remain stuck at the stage of merchant capitalism.[80]

Does Russia's development really warrant such pessimistic conclusions? It is not difficult to understand why the analysts who confront today's bleak reality conclude that the present underdevelopment and merchant capitalism are the final outcomes of the Russian transition. Taking into account, however, that Russian market reforms are less than three years old, analysts should not expect too much too soon, and should avoid the temptation to overgeneralize on the short-term patterns of change dominated up to now by the phenomena of the old order's destruction rather than of the emergence of a new social system. As Braudel has already warned, "it would be however a mistake to imagine capitalism as something that developed in a series of stages or leaps— from mercantile capitalism to industrial capitalism to finance capitalism, with some kind of regular progression from one phase to the next, with 'pure' capitalism appearing only at the late stage when it took over the production and the only permissible term for the early period being mercantile capitalism or even 'precapitalism'."[81]

Summing up our analysis of the social and economic changes now underway in Russia, it is possible to come to the following conclusions. With the destruction of the redistributive state, its main beneficiaries, such as the military-industrial complex and the Far North development, have also entered a stage of deep crisis. The reproduction of the state-dependent type of worker has been definitely disrupted. Privatization is proceeding relatively quickly. New social structures have arisen in which new market groups move ahead and receive more and more room for self-realization. The phenomenon of shop-floor domination of the production process and the logic of confrontation which accompanies it is declining, while the search for the means of social partnership as a way to solve the crisis is expanding. A new system of relations between the center and periphery is forming, which is closer to the real federalism than in any previous period in Russian or Soviet history. The changing structure of prices is creating the basis for the future integration of Russia into the world market. Russian society exists and will continue to exist in a state of unstable transition, but has already made a large step forward in the direction of social self-organization. While it is impossible to exclude the possibility of some catastrophic developments and scenarios, Russian society has a good chance of achieving socioeconomic stabilization and evolving into a modern society whose population enjoys a decent standard of living.

Notes

1. Mikhail Gefter, *Iz tekh i etikh let* (Moscow: Progress, 1991), p. 248.

2. M. Djilas, *Conversations with Stalin* (New York: Harcourt Brace, 1962), p. 114.

3. T. H. Rigby, *The Changing Soviet System: Mono-organizational Socialism from Its Origins to Gorbachev's Restructuring* (Brookfield: Edward Elgar, 1990); Alec Nove, *The Soviet Economic System*, 3rd ed. (London: Routledge & Kegan Paul, 1986).

4. Kenneth Jowitt, *New World Disorder: The Leninist Extinction* (Berkeley: University of California Press, 1992), pp. 245–253.

5. This is true even if terror always remained a major resource of the Soviet regime and an instrument of intimidation by "shaping people's perceptions of what could happen to them if they were to overstep the boundaries of acceptable behavior" (Donna Bahry and Brian Silver, "Intimidation and the Symbolic Uses of Terror in the USSR," *American Political Science Review*, Vol. 81, No. 4, 1987, p. 1067).

6. Ferenc Feher, Agnes Heller, Gyorgy Markus, *Dictatorship over Needs* (New York: St. Martin's Press, 1983).

7. Karl Polanyi, *The Great Transformation: The Political and Economic Origins of Our Time* (Boston: Beacon Press, 1957); George Dalton, ed., *Primitive, Archaic and Modern Economies: Essays of Karl Polanyi* (New York: Doubleday, 1968).

8. S. G. Kordonsky, "Sotsial'naia struktura i mekhanizm tormozheniia," in F. Borodkin, L. Kosals, R. Ryvkina, eds., *Postizhenie* (Moscow: Progress, 1989), p. 39.

9. R. Ryvkina, "Sovetskaia sotsiologiia i teoriia sotsial'noi stratifikatsii," in F. Borodkin et al., *Postizhenie*, p. 33.

10. See, for example, Mikhail Voslenskii, *Nomenklatura: The Soviet Ruling Class* (New York: Doubleday, 1984); Konstantin Simis, *USSR: The Corrupt Society* (New York: Simon and Schuster, 1982); Mervyn Matthews, *Poverty in the Soviet Union*

(Cambridge: Cambridge University Press, 1986); Mervyn Matthews, *Patterns of Deprivation in the Soviet Union under Brezhnev and Gorbachev* (Stanford: Hoover Institution, 1989).

11. T. Zaslavskaia, R. Ryvkina, *Sotsiologiia ekonomicheskoi zhizni* (Novosibirsk: Nauka, 1991), pp. 407–410.

12. A. Kochetov, "Istoki 'novoi' sotsial'noi struktury," *Svobodnaia mysl'*, No. 9, 1993, p. 68.

13. Aron Katsenelinboigen, "Coloured Markets in the Soviet Union," *Soviet Studies*, Vol. 29, No. 1, 1977.

14. Gregory Grossman, "The 'Second Economy' of the USSR," *Problems of Communism*, No. 5, 1977.

15. L. Beliaeva, "Stanovlenie smeshannoi ekonomiki v Rossii i transformatsiia sotsial'noi struktury obshchestva," in *Smeshannaia ekonomika: sotsiokul'turnye aspekty* (Moscow: Ranion, 1994), pp. 129–130.

16. T. Koriagina, "Tenevaia ekonomika v SSSR," *Voprosy ekonomiki*, No. 3, 1990; K. A. Ulybin, *Tenevaia ekonomika* (Moscow, 1991); A. Kochetov, "Istoki," p. 70.

17. Victor Zaslavsky, *The Neo-Stalinist State: Class, Ethnicity and Consensus in Soviet Society*, 2nd ed. (Armonk: Sharpe, 1994), chapter 2.

18. The number of closed cities was growing continuously. All capitals of union republics and most cities with populations of one million or more became closed. By the end of Brezhnev's tenure, up to 20% of the urban population lived in closed cities. The country's main resort areas, along the Crimean coast and the Caucasus and the Baltics, were also closed. The closed regime was also established within the thirty-mile-wide band of territory along the borders of the Soviet Union, from Norway all the way to China.

19. V. Zaslavsky, *The Neo-Stalinist State*, chapter 6; G. Episkopov, "K voprosu ob ogranichenii rosta krupnykh gorodov," *Sotsiologicheskie issledovaniia*, No. 3, 1984, pp. 133–134.

20. Georgii Smirnov, *Sovetskii chelovek: Formirovanie sotsialisticheskogo tipu lichnosti*, 2nd ed. (Moscow: Politizdat, 1973).

21. Vladimir Lefebvre, *Algebra of Conscience: A Comparative Analysis of Western and Soviet Ethical Systems* (Dordrecht: Reidel Publishing Company, 1982); James Millar, ed., *Politics, Work, and Daily Life in the USSR* (Cambridge: Cambridge University Press, 1987). See also a special issue of *Social Research*, Vol. 55, Nos. 1–2, 1988, devoted to Central and East European social science and social theory. Also Miroslawa Marody, "The Political Attitudes of Polish Society in the Period of Systematic Transitions," *Praxis International*, Vol. 11, No. 2, 1991, pp. 227–239; Jadwiga Staniszkis, *The Dynamics of the Breakthrough in Eastern Europe: The Polish Experience* (Berkeley: University of California Press, 1991); A. G. Vishnevskii, ed., *V chelovecheskom izmerenii* (Moscow: Progress, 1989). Especially valuable is a major study conducted by the Moscow Center for the Study of Public Opinion. See Yurii Levada, ed., *Sovetskii prostoi chelovek: Opyt sotsial'nogo portreta na rubezhe 90–kh godov* (Moscow: Vtsiom, 1993).

22. Piotr Sztompka, "The Intangibles and Imponderables of the Transition to Democracy," *Studies in Comparative Communism*, Vol. 24, No. 3, 1991, p. 298.

23. Victor Zaslavsky, "Rossiia na puti k rynku: gosudarstvenno-zavisimye rabotniki i populizm," *Polis* (Moscow), No. 5, 1991; Piotr Sztompka, "Civiliza-

tional Incompetence: The Trap of Post-communist Societies," *Zeitschrift für Soziologie*, Vol. 22, No. 2, 1993, pp. 85–95.

24. Quoted in *Ogonek*, No. 16, 1990, p. 6.

25. Andrew Janos, *Politics and Paradigms: Changing Theories of Change in Social Science* (Stanford: Stanford University Press, 1986), p. 121.

26. M. Gefter, *Iz tekh i etikh let*, p. 309.

27. Jadwiga Staniszkis, *The Dynamics of the Breakthrough in Eastern Europe*, pp. 38–52.

28. L. A. Beliaeva, "Rossiiskoe obshchestvo v preddverii rynka: trevogi ozhidaniia, nadezhdy," *Mir Rossii*, No. 1, 1992, pp. 48–52.

29. L. Babaeva, "Rossiiskii predprinimatel': mezhdu vchera i zavtra," *Segodnia*, January 4, 1994, p. 10.

30. V. Naishul', "Liberalizm i ekonomicheskie reformy," *Mirovaia ekonomika i mezhdunarodnye otnosheniia*, No. 8, 1992, pp. 69–81.

31. Svetlana Senina, "ZIL-zavod izmuchennykh limitchikov," *Kuranty*, December 28, 1993, p. 4.

32. Evgenii Starikov, "Ugrozhaet li nam poiavlenie srednego klassa," *Znamia*, No. 8, 1990, pp. 192–196.

33. Blair Ruble, "The Social Dimensions of Perestroyka," *Soviet Economy*, 1987, Vol. 3, No. 2, pp. 171–183.

34. Lev Gudkov, "Intelligenty i intellektualy," *Znamia*, Nos. 3–4, 1992, p. 217.

35. Boris Dubin, "Zhurnal'naia kul'tura postsovetskoi epokhi," *Novoe literaturnoe obozrenie*, No. 4, 1993, p. 307.

36. Lev Gudkov, *"Intelligenty i intellektualy,"* p. 203.

37. Ibid.

38. According to Russian students of industrial relations, many "highly skilled and educated workers of the military-industrial complex feel that the benefits of their previous position in the Soviet system outweigh the abstract, uncertain benefits of freedom and the market." L. Gordon, E. Gruzdeva, V. Komarovsky, *Shakhtery–92: Sotsial'noe soznanie rabochei elity* (Moscow: Progress-Kompleks, 1993), p. 21.

39. In an interview printed in *Literaturnaia gazeta*, Yegor Gaidar proudly admitted that during the time his government was in power the production of tanks dropped by a factor of 38 (*Literaturnaia gazeta*, January 12, 1994, p. 3).

40. Vladimir Gurevich, "Lobbies: tabel' o rangakh," *Moskovskie novosti*, February 20–27, 1994, p. B1.

41. Erik Whitlock, "Defense Conversion and Privatization in St. Petersburg," *RFE/RL Research Report*, Vol. 2, No. 24, 1993, p. 22.

42. A good example is represented by military enterprises of the previously closed town of Sverdlovsk–44, with its unique plant for the production of enriched uranium. See Andrei Treivish, "Industrial'nyi landshaft Rossii: krizis i modernizatsiia," *Segodnia*, January 4, 1994, p. 3.

43. Igor Birman, *Ekonomika nedostach* (Benson: Chalidze Publications, 1983). On the value-destroying nature of the Soviet economy see Richard Ericson, "The Russian Economy Since Independence," in this volume.

44. Z. V. Kupriianova, "Vtorichnaia zaniatost'," *Ekonomicheskie i sotsial'nye peremeny: Monitoring obshchestvennogo mneniia*, No. 4, 1993, p. 27.

45. Z. V. Kupriianova, "Rabotniki s vysokoi i nizkoi samootsenkoi," *Ekonomicheskie i sotsial'nye peremeny: Monitoring obshchestvennogo mneniia*, No. 3, 1993, pp. 23–28.

46. L. A. Khakhulina, "Otnoshenie naseleniia k differentsiatsii dokhodov i sotsial'nomu rassloeniu," *Ekonomicheskie i sotsial'nye peremeny: Monitoring obshchestvennogo mneniia*, No. 4, 1993, p. 6.

47. Ibid., p. 7.

48. T. Zaslavskaia, "Transformatsiia rossiiskogo obshchestva kak predmet monitoringa," *Ekonomicheskie i sotsial'nye peremeny: Monitoring obshchestvennogo mneniia*, No. 2, 1993, p. 6.

49. L. Khakhulina, *"Otnoshenie,"* pp. 6–7.

50. *Ekonomicheskie i sotsial'nye peremeny: Monitoring obshchestvennogo mneniia*, No. 2, 1993, p. 6.

51. L. A. Gordon, *Ocherki demokraticheskogo rabochego dvizheniia v poslesotsialisticheskoi Rossii* (Moscow: Progress-Kompleks, 1993). See also Donna Bahry, "Society Transformed? Rethinking the Social Roots of Perestroika," *Slavic Review*, Vol. 52, No. 3, 1993, especially pp. 534, 542.

52. Vera Tolz, "Russia's Parliamentary Elections: What Happened and Why," *RFE/RL Research Report*, Vol. 3, No. 2, 1994, pp. 4–5.

53. Boris Dubin, "Zertsalo iunosti", *Svobodnaia mysl'*, No. 9, 1993, p. 60.

54. See, for example, Charles Maier, "Is It 1933 All Over Again?" *The International Herald Tribune*, December 18, 1993, p. 15; Martin Malia, "Another Weimar?" *Times Literary Supplement*, February 25, 1994, pp. 24–25.

55. Victor Zaslavsky, "Russia and the Problem of Democratic Transition," *Telos*, No. 96, 1993, pp. 42–43.

56. Piotr Sztompka, "The Intangibles and Imponderables of the Transition to Democracy," *Studies in Comparative Communism*, Vol. 24, No. 3, 1991, p. 299; see also Marc Garcelon, "The Shadow of the Leviathan: Public and Private in Communist and Post-Communist Societies," in Jeff Weintraub and Krishan Kumar (eds.), *Public and Private in Thought and Practice* (Chicago: University of Chicago Press, 1994).

57. Gail Lapidus, ed., *Women in Soviet Society: Equality, Development and Social Change* (Berkeley: University of California Press, 1978).

58. *Sotsial'no-ekonomicheskie preobrazovaniia v Rossii: Sovremennaia situatsiia, novye podkhody* (Moscow: Otdelenie ekonomiki RAN, 1994), p. 10.

59. G. Gendler, M. Gildingersh, "A Socioeconomic Portrait of the Unemployed in Russia," *RFE/RL Research Report*, Vol. 3, No. 3, 1994, pp. 28–35; *Sotsial'no-ekonomicheskie preobrazovaniia v Rossii*, p. 10.

60. L. A. Gordon, *Ocherki*.

61. L. A. Gordon, E. Gruzdeva, V. Komarovsky, *Shakhtery–92*, pp. 18–27; L. A. Gordon and E. Klopov, "Rabochee dvizhenie v postsotsialisticheskoi Rossii," *Mirovaia ekonomika i mezhdunarodnye otnosheniia*, No. 5, 1993, pp. 5–15.

62. Viktor Yaroshenko, "Popytka Gaidara," *Novyi mir*, No. 3, 1993, p. 111.

63. Donna Bahry, "Society Transformed?" p. 554.

64. Michel de Certeau, *The Practice of Everyday Life* (Berkeley: University of California Press, 1984).

65. *Novoe vremia*, No. 1, 1993, p. 19.

66. Yurii Levada, "Vektory peremen: sotsiokul'turnye koordinaty izmenenii," *Ekonomicheskie i sotsial'nye peremeny: Monitoring obshchestvennogo mneniia*, No. 3, 1993, p. 9.

67. *Ekonomicheskie i sotsial'nye peremeny: Monitoring obshchestvennogo mneniia*, No. 6, 1993, p. 12.

68. For a useful review of these surveys see Lev Gudkov, "Otsenki ostroty otdel'nykh problem," *Ekonomicheskie i sotsial'nye peremeny: Monitoring obshchestvennogo mneniia*, No. 1, 1993, pp. 15–18.

69. Ibid., p. 17.

70. *Moskovskie novosti*, February 13–20, 1994, p. 7B.

71. Andrei Illarionov, "Padenie urovnia zhizni: mif ili real'nost'," *Izvestiia*, February 17, 1994, p. 4.

72. Yurii Levada, "Vektory peremen," p. 9.

73. A. Illarionov, "Padenie," p. 4.

74. Michel de Certeau, *The Practice*, p. xvii.

75. Vladimir Gurevich, "Lobbies," p. B1.

76. See L. A. Khakhulina, "Tri goda ekonomicheskikh reform: izmeneniia v otsenkakh i mneniiakh naseleniia," *Ekonomicheskie i sotsial'nye peremeny: Monitoring obshchestvennogo mneniia*, No. 1, 1993, pp. 20–22. At the same time negative stereotypes concerning private property of large enterprises are still widely held, while the percentage of those who consider foreign investors and entrepreneurs a major threat to Russia's natural resources has even grown.

77. Fernand Braudel, *The Perspective of the World: Civilization and Capitalism, 15th–18th Century*, Vol. 3 (New York: Harper and Row, 1984), p. 631.

78. Mary McAuley, "Politics, Economics and Elite Realignment in Russia: A Regional Perspective," *Soviet Economy*, Vol. 8, No. 1, 1992.

79. Michael Burawoy and Pavel Krotov, "The Economic Basis of Russia's Political Crisis," *The New Left Review*, No. 198, 1993, p. 64; see also Michael Burawoy and Pavel Krotov, "The Soviet Transition from Socialism to Capitalism: Worker Control and Economic Bargaining in the Wood Industry," *American Sociological Review*, Vol. 57, No. 1, 1992.

80. M. Burawoy and P. Krotov, "The Economic Basis," p. 69.

81. Fernand Braudel, *The Perspective of the World*, Vol. 3, p. 621.

5

Russia, the "Near Abroad," and the West

Andrei Kortunov

The disintegration of the Soviet Union in December 1991 was overwhelmingly supported by opinion-makers and decision-makers of the former superpower. Among those trying to evaluate the inevitable costs and potential side effects of the Soviet collapse, very few could be characterized as old-thinkers and defenders of a totalitarian empire. The political leaders of the fifteen newly independent states, who disagreed on virtually everything, were unanimous at least on one issue: they promised their respective constituencies that independence would bring not only individual freedom and economic prosperity, but also national renaissance and spiritual renewal.

Russian President Boris Yeltsin was no exception. In fact, one of his most spectacular political achievements in 1990–1991 was the skillful separation of the notion of "Russian" from the notion of "Soviet." Yeltsin managed to convince many Russians, if not all the other subjects of the Soviet Union, that Russia itself throughout the seventy years of Soviet power had been economically exploited, politically oppressed, and deprived of its historical traditions and national statehood by the omnipotent, transnational Communist elite.

Some of Yeltsin's supporters even argued that during the Soviet period Russia had suffered more than the other republics: all others had at least been allowed to keep some symbols of sovereignty (for instance, republican Academies of Sciences or republican Communist Parties), while Russia had been doomed to dissolve completely within the Soviet Union, serving as the glue that kept it together. Moreover, they claimed, it was the Russians who dealt the fatal blow to the Soviet state in August 1991; therefore Russians had more reason to be proud of themselves than others who had merely sat waiting for the outcome of the drama in Moscow.

In terms of foreign policy the distinction between "Russian" and "Soviet" was crucial in interpreting the outcome of the Cold War. The Russian leaders—from Yeltsin to Speaker of Parliament Ruslan Khasbulatov to Foreign Minister Andrei Kozyrev—repeatedly stressed that the Soviet empire, the superpower, or "the system" had been defeated in the Cold War, but this was not tantamount to the defeat of the Russian nation. Actually, they pointed out, the opposite might be true: the dismantling of the empire created opportunities for the Russian nation to use its enormous creative potential, which had been crippled by the burdens of the totalitarian system. The Russian tragedy happened in 1917, not in 1991, they stated. If the stamina of the nation was not spent, it now had a historic opportunity to create a healthy and viable society—and to meet the geopolitical challenge of the post-Cold War period.

The question of who suffered more under Soviet rule hardly makes any sense now. Each nation of the former USSR can advance arguments and evidence to support its case and to claim special rights or special treatment from the West. For many ethnic groups in the USSR Russians have been the embodiment of Soviet power, the bearers of the imperial ideology, oppressors and occupants directly responsible for all the evil that the Communist regime brought with it. But it would not be fair to dismiss Yeltsin's logic as entirely one-sided or self-serving. The Soviet Union in many respects was a cosmopolitan empire; the results of the forced collectivization were in no way less horrible in central Russia than they were in Ukraine, and the Russian intellectual elite was clearly not spared or given more favorable treatment during the political purges of the 1930s.

As far as economic relations among the Soviet republics are concerned, any unbiased analysis would demonstrate that during the Soviet period Russia was turned into an "internal colony" of the Soviet Union: for decades Russian oil, natural gas, gold, and other raw materials that could have been marketed abroad to bring Russia hundreds of billions of dollars were provided to other Soviet republics at heavily subsidized prices in exchange for low-quality consumer goods and services. One can argue, of course, that it was the "Russian" center which imposed such economic relations on all the republics, but the argument does not change the basic fact: in economic terms Russia got very little (if anything) out of this; from the very beginning the Soviet Union had been a constant drain on its resources.

The apparent enthusiasm with which most Russians (the intellectual elite included) participated in the demolition of the Soviet state indicates that they did not consider it a Russian state or even as something that met Russian needs and interests. One has only to look at the situation in Yugoslavia to realize that a multi-ethnic Communist state will not disintegrate without violence if the core nation is intent on keeping it. However, even in 1991 the euphoria of revolution and Yeltsin's incredible popularity could not hide one simple fact: Russians have never been just another people of the Soviet Union.

Throughout much of its history Russia has been the center of an empire. This is why the dissolution of the Soviet Union and its replacement by the Commonwealth of Independent States (CIS) in December of 1991 presented Russians with problems very different from those facing other nationalities of the former USSR. Though it is clear that Russians were not willing to be the "imperial people" and to pay a price for the maintenance of the empire, the end of the USSR brought about a national identity crisis for Russians that has no analog elsewhere within the post-Soviet area.

After the August coup many Russian scholars and politicians (not necessarily from the political "right") repeatedly warned that a dissolution of the Soviet Union would result in a disastrous loss of Russian identity.[1] The current Russian identity crisis is a complex problem, and here we intentionally limit the discussion to just one dimension—conflicting perceptions of a future Russian role in the so-called "near abroad," the successor states of the Soviet Union, based on different conceptions of the Soviet and imperial Russian legacies for the newly born Russian Federation. To what degree should (and can) Russia profess to be the legitimate heir of the Soviet Union, claiming all the territory of the former superpower as the sphere of its vital interests? Is the "new political thinking" of the Gorbachev years relevant to the Russian strategy toward the "near abroad"? Or should the new Russian state pattern itself on the Monroe Doctrine of an earlier United States? Finally, are smaller republics of the former USSR worth fighting for, or do they deserve benign neglect from the Russian policymakers?

Of course no Russian leadership can arbitrarily choose answers to all these questions. Domestic and international constraints considerably limit the freedom of choice in regard to the near abroad. For example, the gravity of present economic and social problems in Russia essentially prohibits any interventionist, resource-consuming foreign policy even within the borders of the former Soviet Union—at least in the medium term. The vast nuclear complex that Russia inherited from the Soviet Union, along with the lion's share of Soviet debts and assets abroad, ties Russian diplomats, arms controllers, and financial experts to their Soviet predecessors and defines Russian approaches to other former Soviet republics' claims in these spheres. The geostrategic position of the Russian Federation today resembles that of Russia at the end of the seventeenth century, prompting the reemergence of an old concern of foreign-policy makers—free access to the Baltic and Black seas. This concern, however, does not necessarily mean that Russia will have to use "traditional" means—i.e., wars and annexations—to reestablish access. Still, within certain constraints, Russia's foreign policy toward its closest neighbors may reflect varying degrees of prudence or adventurism, transparency or secretiveness, liberalism or nationalism. Moreover, some of the radical opposition leaders, were they to come to power, might try to ignore or overcome the existing constraints. This is why their views, no matter how utopian or removed from reality, cannot be simply ignored.

It should be noted that the Russian policy toward the former Soviet republics as well as Russian foreign policy in general is still in the formative stage. Kozyrev persistently avoided formulating a strategic doctrine guided by explicit principles and goals. He assumed that Russian foreign policy should be reactive and responsive to particular situations abroad.[2] The near abroad was for some time on the periphery of Russian foreign policy, which emphasized relations with the West in order to integrate Russia into the "community of civilized nations."[3] During the first years of Russia's independence numerous fluctuations, inconsistencies, and contradictions were evident in its policy toward the near abroad (just as the policy of the other former Soviet republics toward Russia in most cases lacked strategic vision and consistency).

A very serious complicating factor in Russian strategy toward the near abroad has been an unclear decision-making process. The Soviet Foreign Ministry was one of the most conservative and rigid governmental agencies, with very strict rules and procedures. Personnel changes at the top were rare, diplomatic careers were slow and predictable. Even Eduard Shevardnadze's relatively modest innovations were interpreted by many ministry bureaucrats as a revolution and a "collapse of the ministry's foundations." However, the real revolution came when the Soviet Foreign Ministry was transformed into that of the Russian Federation. Many senior diplomats had to resign or were forced into early retirement because of their alleged support of the August 1991 coup. Some of "the best and brightest" of the younger generation left to look for opportunities in the private sector. Newcomers with no diplomatic credentials made fantastic careers almost overnight, both in the ministry itself and in Russian embassies abroad.

The same processes, though less visible, were reshaping the Defense Ministry, the General Staff, Foreign Intelligence, and other agencies involved in foreign policy decision-making. The role of academic research institutes, which had actively advised Gorbachev on foreign policy matters, especially during his first years, declined mainly because of inadequate funding and defections of gifted scholars. Problems of personnel and expertise were gravest in the areas related to the near abroad because here relations had to be started from scratch. Moreover, in the Ministry of Foreign Affairs and other government agencies, at least at the beginning, work on the near abroad did not bring with it much prestige or many career opportunities. In fact, the near abroad divisions were often perceived as second-rate in comparison with the "far abroad"; they were often staffed with pre-retirement officers who had failed in other foreign policy fields.

A number of new and powerful foreign policy institutions emerged that had no analogs in the Soviet Union. The most spectacular was the rise of the Russian Supreme Soviet and its Committee on Foreign Affairs and Foreign Economic Relations. On many occasions and especially on a number of crucial near abroad issues the committee acted as a rival to the Ministry of Foreign Affairs, challenging its key decisions and basic approaches. The parliamentary involvement in foreign policy issues widened the circle of participants in international affairs discussions in the Russian Federation. New presidential bodies were also created—the Inter-Agency Foreign Policy Commission of the Security Council, established by Yeltsin in December 1992, and the Presidential Council, established in February 1993.[4]

Changes in foreign policy decision-making notwithstanding, many of the old Soviet deficiencies were not overcome; indeed some of them were aggravated. After the Soviet disintegration many observers had hoped that foreign policy decision-making would be an open process, involving not just top bureaucrats, but also the Parliament, leading political parties, the media, the public, independent experts, and lobbies. Unfortunately, nothing of the sort has happened so far. There seems to be neither a clear chain of command nor established procedures in this sphere. The lack of open discussions, information feedback, and independent opinion is evident. Sometimes decisions seem impulsive, marked by pure ignorance about the situation in some part of the former Soviet Union; at other times they reflect a lack of coordination among major ministries and cabinet members. Under the circumstances, the influence of even relatively minor domestic factors on foreign policy formation can be crucial.

This chapter concentrates on a comparative analysis of four competing approaches of Russian policy toward the near abroad: (1) "confederalist," (2) "imperialist," (3) "isolationist," and (4) "selective engagement." It evaluates their influence on the specific strategies pursued and their potential impact on relations between Russia and the West.

Illusions of a Eurasian Confederation

The Eurasian confederation idea was a direct result of desperate attempts by mostly Moscow-based liberals to preserve a renewed Soviet Union. Most Russian liberals, raised to political power and high visibility during the Gorbachev reforms, welcomed the Minsk and Alma-Ata agreements of December 1991 precisely because they interpreted them as a way to rebuild the Soviet Union on a market-oriented economic and democratic political base.[5] Though the exact forms of this new union remained unclear, the dominant perception among Moscow liberals was that the prime obstacle to cooperation in the fall of 1991 had been Mikhail Gorbachev's attempt to mediate inter-republican relations. Without Gorbachev and the discredited "center," it would be easier to maintain a looser union.

These views of the "confederalists" were widely shared at the highest political levels, at least in 1991 and early 1992. One of the most articulate advocates was the newly appointed secretary of state, Gennadii Burbulis, who many believed was the mastermind behind the Minsk and Alma-Ata agreements. In the Foreign Ministry his views were strongly supported by Kozyrev and his deputy on CIS affairs, Fedor Shelov-Kovediaev. A confederalist faction in the Supreme Soviet was represented by Viktor Sheinis, Sergei Yushenkov, Vladimir Kuznetsov, Gleb Yakunin, and Galina Starovoitova; in the media, by Evgenii Kiselev, Yegor Yakovlev, Otto Latsis, Yurii Kariakin, and others.

In the military sphere the confederalists started from the assumption that the new commonwealth made it possible to preserve a relatively stable post-Soviet common defense space, embracing most if not all of the former Soviet Union, with a doctrine shared by all the members of the CIS. The defense postures of Russia and other republics were to be founded on two parallel doctrines: republican doctrines reflecting the specific defense needs of each republic, and an interstate military doctrine of the commonwealth. Most civilian strategists saw Russia as the nucleus of the CIS security system, with special responsibilities (the major share of the commonwealth defense expenditures) and rights (a special role in decision-making at the operational level). In many regards this military-political alliance would have been similar to what Gorbachev had proposed in his last version of the Union Treaty in October 1991—with one important difference: Russia would replace the Soviet center.

In terms of economic cooperation the confederalists saw the future CIS as another European Community. Here the basic assumption was that the highly interdependent Soviet economies, after seventy years of integration (some of which in fact went much further back), would glue the republics together. Even those who recognized the perils of republican nationalisms thought that sooner or later centrifugal tendencies would be overtaken by the common quest for economic performance and welfare; and the charismatic and ideological republican elites of the *perestroika* period would be replaced by new transnational-minded technocrats who would have no choice but to closely cooperate with each other and, above all, with the Russian Federation.

From the confederalist viewpoint, the incentives to cooperate would be reinforced by easily predictable failures of all republics (with the possible exception of the Baltic states) to integrate into other regional (i.e., West European) economic structures. There also was a widely shared perception that all CIS states (and possibly the Baltic states as well) would have to operate within the Russian financial system—the "ruble zone." The economic reintegration would in turn inevitably promote political reintegration, since the politics of coming decades (seen by many Moscow liberals in terms not unlike those of Francis Fukuyama's "end of history") would be centered primarily around economic issues. Within ten or fifteen years the commonwealth would turn into a prosperous economic community that could even be joined by a number of Central European countries. This approach may be called neo-Marxist, for it implies the primacy of economic factors for the formation of elites as well as for political rules between states. Here again Russian liberal thought showed the birthmarks of the Soviet period, though Russian liberals earlier had sharply criticized Gorbachev for attempting to introduce economic reforms without changing political institutions.

Finally, Russian confederalists expected all or almost all the newly independent states to share basic democratic values. They believed that other republics would in the very near future undergo the same transformations Russia had gone through in fall 1991: the Communist bureaucrats would be ousted, the liberal media would rein in nationalism, and government agencies would be purged.

The strong support of Russian liberals for a renewed union was somewhat paradoxical. On many occasions before the Soviet collapse, they had claimed that Russia would make a strong state in its own right, that it was much the most viable among the Soviet republics, and that interrepublican trade had been extremely disadvantageous for Russia. Why then should they support the preservation of a union? The most common explanation is that Russian liberals were and still are to some degree imbued with the Russian imperial mentality and are therefore reluctant to recognize the collapse of the empire, especially the separation of the other Slavic republics—Belarus and Ukraine—from Russia. This explanation, most frequently voiced by Ukrainian politicians and scholars, is not unreasonable: the division of the Slavic core of the country was perceived by many Russian liberals in distinctly apocalyptic terms.[6]

Other explanations are more practical: for instance, liberals in Moscow were concerned that without a renewed union large numbers of Russians and Russian-speakers residing elsewhere would take refuge in the Russian Federation, thus creating countless economic, social, and political problems; among other things, new immigrants could provide a fertile soil for anti-liberal nationalist and even totalitarian movements. Also, a rapid and uncontrolled disintegration of the Soviet Union could trigger the same process in the Russian Federation, thus increasing pressures for self-determination on the part of the numerous autonomous republics.[7]

Yet another explanation was that even after the August coup, most Russian liberals remained Soviet-type liberals.[8] They never tried to develop a liberal Russian national agenda; and one is tempted to say that they were never particularly interested in defining Russian national interests. As Soviet intellectuals, they were cosmopolitan in outlook, and the mere notion of nationalism was alien to them; moreover, it had a distinctly derogatory connotation. During the whole Gorbachev era liberal intellectuals had never been very interested in defining the state interests of the Soviet Union; for them the whole idea of the state was obsolete if not irrelevant. Much more attention was paid to concepts of the "new world order," UN reform projects, and the analysis of "transnational" trends in global politics. In a sense, like their most consistent opponents from the Marxist-Leninist camp, liberal intellectuals were pure "ideologists" basing their concepts on values and beliefs rather than facts and interests.

After the Soviet collapse Russian liberals suddenly faced the prospect of living in a nation-state—and found it unappealing. They were not ready, intellectually or psychologically, for political competition with Russian nationalists. The CIS, with all its deficiencies, was a promise of something more than a nation-state, where liberals could play a significant role. It was no accident that after the August coup Moscow liberals persistently promoted all-union political movements that could transcend republican borders and present a viable alternative to the old Communist Party.

From the liberals' point of view, the choice between the last Union Treaty proposed by Gorbachev in the fall of 1991 and the CIS was not merely a choice between a confederation and a commonwealth of nations. Under Gorbachev's Union treaty, the Russian Federation might have ended up in a confederation with six Muslim republics and perhaps Belarus. This composition would not only have moved the center of gravity of the new Union to the East, from Europe to Asia; it would also have shifted the balance of power within it in favor of the old Communist elites, who even after the coup continued to rule most of the Soviet Asian republics. The creation of the CIS with Ukraine, Belarus, Moldova, and Armenia participating led to hopes that a more West-oriented and more liberal union would emerge on the territory of the former USSR.

As further developments have shown, Moscow-based liberals (including many of Yeltsin's advisors) evidently underestimated republican nationalisms and overestimated the driving force of economic interdependence among the newly independent states.

First, nothing like a new political and military union emerged from the Commonwealth.[9] A new NATO-type alliance system covering the entire territory of the former Soviet Union or even its European part, as proposed by Yeltsin to his colleagues from other republics in Minsk and Alma-Ata in December 1991 and persistently promoted by the Commonwealth and Russian military leaders, did not come about. It was impractical not only because of the Ukrainian and Azerbaijani quests for unfettered independence in military decision-making; it was also impractical because of divergent security interests that now tore apart the "common defense space" of the former USSR.

A defensive alliance system presupposes that its members share significant common or at least overlapping security interests. Moreover, a stable security mechanism that would include appropriate political and military institutions, a legal framework, burden sharing, and strategy planning procedures, can be created only if these interests are lasting. Otherwise the participating states can afford only temporary coalitions aimed at achieving specific security objectives (such as the anti-Hitler or anti-Iraq coalitions). Having accomplished their functions, such coalitions tend to disintegrate.

In the case of the former Soviet republics there were no long-term common interests important enough to overcome mounting nationalism. It should also be kept in mind that political and social instability in many of the republics made it difficult to define their respective long-term security interests and foreign policy orientations, which were therefore subject to considerable fluctuation.

The republics' leaders did recognize, of course, that they shared the task of dealing with the inherited Soviet military potential in such a way as to preclude its uncontrolled decomposition, accidents, or military coups. This, however, was a temporary issue, a problem of the past, not of the future. Besides, liberals typically failed to see that this problem was a double-edged sword: it could unite state leaders but also separate them, possibly provoking sharp conflicts over the "fair share" of each republic within the overall Soviet military heritage. As Russian-Ukrainian disputes over the Black Sea fleet have demonstrated, the problem turned out to be extremely sensitive, explosive, and difficult to solve.

At the same time, to preserve the military structure of the nonexistent Soviet state would have been politically dangerous for the leaders of newly independent states: until they got full control over troops and weapons deployed on their respective territories, the possibility of military backlash, such as a coup aimed at the forcible restoration of the Soviet Union, could not be excluded. Given the weak political structure of the CIS, the Commonwealth armed forces could easily slip out of political control, thus becoming independent political actors. Even if a Commonwealth summit took a decision, the military establishment would have been able to question or sabotage it in a variety of ways. For example, in September 1991 the command of the Soviet Baltic military district openly declared that it would not obey Gorbachev's orders to withdraw from Lithuania until an adequate infrastructure was ready in the new regions where its forces were to be deployed.

Yet another fear in non-Russian republics was that a "united Commonwealth armed forces" would turn out to be nothing but a euphemism for the Russian army. The initial Russian commitment to the concept of integrated armed forces of the CIS was politically self-defeating because it immediately raised old suspicions of Russian imperialism and domination. In short, the Commonwealth in 1992 did not look like the NATO alliance of 1949: there was neither a common enemy nor a clear understanding of common values. Moreover, while the Alma-Ata agreements envisaged the preservation of the "common military-strategic space," from the very beginning Ukraine, Azerbaijan, and Moldova dropped out of this space, while Uzbekistan and Turkmenistan insisted on building their national armies before any military integration with other states of the CIS. In May 1992 Russia itself was obliged to announce that it had begun the formation of its own national army beyond the structures of the CIS Supreme Command. At least for the time being, the idea of an integrated armed force was put aside. True, a number of important documents were signed in the security sphere in 1992 and 1993. Among them were the agreement on peacekeeping (joined by Armenia, Belarus, Kazakhstan, Kyrgyzstan, Moldova, Russia, Tajikistan, and Uzbekistan) and an agreement on collective security (signed by Armenia, Kazakhstan, Kyrgyzstan, Russia, Tajikistan, and Uzbekistan); but neither agreement was implemented.

The second hope of Russian liberals—the division of labor within the former USSR—did not work either. In large measure, the interdependence among the republics of the former USSR had been artificial, imposed on them by the Soviet administrative-command system. In the absence of real market mechanisms, immense price distortions favored some and punished others. For example, domestic prices for fuel and raw materials were artificially kept much lower than world prices. Conversely, prices for finished products were higher. Fuel was especially cheap, even compared to other raw materials. Ukraine and Kazakhstan bartered one ton of their wheat for three tons of Russian oil, although elsewhere in the world one ton of crude oil would be more than enough to acquire one ton of grain.

With no market mechanisms to evaluate the "fair share" of each republic in the overall Soviet GDP, all the states, from the Baltic to Central Asia, had reason to believe that they were being exploited and colonized, giving more to the "Center" than receiving from it. Consequently, they expected to be better off by "going it alone." Those republics that were relatively more affluent proved most resistant to the idea of close economic integration. For example, the nationalist mood in Ukraine was greatly strengthened by the evident gap between its own consumer goods market and that of Russia. With all its shortcomings and problems, the economic situation in Ukraine in 1991–early 1992 appeared much more stable, with lower prices and a wider choice of food products. Protectionist sentiments were one of the reasons why most ethnic Russians living in Ukraine supported its independence in the referendum of December 1, 1991; in heavily Russian Donetsk 80% of the voters supported independence, and in the largely Russian Black Sea port of Odessa the figure was 86%.

The economic ambitions of new political elites in the "near abroad" (and, we should add, their very poor knowledge of economic realities) prevented any kind of Eurasian Economic Community from emerging on the territory of the former USSR. The only major achievement in terms of synchronizing the economic transition in all the republics was the more or less simultaneous price liberalization in January 1992. This, however, was not the result of independent decisions taken by the non-Russian republics but a reflection of their inability to isolate their consumer markets from Russia's. On two other main elements of economic reform—privatization and demonopolization—no agreement was reached. Moreover, within just days after the Alma-Ata accords were signed, the Russian government banned the export of sixty consumer goods and food products in retaliation against alleged restrictions on the exports of consumer goods to the Russian Federation imposed by other CIS states.[10]

Despite all the attempts to reverse the trend toward protectionism and economic isolationism, inter-republican trade declined sharply in 1992–1993 (just as had happened with COMECON trade in 1991 after the latter had been converted to world market prices and a hard-currency base). The decline turned out to be even more dramatic because some of the former Soviet republics introduced (or tried to introduce) numerous non-trade restrictions based on political considerations. The deepening economic crisis exacerbated political conflicts rather than leading to a new union. In short, by 1992 it became clear that economic factors could hardly take precedence over trends toward political and strategic disintegration.

All attempts in 1992–1993 to preserve a "common economic space" on the territory of the former USSR revealed one more problem: how to maintain a viable economic union (and political union, for that matter) in which one member was more powerful than all the others taken together? If the votes were allocated on the basis of the economic and financial potential of the participants, Russia would receive an absolute majority and consequently would be in a position to impose its will on the whole of the CIS. If the principle was "one state, one vote," smaller republics that account for only a fraction of the Commonwealth's population and resources could form a voting bloc able to act against the interests of the larger republics.

Finally, the expectation that the old communist ideology would be easily replaced by common democratic values proved to be naive or, at the very least, premature. All attempts to maintain transnational liberal political movements (such as the Movement for Democratic Reforms) ultimately failed. Russian liberals were not prepared to face the fact that their former allies from other Soviet republics, with whom they had joined in the common fight against communism and the Soviet center for at least three years, had suddenly turned their backs on Russia. Especially frustrating was the nationalistic transformation of the Latvian and Estonian political elites and their political and economic discrimination against the Russian minorities; the consistency of the democratic orientations of the Baltic independence movements may have been questionable from the very start, but Moscow liberals had preferred not to notice it. To defend the rights of Russians and Russian-speakers abroad was an entirely new challenge for the liberals. They had been used to reducing the human rights problem to the totalitarian nature of communism and the Soviet state; once both were gone, human rights were expected to flourish.

An important attempt to preserve the "common political space" of the former Soviet Union was made in February 1992, when the conference of heads of supreme soviets of the CIS discussed a proposal to start an Interparliamentary Assembly to coordinate economic and political reforms on the territory of the former USSR. Despite vocal opposition from those who considered such an Assembly an attempt to restore the old USSR Supreme Soviet, the idea took root, and in March 1993 the Interparliamentary Assembly was officially launched by Armenia,

Belarus, Kazakhstan, Kyrgyzstan, the Russian Federation, Tajikistan, and Uzbekistan.

Theoretically the Interparliamentary Assembly could have served as an important mechanism to synchronize the transition of newly independent states to political democracy and market economy. With its five commissions—legal affairs, economy and finance, social policy and human rights, environmental problems, and security matters—the Assembly covered a wide range of problems common to all CIS states. Ruslan Khasbulatov, head of the Russian parliament, made it clear that the long-term goal of the Assembly was to promote integrationist trends on the territory of the former USSR in the direction of a future confederation.[11]

However, the widening rift between the executive and the legislative branches in Moscow turned the Interparliamentary Assembly into a hostage of domestic Russian politics. Instead of promoting cooperation within the CIS, the Assembly got involved in futile competition with the similar coordinating body of the top CIS executives, the Council of the Heads of State. Khasbulatov was constantly accusing Yeltsin of being incapable of handling CIS problems properly and responding to growing public support for integrationist trends; and Yeltsin, in turn, completely ignored most of the decisions made by the Interparliamentary Assembly.

Thus the initial high hopes of the Russian liberals turned out to be illusory. The Commonwealth partnership was flawed from the moment of its creation in December 1991. The documents, signed by the republican presidents, in many cases appeared to be declarations of intent rather than binding agreements. The subsequent Russian-Ukrainian dispute over the future of the Black Sea Fleet and definitions of "strategic forces" brought to the surface all the fragility of the Commonwealth. The CIS Charter, which in the view of many "confederalists" should have cemented the new alliance, was not signed until January 1993, with only seven states agreeing to full membership (Armenia, Belarus, Kazakhstan, Kyrgyzstan, Russia, Tajikistan, and Uzbekistan). Moreover, after a year of deliberations the Charter had turned into a very loose document, subject to further reservations and amendments to be introduced at the stage of ratification by the legislatures of the several member-states.

Summing up, one can assert that the collapse of the Soviet Union and Communist ideology, and the emergence of new problems and new "rules of the game" within the CIS, were bound to lead to a rapid decline of liberal, Western-oriented political thought in Russia. Deprived of their prime enemy, liberal "ideologists" very quickly lost both public appeal and their own sense of direction. After all, their major mission had been destructive rather than constructive. Liberal "ideologists" who emerged during the Gorbachev years helped destroy the Cold War international order, the old Soviet alliance system, the rigid ideological myths and dogma. They were mostly outsiders to the traditional Soviet foreign policy establishment and therefore not inoculated with Gromyko's "professionalism."

After the collapse of the Soviet Union—though some remnants of the Cold War era remained—the mission of destruction was basically accomplished. It was clear that the world would never be the same as it had been in the mid–1980s. The new foreign policy agenda of the Russian Federation had to be creative rather than destructive. How could the delicate balance of power on the territory of the former Soviet Union be preserved? What role, if any, was Russia to play in Central Asia? How was it to get into the Western international financial system without damaging its traditional ties with the countries of the "near abroad"? What sectors of the Russian economy were to be protected from CIS competition, and in what sectors could Russia afford to embark on free trade?

To cope with these problems one needed not so much political courage as political wisdom and the knowledge of the nuts and bolts of the modern international system, and, above all, the new international system emerging in Eurasia. The concept of a "Eurasian confederation" turned out to be naive and impractical, reminiscent of the idea of a "common European home," espoused earlier by Gorbachev. The Russian political class sensed that in its relations with the "near abroad" the "new thinking" was of very little use. Everything needed to be different: the style, the decision-making process, the people who handled it. Broad political slogans needed to be replaced by elaborate multi-stage programs, radical initiatives had to be abandoned for a cautious step-by-step approach. Idealistic and messianic rhetoric had to yield to a pragmatic, perhaps even a cynical approach.

In short, the disintegration of the Soviet Union and the collapse of the Communist ideology signaled that the holiday of revolution was coming to an end. And if the time had come for "business as usual," revolutionaries and romantics in politics had to pass their responsibilities on to cold-blooded businessmen and pragmatists. That is why when Andrei Kozyrev tried to act as a "Russian Shevardnadze" in 1992, using the "new political thinking" in relations with both the "near" and "far abroad," he was sharply criticized by exactly the same journalists and academics who had enthusiastically supported Eduard Shevardnadze in 1985–1990.

By mid–1992 the ideas of a "Eurasian confederation" had lost a lot of their initial appeal, giving way to other concepts of Russian foreign policy toward the "near abroad." Among these the most influential were the concepts of a new Russian Empire and that of Russian isolationism.

Aspirations for a New Russian Empire

From the very start, the Russian proponents of an imperialist policy toward the republics of the former USSR could be divided into two groups: those who were still defending the Soviet Union and those who considered the CIS to be a major defeat for Russian diplomacy. The first stuck to the traditional Soviet legacy, while the latter reverted to older Russian imperial aspirations. Within the first group perhaps the most vocal was the Soiuz faction from the former USSR Supreme Soviet (led by "black colonels" Viktor Alksnis and Nikolai Petrushenko), who strongly denounced the Minsk and Alma-Ata agreements as "a coup d'etat" and "a pact among newly arisen appanage princes." Soiuz predicted "countless misfortunes" that would result from the collapse of the Soviet Union.[12]

The "pro-Soviet" critics of the CIS made the most of the fact that the initial Minsk meeting included only Russia, Ukraine, and Belarus, and that the media described it as an attempt to create a separate "Slavic union" based on ethnicity or religion. Sergei Baburin, a leader of the conservative opposition in the Russian parliament, declared during the hearings on December 12, 1991 that the creation of the CIS would "set the Slavic world against the Turkic-Muslim world and lead to the complete disintegration of the country and a final break between peoples."

The "pro-Russian" critics included the leader of the Democratic Party of Russia, Nikolai Travkin, and the Chairman of the Constitutional Democratic Party of Russia, Mikhail Astaf'ev. The creation of the CIS, Travkin claimed, marked a clear defeat for Russia and a victory for Ukraine, which managed to get the most out of the agreement. The most dangerous result for Russia, in his view, would be an increase of centrifugal tendencies among Russia's autonomous areas and regions and a heightened danger that Russia itself would be the next state to break apart.[13]

Indeed, the creation of the CIS had not prevented the growth of centrifugal trends within the Russian Federation. Tatarstan, for example, stated its intention to join the CIS as an independent participant, separate from Russia. Nationalist leaders in other "autonomies" voiced similar intentions. The way in which the CIS was created undermined the notion that constitutional law and legal procedures should govern the process of self-determination, wrote Stepan Kiselev, deputy editor of *Moscow News*, after the Alma-Ata agreements were signed.[14]

Far-right nationalistic groups could not support the creation of the CIS either. For them the collapse of the Soviet Union should have logically led to the restoration of the old Russian Empire rather than to a new Commonwealth. For example, the Party of Russian Nationalists, a small but vocal Moscow-based political group, argued in early 1992 that Russia should declare null and void all Soviet legislative acts creating national republics and autonomous regions and districts on the territory of the Russian Empire. This newly-configured Russian federation should adopt legislation that would, above all, reflect its security interests, as well as the interests of Russian-speakers in the periphery, by sharply restricting the right of secession. Not surprisingly, the main ideas of such legislation were very close to the notorious law on secession passed by the USSR Supreme Soviet back in 1990.[15]

The most consistent criticism of the CIS as a "direct continuation of the Soviet anti-Russian ethnic policies" can be found in the documents of the so-called Russian National Council *(Russkii Natsionalnyi Sobor)* formed in early 1992. In its appeal to the sixth Congress of People's Deputies of the Russian Federation, the Council stated that "the decision to create the CIS was the continuation of a purposeful strategy to destroy a thousand-year-old Great Power. One stroke of the pen erected formerly nonexistent state boundaries, perfidiously broke into pieces the united and indivisible Russian people, cut off almost 30 million Russians from their nation. These millions were turned into outcasts, second-class citizens. They are forced to change their faith, convictions, language, and life-style. Though well informed about discrimination against Russians in the Baltic states and Moldova, Boris Yeltsin has accepted these policies by concluding with these states political, economic and trade agreements disadvantageous for Russia."[16]

Probably the most flamboyant proponent of the restoration of the Russian Empire was the leader of the Liberal-Democratic Party, Vladimir Zhirinovsky. Even before the Soviet collapse he had advocated the imperial past rather than the communist present. As Zhirinovsky declared in the fall of 1991, "I reject the decision of the USSR State Council to recognize the independence of the Baltic States. When I become president of the confederation, I will annul this decision. If we are liquidating the totalitarian system, we should return to the borders of September 1917, when we had only the Baltic provinces. There was no Lithuania, Latvia, or Estonia." (TASS, September 9, 1991.)

The statement, "We want the Soviet Union back!" that was so popular in 1992, was based on the assumption that the USSR had not "collapsed on itself" because of its intrinsic flaws and deficiencies—stemming from the authoritarian political system and economic mismanagement to its self-defeating foreign policy and the lack of personal rights and freedoms—but had been sold out, betrayed and destroyed by Gorbachev and his political successors, first and foremost Boris Yeltsin. Moreover, the Soviet disintegration was often explained in terms of a "conspiracy theory": all that happened in the USSR after 1985 had allegedly been planned, directed and financed by the West (by Washington, to be exact) as a long-term program of subversive activities. The goals of the "conspiracy" were more than obvious: to destroy the USSR as the main obstacle to American world domination, to reduce the role of Russia and other Soviet republics to that of suppliers of cheap raw materials and labor for the West, and eventually to eliminate their sovereignty, culture, traditions, and languages.

That is why for many defenders of the Soviet Union the Minsk and Alma-Ata agreements were the "moment of truth" that finally exposed the conspirators and the conspiracy itself. Who but "foreign agents" would act as Yeltsin, Kravchuk, and Shushkevich did, taking one destructive step after another against their countries' best interests and, finally, dividing the USSR into a score of quasi-states? The "Soviet patriots" hoped that the shock caused by the "treason" would mobilize the public, the army, and the power structures, and that the communist party would regenerate itself for a swift comeback.

But these hopes were soon dashed. After the Soviet collapse the communist "ideologists" were pushed aside; they lost their power base, many of their media, and their mechanisms to influence state policy. Since the policies of "proletarian internationalism" had been no more popular in Russia than foreign aid programs were in the United States, the Marxist-Leninist orthodoxy could not generate any public support for its foreign policy ideology in the absence of coercive state power. So the communist-dominated power structures, the armed forces included, switched their political allegiance and their political rhetoric literally overnight. While anti-Western and anti-American rhetoric had long had a clear appeal for some social groups in Russia, the communists had never had a monopoly on these slogans and ideas, which were lately most vociferously propagated by numerous rightist, xenophobic political movements. As the remnants of communist orthodoxy began to forge an uneasy alliance with the nationalists, the rhetoric of Gennadii Ziuganov and his Communist Party of the Russian Federation was transformed from that of "socialist internationalism" to that of Russian nationalism. By mid–1992 "Soviet" and "Russian" imperialist groups had essentially merged, both intellectually and politically. Proponents of the Soviet restoration became junior partners of the Russian imperialists.

The Russian nationalists themselves have never constituted a united group. Their numerous differences and contradictions notwithstanding, nationalists were able to create a vast network of organizations, associations, media, and even think-tanks. In the Russian Supreme Soviet they formed a powerful bloc called "Russian Unity"; outside the parliament most of the numerous nationalist organizations rallied around the "National Salvation Front."[17] The imperialists' political outlook was supported by a part of the Slavophile intellectuals and writers, such as Aleksandr Prokhanov, Stanislav Kuniaev, Vassily Belov, Vadim Kozhinov, and Ilia Glazunov.[18]

During 1992–1993 the imperialist political groups tried, with some success, to win the support of the Russian legislature. The position of the Russian Supreme Soviet on CIS issues was never consistent. At some points, it clearly supported the "confederalist" approach.[19] On other occasions, the Supreme Soviet took very rigid nationalist positions. For instance, on July 9, 1993, a joint session of the Russian Supreme Soviet adopted a resolution calling for the reassertion of Russian sovereignty over the Crimean port of Sevastopol' and overturning the Yeltsin-Kravchuk agreement to divide the Black Sea Fleet. Nor were "imperialist" sentiments alien to the Russian military. The military establishment in Moscow expressed concern that if Russia left the "near abroad" politically and militarily, the power vacuum would be filled by other countries to the detriment of long-term Russian interests.[20]

Oddly enough, this logic was echoed in a statement of Foreign Minister Andrei Kozyrev. Speaking at a meeting with ambassadors from the CIS and the Baltic states in early 1994, Kozyrev emphasized the need to preserve the Russian military presence on the territory of the former USSR; he argued that proposals to withdraw militarily were "extremist" because, if Russia left the "near abroad," the security vacuum there would inevitably be filled by other powers "not always friendly, and in many cases hostile, to Russian interests."[21]

In fact, the gap between the "confederalist" and imperialist approaches has never been all that wide. Both concepts have stressed the perils of national isolation; both favor greater integration between Russia and its immediate neighbors. The only question was who would set the rules for the integration, who would control the process, and what were its ultimate goals. Since many of the "confederalists" assumed that Russia by virtue of its sheer size and power was bound to have some special rights and responsibilities in a new Eurasian confederation, and "moderate" imperialists recognized that other CIS countries and the Baltic states were entitled to some role in the decision-making of a neo-imperial system, centrist politicians, journalists, and scholars could drift from one concept to the other with relative ease.

Of course, the most radical versions of imperialist policies were emphatically rejected by the Russian executive branch and by moderates in the Supreme Soviet. However, in 1992 and especially in 1993, the Kremlin leaders, seemingly disappointed by the failure of attempts to build a Eurasian confederation, betrayed an inclination to utilize at least some imperialist ideas without going to extremes. Different degrees of "moderate" imperialism were characteristic of Russian Vice President Alexander Rutskoi, chairman of the Supreme Soviet Ruslan Khasbulatov, chairman of the Russian Democratic Party Nikolai Travkin, head of Russia's Industrial Union Arkadii Volskii, and head of the parliamentary Constitutional Committee and of the Social-Democratic Party Oleg Rumiantsev. Within the executive branch these positions were supported by the leaders of the military-industrial complex and branch ministries (energy, transportation and others). The chief of the Security Council Yurii Skokov and Vice Premiers Oleg Lobov and Mikhail Malei implicitly or explicitly supported the moderate imperialist vision of Russian–"near abroad" relations. Intellectuals who were also proponents of this position included Sergei Karaganov, Andrei Zubov, Sergei Stankevich, Andranik Migranian, and Aleksandr Tsipko.

A typical "moderate imperialist" is the former Chairman of the Supreme Soviet Committee for International Affairs and Foreign Economic Relations, Evgenii Ambartsumov. He has been critical of the CIS but had never opposed its creation.[22] On the one hand, he asserts that Russia should base its relations with other former Soviet republics on universal principles of non-interference, national sovereignty, and the inviolability of borders. On the other hand, he insists on Russia's having special rights and responsibilities on the territory of the former Soviet Union.[23]

Another manifestation of the "moderate neo-imperialist" position can be found in "A Strategy for Russia," developed in the summer of 1992 by the Moscow-based Council for Foreign and Defense Policy (a group of influential politicians, academics, generals, and businessmen). The report calls on Russia to pursue an "enlightened post-imperial integrationist course" in its relations with the former Soviet republics. It assumes that Russia can be the only major factor of stability in this region and calls for "an active (if possible, internationally sanctioned) participation in preventing and ending conflicts, if necessary even with the help of military force, and preventing any mass and gross violations of human rights and freedoms."[24]

To be sure, such statements reflect not only perceptions of Russian national interests but also the institutional interests of the Russian military. Liberal intellectuals have frequently accused the military of wasting national resources, denied any positive function to the army, and demanded drastic reductions of the Russian armed forces irrespective of possible social and political consequences. For consistent "confederalists" the Russian military presence in the "near abroad" has in most cases been unjustifiable, raising suspicions about Russian intentions, whereas "moderate imperialists" have maintained that a complete withdrawal of the Russian military from the "near abroad" would be dangerous and short-sighted. The latter group has tried to rationalize the stationing of a relatively high number of Russian armed forces abroad and to give them a new sense of mission.

"Moderate neo-imperialists" like Ambartsumov would like to have the best of both worlds: to secure the right of the Russian Federation to interfere in the former Soviet republics and, at the same time, to ensure international political and financial support of Russian actions in the "near abroad." To the "moderate neo-imperialists," this does not appear to be a contradiction. Russian attempts to bring "law and order" to the highly explosive regions of Eurasia, they argue, serve not only Russian national interests but also the strategic interests of the global community. Russia alone can absorb destabilizing impulses coming from the Caucasus, Central Asia, and other regions of the former Soviet Union; therefore, Russia is entitled not only to Western recognition of its special role, but also to substantial Western support.

On the level of rhetoric, this position was substantially endorsed by the Yeltsin government. In February 1993, in a speech to the Civic Union, Yeltsin stated that "Russia continues to have a vital interest in the cessation of all armed conflict on the territory of the former USSR. Moreover, the world community is increasingly coming to realize our country's special responsibility in this difficult matter. I believe the time has come for authoritative international organizations, including the UN, to grant Russia special powers as guarantor of peace and stability in this region."[25] Later the Foreign Ministry officially asked the UN and the CSCE to grant Russia special peacekeeping rights in the "near abroad."

Since the initial reaction of the international community to these claims was, at best, ambiguous (most of the target countries emphatically rejected Yeltsin's idea), the Russian leadership tried to modify the initial formula by placing greater emphasis on multilateral CIS peacekeeping operations.[26]

It is not clear whether Yeltsin will be in a position to fine-tune a "moderate" approach to the "near abroad," considering the growing pressure from radical imperialists, which became more focused after the elections to the Russian parliament in December 1993. In the newly elected State Duma, Zhirinovsky's Liberal-Democratic Party gained control over the newly formed Committee on Geopolitics (chaired by Viktor Ustinov); the Committee on Security was handed to the communists (chaired by Viktor Iliukhin). The Committee on International Affairs, led by Vladimir Lukin, from the "Yabloko" bloc, appears to be more moderate, though Lukin has more than once criticized Foreign Minister Kozyrev for his allegedly pro-Western and pro-American policies. The only chance for the executive branch to withstand the pressure of the State Duma (if, of course, Yeltsin cares about the legislature at all) is to profit from the inevitable differences and conflicts among communists, imperialists, and moderate nationalists on foreign and defense policy.

And yet, in spite of the political successes of the proponents of a new "Russian Empire," the period since December 1991 has demonstrated that their perceptions of probable developments on the territory of the former USSR are no closer to reality than those of the "confederalists." First of all, they expected that 25 million Russians living outside the Russian Federation would be brutally oppressed and discriminated against by local nationalist leaders, turning them into a powerful political and social force for the imperial comeback. But with the notable exception of the Baltic states, Russians and Russian-speakers have received all the political and economic rights enjoyed by the so-called titular nationalities.

In Ukraine, no serious attempts were made to introduce new legislation on languages in order to replace Russian by Ukrainian in the (more heavily Russified) Eastern regions and the Crimea. In Belarus Russian remained more widely spoken than Belarusian. In Central Asia local authorities did their best to make Russians stay, since they provided a large and irreplaceable share of skilled labor.

This is not to say that Russians in the "near abroad" experienced no problems at all. In many former Soviet republics, Russians occupying key positions were gradually replaced by locals, and all sorts of low-profile discrimination and random threats from extreme nationalist or fundamentalist groups were reported. But the deterioration of the social, political, and economic status of the Russian population, when it took place, was relatively slow and gradual. So the Russian national explosion, which the imperialists had counted on, never happened in any of the successor states.

Second, the "imperialists" overestimated the potential scale of military conflicts or of economic and social catastrophes on the territory of the former USSR. True, during the past several years a number of bloody wars broke out in the "near abroad"; in Moldova, Tajikistan, and the Caucasus losses of human lives and economic damage were severe. But these civil conflicts and interstate wars, as tragic as they were for particular regions and ethnic groups, cannot even remotely be compared to those that occurred after the collapse of other great empires.

For instance, the slow decline and ultimate collapse of the Ottoman Empire in 1832–1914 was accompanied by four major European crises, two all-European wars and a number of smaller-scale military conflicts.[27] The collapse of Austria-Hungary not only provoked the first World War but also left a profound power vacuum in Central Europe that undermines regional stability to this day. It would not be too much to claim that the current military confrontation on the territory of former Yugoslavia, the disintegration of Czechoslovakia, the conflict potential in Hungarian-Romanian relations, as well as the general instability in the Balkans are all manifestations of the inability of nations, cultures, and political elites of the region to transform the imperial system of international relations (Ottoman-Austrian-Russian) into a system based on the interaction of national states.

The withdrawal of the West European colonial powers from Asia and Africa, though planned long beforehand and in most cases carried out in an orderly fashion, still resulted in numerous wars with huge losses in human life and wealth. At least five regional wars (Cambodia, India-Pakistan-Bangladesh, Nigeria, Sudan, Vietnam) cost more than one million lives each. In eight other cases (Angola, Burundi, Indonesia, Lebanon, Mozambique, Rwanda, Uganda, Zaire) the toll exceeded a hundred thousand.[28] The cost of decolonization thus turned out to be very high, and in some regions formerly ruled by the European powers, political and military stability has never been restored.

One might think of different explanations of why, by comparison, the Soviet disintegration has been so smooth and relatively peaceful. A communist would argue that the Soviet Union was never a "classical" empire and therefore the rules of imperial collapse do not apply. A liberal would state that the Gorbachev period did bring about at least some elements of a civil society in most of the constituent republics, and it was this civil society that precluded large-scale violence. A Russian nationalist would probably attribute the lasting peace to the "historic patience" of the Russian people, the non-imperial psyche of Russians, and their false sense of guilt, which is being exploited and abused by other nations of the former USSR. A historian would emphasize that the Soviet collapse differs from that of the Ottoman Empire or the Austro-Hungarian Empire, among other things, in that no major external power has been interested in exploiting the opportunities created by the Soviet disintegration; the whole international community (with minor exceptions) has demonstrated a clear intention to contain the Soviet collapse within the borders of the former superpower and to prevent any geographical explosion of political and military instability.

But no matter which explanation is more accurate, the apocalyptic scenarios of Soviet disintegration sketched by many Russian and foreign politicians and scholars in 1991–1992 have not come true. Not only have there been no large-scale wars, disastrous nuclear accidents, or outbursts of political terrorism; despite the steady deterioration of the economic situation, there have been no mass famines on the territory of the USSR, no lethal epidemics of national or regional scope, no catastrophic failures of the urban infrastructure. A pessimist would maintain that all these calamities are just around the corner, and the peoples of the former USSR are fortunate only because the old social and economic systems, though decapitated, are still operating. Even if this were the case, the relative tranquility and the widespread sense of normalcy and lassitude, or at least of the inevitability of current changes, are not the best environment for generating imperialist moods.

Finally, the imperialists overestimated the psychological impact of the Soviet disintegration on the Russian people within the Russian Federation. The conviction that Russians "would never tolerate" Ukrainian independence, that the whole society would mobilize to "rescue" the Russian minority in Moldova, that radical nationalist slogans could easily inflame public opinion turned out to be essentially groundless. True, the Russian public did not demonstrate total immunity to nationalism, giving some support to Zhirinovsky and his party in the December 1993 elections. But in more practical terms, the Soviet disintegration was accepted by Russians more or less indifferently: no crusades were launched, no border clashes were provoked, no powerful rightist organizations were formed around the core of Russian repatriates from other republics.

Here, again, one can suggest a couple of different explanations. Some argue that in the post-communist context, as during the whole of Russian history, public opinion and political behavior have been characterized by a strong commitment to the maintenance of the status quo, rooted in economic parochialism, lack of social mobility, and intellectual conservatism. After centuries of slavery, decades of totalitarianism, and years of *perestroika*, people accept innovations, revolutions, and disasters coming to them mostly "from above" fairly enigmatically, because they lack a firm personal stake in the outcome and faith in change. They would sabotage any political program, good or bad, by keeping aloof and remaining uncooperative.

A more flattering explanation argues that Russian society is already mature enough successfully to resist primitive nationalist forms of political mobilization. There are many new group identities in Russia (professional, political, cultural, religious, regional) that can successfully compete with national identity. Besides, economic reforms have channeled people's energies—in particular, younger Russians'—into more constructive undertakings than futile outbursts of nationalism.

In any case the Russian public failed to live up to the imperialists' expectations. After the first two years of its independent existence Russia was still looking mostly inward, not outward, more ready to accept an isolationist than an imperialist policy toward the "near abroad."

Temptations of Isolationism

Russian isolationism is not an entirely new phenomenon. It existed during most of the Soviet period as a reaction to the alleged economic, political, and cultural discrimination against Russia within the Soviet state. The slogan "Russia first" was actively and very successfully used by Boris Yeltsin in his power struggle against Gorbachev in the late 1980s. After the Soviet disintegration, isolationist sentiments were exacerbated by the failure of Russia's attempts to achieve any significant economic, political, and military integration within the CIS structures. A widespread perception that Russia was not being treated fairly by its neighbors (who, it was alleged, were trying to suck up its resources while ignoring Russia's legitimate interests and concerns) also encouraged the trend.

The core of the isolationist approach to the former republics of the Soviet Union is economic in nature. It is a fact that Russia has always been, and still is, subsidizing the smaller and weaker economies of its neighbors. If such subsidies were deemed tolerable during the Soviet period, they were considered an impermissible waste of scarce resources after the Soviet collapse. Indeed, despite all the political and strategic disagreements with its CIS partners in 1992, in trade with them Russia ran a combined surplus of some 1.5 trillion rubles, that is, some ten percent of its gross domestic product.[29]

Even though other republics sold their goods to Russia well below world market prices, the structure of Russian trade with most of the CIS members (with Russian exports dominated by energy and raw materials, and Russian imports composed mostly of food and consumer goods) led to relative trade disadvantages for Russia. The Russian Ministry of the Economy claimed, for example, that in 1992 the average cost of the goods it imported from Kazakhstan was about 60–70% of world prices, while Russia's own exports to Kazakhstan averaged only 30–40% of world prices.[30]

Another constant irritant for Russian politicians and especially economists was the so-called common "ruble zone" that until the fall of 1993 covered most of the former Soviet territory. Though the preservation of the ruble zone was often interpreted by the Kremlin leaders as a success of their integrationist policies toward the "near abroad," in fact the zone steadily drained Russian financial resources and exacerbated inflation. The national banks of newly independent republics were issuing massive ruble credits to their enterprises without any coordination with the Russian Central Bank, which did not seem to object. No rules of the game were agreed upon, and the CIS countries were competing with each other in running up large budget deficits.

All Russian attempts to handle the problem through routine mechanisms were not successful. For example, in 1992 Russia tried to offset the negative trade balance by cutting down on the quantities of oil, gas, and other raw materials that it supplied to other CIS countries. But Russia's trade partners were even faster in reducing their exports. According to Mashits, in 1992 they supplied Russia with only 18–58% of the products they had promised, while Russia supplied them with 60–75%. Likewise, an attempt to convert all trade imbalances into technical credits led only to a rapid accumulation of debts to Russia by the CIS countries, with no realistic prospect of repayment.

Clearly this problem in Russian-CIS relations could not go unnoticed. The main slogan of the "isolationists"—"Down with the spongers!"—has been very popular with the general public. Before the velvet revolutions in Central Europe in 1989, it was widely used by those who considered the Soviet empire to be a liability rather than an asset for the Soviet Union. They claimed that the Central European economies had turned the USSR into their colony, securing cheap natural resources and in return flooding the Soviet domestic market with expensive, low-quality consumer goods. But in the Soviet years the "isolationists" for obvious reasons could not have any serious impact on foreign policy decision-making. Besides, their arguments were very shaky even if appealing: no reliable statistics were published on USSR-Central European relations, and the question of who was exploiting whom remained in dispute.

After 1991 the "isolationists" became much more vocal. Politically they represented a very mixed coalition ranging from principled liberals to ultra-nationalists. They all cheered the Soviet disintegration precisely because they felt that Russia had been exploited and abused economically, if not politically, by the other republics. Furthermore, "isolationists" found it outrageous that the countries of the "near abroad" were allowed to enjoy all the political benefits of independence without bearing its economic burdens.

It should be noted that "liberal isolationists" and "nationalist isolationists" had different views on the possible (and desirable) consequences of a more rigid Russian economic policy toward the "near abroad." For liberals, more "natural" economic relations with the CIS countries, based on world market prices, should push the latter in the direction of more radical economic reforms and structural changes and, after some time, would lead to a healthy market-oriented integration on the territory of the former USSR.

For nationalists, the "near abroad" countries were highly artificial creations that were not able to sustain themselves politically, economically, or militarily, and their only salvation lay in open or covert Russian subsidies and Russian support. To withdraw economic subsidies and Russian political and military support would mean letting these quasi-states go bankrupt, so that they could later be absorbed by Russia.[31] In other words, for liberal "isolationists" this policy is an uneasy but necessary step in the direction of true, mutually beneficial integration; for nationalist "isolationists" it is also an interim solution on the way to the restoration of the empire.

The only major practical difference between liberal and nationalist isolationists was that the former argued for humanitarian assistance to the "near abroad" to help people cope with natural disasters (famines, epidemics, earthquakes, and storms), while the latter (e.g., the Liberal-Democratic Party) opposed even these limited actions to help societies in the "near abroad."

No matter how "isolationist" approaches are justified, they reflect a real conflict of interest between Russia and the "near abroad" which became graphic after Yegor Gaidar and his team of radical reformers came into office in Moscow. As Gaidar and later Boris Fedorov saw it, Russia's immediate task was to continue with radical economic reform, emphasizing macroeconomic stabilization. In their view, to preserve its financial system and avoid hyperinflation Russia simply could not afford any integration with the "near abroad" in the immediate future. Any real economic reintegration of the CIS was feasible only once Russia had resolved its domestic economic problems and could serve as a locomotive for the weaker economies of its neighbors. For most of the CIS countries, on the other hand, economic cooperation with Russia (which essentially meant preferential terms of trade, cheap Russian credits, and unlimited access to Russian raw materials, energy, and markets) was especially important now that these countries were trying to establish their statehood. In the longer range all of them hoped to reduce their economic dependence on Russia and, if possible, to plug into other regional integration structures.

There is also a widespread perception in Moscow that because of the size of its domestic market Russia could afford economic isolationism to a degree no one else in the CIS could. Indeed, prior to the Soviet collapse the relative level of Russian involvement in inter-republican trade was lower than that of other republics: it accounted for approximately 12.5% of Russian GNP, while for other Soviet republics it was in the range of 30–50%.[32] Russia, all current economic problems notwithstanding, accounts for more of the former Soviet gross national product than all the "near abroad" taken together, and while not totally self sufficient, Russia is much better placed than other former Soviet republics to "go it alone."

In any case, in 1993 "isolationist" moods began to weigh heavily on

Russian economic policy toward the "near abroad." First, the Russian government announced that any energy exports not covered in bilateral agreements would be sold to the "near abroad" at world prices. As for bilateral agreements, Russia raised prices on oil to 55–65% and on gas to 40–45% of world market prices.[33] Second, Russia suggested that its neighbors repay their debts, using industrial property as collateral and, in the Ukrainian case, military hardware and the long-term lease of naval bases and other facilities. Finally, the Russian government proposed a number of preconditions for countries wishing to remain within the "ruble zone"; if accepted, these preconditions would lead to almost complete subordination of the republics' national banks to the Russian Central Bank and Finance Ministry.

Of course, these changes could be interpreted as manifestations of imperialist rather than "isolationist" trends in Russian policy. The "oil whip" could be used to discipline the ranks of the former Soviet republics, to obtain concessions from them at the moment of their greatest economic weakness, and to nail down Russia's dominant position in Eurasia. One cannot exclude such intentions on the part of the Kremlin leadership. But it is worth noting that Moscow's decision to turn to world prices in the oil trade was accompanied by a statement that henceforth Russia would not link economic relations with CIS countries to political or military relations.[34]

The CIS member states, confronted with a new policy from Moscow, tried to retaliate by all the means at their disposal. Ukraine started to charge Russia world market prices for the transit of Russian oil and gas through its territory. Kiev also radically raised the prices on beet sugar it ships to Russia. Kazakhstan similarly raised prices on wheat exported to Russia to levels well above world market prices, and Uzbekistan did the same with cotton exports. A matter of special concern to Russians was the attempt by Ukraine and Georgia (under Zviad Gamsakhurdia) to form a transit and economic union, with a clear intention of creating a buffer zone between Russia and foreign countries in the south and west. But all these attempts were ineffective: Russia started to build another gas pipeline to Western Europe through Belarus and Poland, and sugar, grain, and cotton are in abundance on the world market. As a result of the "trade wars" some of the "near abroad" countries lost their traditional positions in the Russian market, yielding to other suppliers from the "far abroad."

At first, isolationism was limited to economic relations between Russia and the countries of the "near abroad." However, some signs of an "isolationist" mood can be traced beyond the economic sphere. One of the earliest symptoms of political and military isolationism was the almost unanimous disapproval by both the Democratic Russia movement and the Russian Supreme Soviet of Yeltsin's decision to use military force to handle the Chechen proclamation of independence in November 1991. Facing a powerful opposition, Yeltsin immediately had to back down. The president also faced mounting opposition to the Russian military presence in Nagorno-Karabakh, with inevitable casualties and high material costs. Despite an evident intention to preserve Russian influence in this part of the former Soviet Union, in the spring of 1992 Yeltsin had to order the Russian (at that point still nominally CIS) troops out of Nagorno-Karabakh and simultaneously ask for the deployment of NATO troops as a peacekeeping force there. Furthermore, not only did the Russian side not try to prevent mediation efforts by Turkey and Iran in the Armenian-Azerbaijan conflict, but it actively encouraged these efforts.

The negative public reaction did not prevent the Russian military involvement in Tajikistan in 1992, but this commitment further fueled isolationism.[35] Practically none of the other CIS members showed any inclination to help Russia in its peacekeeping efforts.

Other republics also showed their distinct unwillingness to participate in any of the Russian-led economic assistance programs to poorer members of the CIS. Neither Ukraine nor Belarus was able to allocate any substantial resources to help deal with the consequences of the Armenian earthquake of 1988 or with the problems of the Aral Sea. Such economic egotism, quite explicable given the general economic situation in Ukraine and Belarus, nevertheless caused a lot of irritation in Moscow.

The typical isolationist position on conflicts in the "near abroad" can be summed up in the following way. First, no Russian government, no matter how powerful or popular, will be able to maintain public support for large-scale military involvement in the "near abroad"; the public remembers Afghanistan and will resolutely oppose any actions that could lead to another Afghan war. Second, the Russian army is not ready to engage in peace-keeping and peace-building operations in the "near abroad." To perform such functions, the armed forces have to be retrained and re-equipped—a process that will inevitably take time and money. Third, Russian diplomacy is not mature enough to mediate in "near abroad" conflicts: it tends to take sides and to miscalculate situations. Moreover, given past experience, even if Russians could act as "honest brokers" in these conflicts, they would be looked at with suspicion and mistrust at least by some of the parties to the conflicts. Fourth, instead of providing for greater security, such an involvement would create more insecurity for Russia: its enemies in the "near abroad" might try to retaliate by promoting secessionist trends in autonomous republics on Russian territory, or by launching acts of terrorism in Moscow and St. Petersburg. Finally (this is a point made by liberal isolationists), a considerable military involvement abroad cannot but undermine democratic values and institutions in the country, making a new dictatorship more probable.

Isolationist moods ran high during the elections to the Russian parliament in December 1993. Most political parties, liberal and nationalist alike, from Gaidar's Russia's Choice to the Liberal-Democratic Party of Zhirinovsky, introduced at least some isolationist slogans in their election platforms. After the elections two events demonstrated that isolationism was on the rise in Russia. The first was the political debates around the Russian-Belarus agreement to embark on a closer economic union with the unification of financial systems of the two countries. The agreement, signed by the heads of governments and central banks of the two countries, meant that Russia would accept Belarus into its "ruble zone."

It might have seemed that the Russian government had achieved a major foreign-policy victory or even taken the first step toward a new Russian empire. However, the decision, taken in January 1944, caused a storm of criticism in Moscow. Yegor Gaidar even cited it as one of the key reasons for his resignation. The reason for the criticism was simple: the financial unification promised to be an expensive commitment for Russia. Belarusian rubles were to be exchanged for Russian rubles at the rate of 1:1, whereas the market exchange ratio was between 5:1 and 6:1. Some experts claimed that the decision would increase the monthly inflation rate in Russia by five percent. Besides, the National Bank of Belarus preserved the right of an independent emission "within limits agreed upon with the Central Bank of Russia"—a very vague formula.

These shortcomings in the agreement were immediately picked up by the isolationists. They did not oppose closer economic ties but emphatically rejected the terms of this agreement. They also accused the Chernomyrdin government of applying "double standards" after it had persistently sought to push Kazakhstan and Uzbekistan out of the "ruble zone."

The second indication of rising isolationism was the mixed reaction in Moscow to the security treaty signed by Yeltsin and Shevardnadze in January 1994. If the Russia-Belarus agreement could serve as a model for the economic absorption of smaller republics by the Russian center, the Russian-Georgian treaty might serve as a case study for the military and political restoration of the Russian empire. Indeed, after two years of desperate attempts to preserve their independence and territorial integrity, after a high wave of self-confidence and nationalism, Georgians had to accept a spectacularly high degree of political and military cooperation with Russia, including the permanent stationing of Russian troops on Georgian soil. Many analysts claim that during 1992–1993 Russia was persistently pushing Georgia in this direction, skillfully using a wide range of methods in order to force it into the role of a client—from the economic blockade and financial isolation of Tbilisi to the covert support of secessionist forces in Abkhazia and South Ossetia.

Even if this logic is correct and Yeltsin did manage to push Shevard-nadze into a corner, the Russian president failed to sell the deal to the public in his own country as a foreign policy triumph. Not that most Russians were anti-Georgian or particularly sympathetic to the cause of Abkhazian and Ossetian secessionist groups. Isolationists simply failed to see why Russia should take responsibility for keeping peace and sta-bility south of the Caucasian mountain chain, or why Moscow should risk the lives of Russian soldiers and assume a substantial financial burden just to keep "old buddy Shevy" in power. Isolationists also main-tained that the pro-Tbilisi position that Russia wound up taking in the civic conflict in Georgia would inevitably create serious problems for Yeltsin with most of Russia's North Caucasian autonomous republics, which enjoy very close cultural, political, and even military ties with the rebellious regions of Georgia.

The Russian president was able to ignore the criticism coming from isolationist groups. However, if Russian troops suffer significant losses in Georgia or elsewhere, or if the economic costs of the Russian involve-ment in the Caucasus climb higher, isolationists will not miss their chance to present the bill to Mr. Yeltsin and Mr. Kozyrev.

No doubt, the current Russian isolationism has its natural limits. An alignment of Gaidar with Zhirinovsky cannot but prove very loose and unstable. Furthermore, Russia is not in a position to turn its back on the "near abroad." The problems of the Russian and Russian-speaking minorities, of stable Russian borders, of the "near abroad" markets for Russian producers, and of reliable communication lines between Russia and the "far abroad" have no answers within the isolationist paradigm. Russia is doomed to an active policy toward the former Soviet republics.

But isolationism in its different forms is likely to be a permanent factor in Russian political life. Isolationism at home will do more than the resistance of the "near abroad" countries or the opposition of the West to tame some of the most aggressive manifestations of Russian neo-imperialism. Instead of blunt attempts to "restore the empire" during the coming years we are far more likely to see a "selective involvement" of the Russian leadership in the countries of the "near abroad."

Toward a Strategy of "Selective Engagement"

A "selective engagement" strategy of the Russian Federation on the territory of the former Soviet Union has not yet been fully worked out by politicians and scholars. It is still taking shape, and to a large extent it borrows concepts from all three approaches discussed above—the "Eurasian confederation," the "Russian Empire," and the isolationist approach.

The basic assumption behind the "selective engagement" strategy, however, is distinctly different from these three approaches. To be "selective" means to apply different rules and patterns to different situations, and to abstain from any universal approaches, blueprints, or guidelines. Advocates of "selective engagement" start from the premise that Russian resources are scarce; it is simply impossible to muster sufficient power and domestic political support to restore the Russian empire or to build a reliable collective security system on the territory of the former USSR. On the other hand, Russia cannot afford an isolationist policy either. In regard to the "near abroad," a Russian "selective engagement" strategy means first and foremost that, instead of a single set of political, economic, military, and other rules of conduct on the territory of the former USSR, it is necessary to develop a variety of regional and sub-regional accommodations with different degrees and types of Russian participation.

The "selective involvement" approach maintains that for Russian foreign, economic, and defense policy it is important to avoid mutually exclusive obligations in different regions as well as disproportionate attention to any one at the expense of others. At the same time Russia should develop a clear set of regional and sub-regional priorities to save scarce resources and avoid imperial overextension. By participating in various multilateral and bilateral alliances and unions, Russia could seek to coordinate the development and security interests of all the former subjects of the USSR to assure both its own interests and Eurasian stability in general.

Advocates of this policy claim that with skill Russia might in five to ten years erect a stable Slavic political and economic community, a Russian-Central Asian defensive alliance, a Russian-Caucasian protectorate or union, and so forth. Specific arrangements and conditions of membership as well as Russian responsibilities in each of these blocs might vary considerably, depending on the security problems in each region, the levels of Russian economic involvement there, political relations with the regional centers of power, and other factors. In the view of proponents of "selective involvement," these overlapping security structures on the territory of the former Soviet Union should be supplemented by the participation of Russia and other republics in wider international security-related bodies, such as various NATO institutions—above all the North Atlantic Cooperation Council and the Partnership for Peace—as well as CSCE mechanisms, and new blocs or regional collective security organizations that may emerge in Southwest Asia or the Asian-Pacific region.

Nobody seems to question the crucial importance for Russia of stabilizing political, military, and economic relations within the Russian-Ukrainian-Belarusian triangle—the "heartland" of the Commonwealth, which contains most of the Soviet military potential, industrial base, and skilled labor. Other actors in this region cannot be ignored by Russia either, but by comparison with the two Slavic states are distinctly subordinate in importance, forming two additional triangles—the northwestern (Russia, the Baltic states, and Belarus) and the southwestern (Russia, Ukraine, and Moldova).

While there are some divergences among the European republics of the former Soviet Union (the Baltic states, Belarus, Ukraine, and Moldova, if the latter survives), the dominant trend in the region most likely will continue to be toward military and political "decoupling" from other republics, independent military decisions, and attempts to integrate into West European economic and Atlantic security structures. For these new countries, such "de-coupling" will be not only a symbol of their newly acquired independence but also a manifestation of their Europe-oriented strategies.

Of course, one cannot exclude serious security concerns in the relations of these states with their Western neighbors. Romanian-Moldovan and Polish-Lithuanian relations are cases in point. But these conflicts are not likely to push the other successor states into a close military union with Russia.

This does not mean that the European "near abroad" countries will lose all military and political ties with Russia. Russia will always be interested in preventing its Western neighbors from becoming bridgeheads or corridors for potential adversaries. The Baltic states, Belarus, and Ukraine, for their part, might be interested in certain military guarantees from Russia (especially in case of political and military instability in Central Europe). Another factor bringing them together will be the defense industries located in these countries: they are broadly integrated into the Russian economy and cannot operate on their own. Some cooperation in arms production is practically unavoidable.

However, the focus of Russian efforts in this part of the former Soviet Union should probably be economic rather than political or military. "Selective engagement" assumes that Russia should be prepared to pay a certain economic price, e.g., to prevent Ukrainian disintegration and to synchronize economic reforms in three Slavic republics.

Belarus

Provided it is able to avoid political blunders, Russia might achieve much more with Belarus than with the other European republics of the former USSR. The cultural and ethnic closeness to Russia and the relatively low level of Belarusian nationalism and of anti-Russian sentiment permit a higher degree of political, economic, and even military cooperation between the two states (including, perhaps, common infrastructure, joint exercises, coordinated military reforms, etc.).

The centrifugal trends and political passions that tore apart the Soviet Union were much less visible in Belarus than in Ukraine or the Baltic states, in large measure because a relatively good economic performance prevented social tensions from running high.

Another specific feature of Belarus was and still is a lack of clear and distinct national identity. Belarus never experienced state independence, and the results of the March 1991 referendum on the preservation of the USSR showed higher than average support for the Union in Belarus.

During the so-called Slavic summit on December 7–8, 1991 in Minsk, where the Commonwealth of Independent States was born, the hosting side assumed the role of an "honest broker" between pushy Russians and stubborn Ukrainians. Since Belarus gained its independence, the transformation of its political system has been much slower and more steady than in Russia and even Ukraine. Still, political changes in the republic are gaining momentum. One can see growing friction between the government and the parliament, between "conservatives" and "democrats," among the newly born "democratic parties" as well as between the institutional power (the parliament and the government) and the non-institutional opposition (political parties and movements, the media, and intellectuals).

The Belarusian Popular Front, which seeks to unite all anti-establishment forces, started collecting signatures in favor of a referendum on the dissolution of the Supreme Soviet and the election of a new, professional parliament, as well as for the resignation of the cabinet—many of whose members go back to the times of the Belarusian Communist Party Central Committee. On the other hand, the Supreme Soviet, which consists of the old nomenklatura, has resisted even a compromise package of economic and political reforms.

The Republic of Belarus, along with Ukraine, has been a member of the United Nations since 1945 and therefore has a number of experienced foreign policy experts and diplomats. Like other European republics of the former USSR, Belarus has declared its intention to integrate into the European Community. It goes without saying that this goal remains very

remote if not illusory. On the other hand, Belarus has been quite successful in dealing with the Baltic states. It managed to distance itself from the
Russian-Baltic tensions and to dispel suspicions that Minsk might be just
another tool in the hands of Moscow. Economic and political cooperation
with Lithuania looks especially promising for Belarus.

Belarus is in the process of choosing between Russia and Ukraine as
its principal partner in international affairs. Each option has advantages
and disadvantages. Being with Russia means reliable security guarantees
and unquestionable economic advantages. Culturally Belarus is also
closer to Russia than to Ukraine, though the Ukrainian influence is very
marked in the southern part of the republic. But at the same time a close
alliance with Russia is perceived by many in Minsk as a real danger to
Belarusian sovereignty, especially when many politicians in Moscow
consider Belarus to be no more than a backyard of Russia and no different from large regions within the Russian Federation itself. A Belarusian-
Ukrainian union promises more equal and balanced relations. For many
Belarusian intellectuals the choice in favor of Ukraine means preference
for a "European" orientation over a "Eurasian" one. Indeed, a closer alliance with Russia would pull Belarus to the East while a drift toward
Ukraine and the Baltic states could accentuate its Central European
nature. If the two Western Slavic republics were able to pool their
resources, they might be in a position to create a formidable economic
and military power capable of balancing the overwhelming might of
Russia in the whole of Eastern Europe. If joined by the Baltic republics,
such a union potentially could even block Russia from the rest of Europe.

If the Moscow leadership does not want to take chances with its qui-
etest Slavic brother, it must not take a close Russian-Belarusian alliance
for granted. Russian policy toward Belarus must be extremely cautious
and fine-tuned to avoid any actions that would provoke a nationalist
response or a pro-Ukrainian bias.

Moldova

There are two possible futures for the newly created Moldovan
state—rapid reunification with Romania or gradual consolidation into a
truly independent entity. Here, too, Russia can influence the outcome.

The reunification scenario might serve certain political interests of the
Russian Federation. A stronger Romania could create a new power
center in southeastern Europe, effectively circumscribing Ukraine's
foreign policy options and pushing it in the direction of closer cooperation with Russia. Moreover, the terms of reunification could exclude the
"Dniester republic" from Greater Romania and thus satisfy the secessionist aspirations of the Russian-speaking population of the area. If an inde-

pendent or semi-independent "Dniester republic" emerged in the process of reunification, Russian influence within this new entity would be quite significant.

However, these prospects look doubtful. First and foremost, there are too many uncertainties about the political future of Romania itself. In any case, it seems highly unlikely that Romania will play a major stabilizing role in Balkan politics in the foreseeable future.

A rapid reunification of the two Romanian-language states would in a number of ways increase domestic instability in Romania. In particular, many in Romania fear that, should Bucharest launch a process of reunification with Moldova, Budapest would undertake similar steps in relation to Transylvania. Such an "exchange" of territories would in no way be profitable for Romania.

Of course, independent Moldova can by no means be considered a stronghold of political or military stability in the Balkans either. But its potential destabilizing impact even at the regional level would be limited. Its armed forces, if and when created, would not influence the regional balance of powers in any significant way.

At the same time, a "Dniester republic," if created, would hardly evolve into a viable state. It could well turn into just another bone of contention between Russia and Ukraine. Moldova's decision to join the Commonwealth (though not without numerous reservations and preconditions) was a clear demonstration that Chisinau considers independence to be more than just a brief transitional period. Still, the pro-independence choice cannot be regarded as final. The future political balance in the republic will be defined by the state of inter-ethnic relations and by the depth of Moldova's economic decline.

For Russia a prudent and realistic policy toward Moldova would be to lend conditional support to the pro-independence Snegur leadership based on its record in protecting the rights of ethnic minorities. In particular, it would be in Russian interests to work toward a political settlement in the Dniester and Gagauz "republics" based on the preservation of the territorial integrity of Moldova and full respect for the minorities' rights on the part of Chisinau (including cultural and linguistic autonomy).

Of course, this policy will meet with serious resistance in both Russia and Moldova. Political pressure on Moscow from the Russian separatists in Moldova is increasing. The leaders of the "Dniester republic" demand official diplomatic recognition from Russia before accepting any settlement. The Moldovan Popular Front is not interested in a settlement with the "Dniester republic" either. But Russia should not support any separatist movements in Moldova, not only because it might provoke a new wave of Moldovan hyper-nationalism, but also because it could be viewed as a precedent for the secession of autonomous areas within Russia itself.

A trilateral agreement should be worked out with Chisinau and Kiev for the Fourteenth Army's withdrawal from Moldova. The Army directly or indirectly supported the separatist movement in the republic and at certain points was even involved in military activities against the central Moldovan government. Though now formally subordinated to the CIS joint command, it is widely perceived in Moldova as a "Russian occupation force" and an instrument of Russian political pressure on the republic.

The Baltic States

There are good reasons to argue that the relations with the Baltic states should not be among the main concerns of the Russian leadership. First of all, the Baltic region can be considered a bastion of political and military stability in comparison with, say, the Caucasus or Central Asia. Territorial disputes are not at the top of the political agenda in any of the states in question. Moreover, economic and political problems within Lithuania, Latvia, and Estonia appear to be more manageable than in the other parts of the former Soviet Union. The three republics have a clear sense of self-identity and a tradition of statehood which is lacking in many of the newly-born independent states. There are long-standing cultural and political ties between the Balts and the West. Finally, the pre-coup record of Russian-Baltic relations was mostly positive. In July 1991 Russia recognized Lithuania as an independent state and on August 26, right after the defeat of the coup, Russia was the first state to recognize the political independence of Latvia and Estonia.

However, with the collapse of the central Soviet power, Russia and the Baltic states lost their common enemy and the common cause that had enabled them to disregard sources of potential conflict between them.

The first source of potential conflict is economic in nature. Trade with Russia has already turned into a major domestic political issue in Latvia and Estonia. A number of ultra-nationalist political parties assert that Russia is following Soviet tactics, using economic pressure to get crucial political concessions from the Baltic states. It is an open question whether the Russian government is in fact purposefully applying its economic leverage to achieve specific political goals in the region. There is little evidence of a direct correlation between oil shipments and Russian political initiatives vis-à-vis the Baltic states. But the core of the problem is that Russian fuel and raw materials can be marketed outside the Commonwealth for hard currency, and the consumer and agricultural goods produced in the Baltic states cannot. Thus the dependence of the Baltic states on the Commonwealth, mostly Russian, markets is very high—from 80% for Lithuania to 95% for Estonia—and there is no real symmetry in the trade interests of Russia and the Baltic states. Moreover, deregulation of prices and privatization of economy in Russia substantially limit the ability of the government to control trade flows. In their quest for lucrative contracts, both private and state-owned enterprises find numerous ways to avoid existing regulations and redirect their shipments to where they can get a higher price.

The second set of problems complicating Russian-Baltic relations involves the timing and costs of troop withdrawals. (In many respects the problems are similar to those of Soviet withdrawals from East Germany, Czechoslovakia, Hungary, and Poland.) Although some progress has been achieved, and the Scandinavian countries have agreed to assist financially, many specific questions remain in dispute. Until the process of withdrawals is over, the "Russian" military presence in the region will continue to complicate political relations with the Baltic states, because it is for Balts a symbol of Soviet oppression and coercion. Some Balts also fear that the command of the Northwestern Group of Forces (the former Baltic Military District) might independently decide to take military action against the Baltic states.

For the future of Russian-Baltic security relations two factors appear to be most important. First, there is the highly sensitive issue of the Russian and Russian-speaking population in Latvia and Estonia. Any political, cultural, or economic discrimination against Russian residents by the Baltic states, as well as any attempts of Moscow to use Russian settlers as a "fifth column," inevitably color all spheres of Russian-Baltic relations and undermine the chances for a stable political and security partnership.

Second, much depends on the ability of the Balts to speed up their own security cooperation. If the Baltic region emerges as a united political and military entity, it will have stronger positions in subsequent negotiations with Russia (and a very significant influence on Belarus) than if it remains divided.[36]

Bilateral security agreements between Russia and the Baltic republics based on mutual interests—possibly modeled on the Austrian State Treaty of 1955—could ease Russian security concerns without compromising the national sovereignty of its neighbors. Security agreements might become more attractive to the Balts if accompanied by preferential economic treaties.

For Russian foreign policy it is extremely important to keep a low profile in the region, and to avoid any attempts to impose on the Balts any far-reaching political and security treaties. Though virulent nationalism in the Baltic states seems to be in decline, the old suspicions and mistrust of Russians are still there. Many politicians in Estonia, Latvia, and Lithuania fail to see any significant difference between the new Russia and the old USSR, or between Yeltsin and Gorbachev. It will take time before a closer Russian-Baltic partnership can emerge.

Central Asia

The independent republics of former Soviet Central Asia, Kazakhstan, and the Caucasus occupy a much less fortunate geostrategic position and should be interested in preserving a more solid political and military alliance with Russia, provided they manage to avoid hyper-nationalism, religious fundamentalism, and total economic and social collapse. Thrust as they are into the chronically unstable international systems of the Middle East and South Asia, these new states will inevitably become objects of political pressure and blackmail on the part of stronger neighbors such as Pakistan, China, Iran and Turkey.

The ethnic maps of these regions are very mixed, and their boundaries primarily reflect the colonial demarcation between the British and Russian Empires in the case of Central Asia, and the Russian, Ottoman and British Empires in the case of the Caucasus. Territorial claims by any of the states of the region can be easily justified on historical grounds and can find considerable domestic support in authoritarian or semi-democratic countries. For example, Afghanistan, which started to decompose once Soviet military and economic support ended, might turn into a bone of contention between Pakistan and the former Soviet Central Asian republics. Tajikistan is especially vulnerable to political and military influence from the south because of the large Tajik minority in Afghanistan. A problem might also emerge in Azerbaijani-Iranian relations due to the presence of at least seven million ethnic Azeris in northern Iran.

Even if the former Soviet republics in these regions consolidate as viable states, they will still be obliged to seek Russian military guarantees against perceived threats from the south. Another possible scenario would involve the creation of an Islamic alliance in which the former Soviet republics could turn into junior partners of Pakistan, Iran, or Turkey, receiving in exchange guarantees of their territorial integrity and some economic assistance. Indeed, Pakistan has already proposed a political and economic "Union of Ten" (Pakistan, Turkey, Iran, Afghanistan, Azerbaijan, the four republics of Central Asia, and Kazakhstan) that would dominate the political and strategic landscape of the region—an idea warmly received in the Central Asian capitals. However, Islamabad can hardly replace Moscow as strategic ally or trade partner, and it is likely that the main struggle for political influence in the region will take place between Turkey and Iran.

It is possible that Turkey and Iran will eventually reach a tacit understanding on the division of "spheres of influence" in the region that would correspond to their respective economic and political interests as well as historic traditions and cultural peculiarities. Turkey might have more opportunities with Kyrgyzstan and Kazakhstan, as these countries are united not only by common Turkic language but also by relatively democratic political systems and Sunni Islam. Azerbaijan is also a natural Turkish client. Iran might get closer to autocratic and less developed Tajikistan and Turkmenistan. Uzbekistan, the strongest power in the area, will most likely try to distance itself from both "protectors."

Russian interests in the Caucasian and Central Asian regions are somewhat contradictory. Russia will remain interested in stability to the south of its borders and therefore in keeping a buffer zone between itself and the explosive Middle East and South Asia. This interest is intensified by the need to protect large Russian and Russian-speaking communities existing in almost all republics of these regions. Numerous politically vocal Turkic-speaking and Muslim ethnic groups within Russia with diverse ties in Central Asia and Kazakhstan are also a powerful lobby preventing Russian politicians from turning their backs on the south. On the other hand, direct involvement in conflicts in the south is not in Russia's interest. After the war in Afghanistan no political leadership in Moscow would be able to generate wide public support or material resources for a military engagement in this area. Russia's interests in the region might be enhanced, though, by a NATO-type multilateral alliance, with Russia playing the role of the United States, and its Central Asian partners that of Western Europe. Such an alliance would not imply any automatic Russian involvement in a conventional conflict or any Russian obligation to mediate in "domestic" disputes and clashes. Any such alliance should be premised on the clear understanding that members of the alliance will have very different social, political, and economic structures, different perceptions of democracy and human rights, etc. In this sense it might have more in common with the Organization of American States than with NATO.

The Caucasus

A multilateral alliance, however, is not likely to solve conflicts in the Caucasus. The "lebanization" of the region is a *fait accompli*, and it is unrealistic to expect any political and military stabilization in the near future. The conflicts tearing apart the Caucasus go deep into history and are now complicated by the disintegration of the former Soviet armed forces. Abandoned by the Moscow General Staff, local commanders have to fend for themselves. They are obliged to strike special deals with local political leaders. Eventually, local units turn into mercenaries ready to sell their support to anybody who is able to pay a good price. They could even try to replace civilian administration and seize political control in some communities or isolated territories.

This dangerous trend toward the disintegration of the armed forces is not limited to the Caucasus. Moldova, with its autonomous Dniester and Gagauz areas, may be the clearest case. Ukraine and Russia also are not immune to these problems. But for the Caucasus, with its immense ethnic, cultural, and political diversity, its still existing tribal and feudal traditions, and the conflicts already raging there, prospects are especially dismal. Political leaders in the region might try to maintain their positions by creating "parallel" or "alternative" armed units of their own, aside from the regular armed forces. The political orientation of such units and their behavior during crises, as in the case of the national guard established by former Georgian President Zviad Gamsakhurdia, are unpredictable. Moreover, there is in the Caucasus a long-standing tradition of private ownership of arms. The Georgian government controls only a part of the weapons in Georgia, the rest being in the hands of the Georgian opposition, South Ossetians, Abkhazians, local political leaders, semi-criminal and criminal groups of various kinds, "self-defense" units of private citizens, and others. Low-intensity conflicts of a tribal character are virtually unavoidable.

For Russia the problem is not to prevent these conflicts or to mediate them: it is too late for the first, and for the latter Russian diplomacy is simply not mature enough and tends to be politically biased and subject to political lobbying from ethnic communities. Probably UN or CSCE mediation would prove to be more efficient in the region. But what Russia can and should do is to stop all arms transfers to the Caucasus and to reach a political settlement with its own ethnic republics in the Northern Caucasus.

The fallback position for Russia might be a retreat from the Northern Caucasus to the traditionally Cossack-populated areas north of Chechnia and Dagestan. The cost of such a policy of withdrawal would be the almost complete disruption of economic ties, a massive outflow of Russians and other refugees from the region, and the permanent danger of the spillover of Caucasian conflicts to the southern Russian territories. To limit the damage and the risks, Russia would have to harness its diplomacy in the region, using economic leverage, backstage diplomacy, and internal regional controversies.

Can the United States Make a Difference?

Current Russian-American relations resemble a somewhat extended honeymoon. The newlyweds are still in an elated mood and shower each other with smiles and compliments, but there is already a pile of dirty dishes in the sink, the refrigerator is empty, the mail-box is full of unpaid bills and, in fact, the party is over. It's time to get down to earth with all its problems, hardships and conflicts.

There are more than enough grounds for a quarrel—Russia's desire to revise the articles of the Paris Treaty on conventional arms in Europe, the reluctance of the Clinton administration to increase significantly its economic aid to Moscow, differences of opinion on the Bosnian problem, a possible conflict of interests on the world arms market—just to name a few. But the definition of Russia's rights and obligations in relation to the other former Soviet republics poses the most serious problem for the West. It could well become the backdrop not just for a quarrel but for a full-blown political conflict.

It is apparent that even if Moscow prefers the strategy of "selective involvement" over an "imperialist" approach, its foreign policy conduct has become tougher. The signs of a new line have become evident in 1994. Thus, the protection of the rights of Russian minorities by diplomatic or other means has become an official strategy. Russian armed forces are being drawn into military operations in other republics, while officials of the Yeltsin administration call for a new Monroe Doctrine for Russia in regard to the "near abroad."

Moscow argues that Russia is guided not only by its own interests but also by those of the whole civilized world in maintaining peace and stability in Eurasia; thus Russia claims to have become an important outpost holding back the waves of religious fundamentalism, nationalism, and political extremism in the Caucasus, Central Asia, and other regions of the former Soviet Union. In other words, Russia serves as gatekeeper for the West, much as Germany did throughout the Cold War.

Of course, leaders in Kiev, Chisinau, and Almaty see Russia's conduct in a very different light. There, calls for a new Monroe Doctrine are viewed as a clear manifestation of imperial thinking. In many cases local officials even refuse to acknowledge the existence of a problem with the Russian population, and the prospect of Russia again becoming Eurasia's policeman is perceived as a way to restore the Soviet Union. This creates serious policy problems for the United States, with conflicting advice from specialists in and out of the government as well as ethnic lobbies in Washington and U.S. allies abroad.

Is it altogether impossible to prevent a Russian-U.S. clash over the "near abroad"? One potential solution could be the "finlandization" of the former Soviet republics: a pledge of the West not to draw these countries into implicitly anti-Russian alliances in exchange for a Russian commitment to abstain from interference in their domestic affairs. Such a formula would considerably lessen the chances for a conflict of interests between Russia and the United States over Eurasian affairs and could stabilize the whole situation in the region. At the same time such an understanding—even a tacit one—would preempt possible manifestations of radical imperialism from the Russian side, rendering impossible any Russian "Monroe Doctrine" in the "near abroad." One of the additional Russian responsibilities based on adequate Western assistance could be its role as an economic balancing wheel in Eurasia (primarily to prevent trade and financial imbalances within the CIS). Finally, Russia could take care of the regional infrastructure, such as financing and maintaining transportation and energy systems and developing information channels and communications.

However, even a tacit Russian-U.S. understanding on the "finlandization" of the "near abroad" appears very unlikely. First of all, neither conservative Republicans nor liberal Democrats in Washington would support it; the very notion of "finlandization" acquired a derogatory meaning in U.S. political elite circles when, during the Cold War, the U.S. fought against the perceived "finlandization" of Western Europe by the Soviet Union. Second, such a solution would mean a new division of Europe, this time along the Western border of the former USSR. It would block attempts to promote a common European political and defense space, setting different rules of the game for the Central European countries, on the one hand, and the Eastern Europeans, on the other.[37]

The other option the United States has in the Russian "near abroad" is to follow the activist policy of an "honest broker" among the former Soviet republics, depriving Moscow of any opportunity to display its imperial instincts. This activist position, including the use of economic and political sticks and carrots, mediation and peace-keeping, would undoubtedly be cheered in the capitals of the smaller successor states. But the option of an active U.S. involvement in Eurasia to keep Russia in check seems to be even less probable than "finlandization." The avoidance of such an involvement is likely given the difficulty that democratic societies have in mobilizing for operations when both the threat to national security and the possible benefits to national security are obscure. Only a very painful shock (such as Pearl Harbor) or a mortal threat to the existence of the democratic society (the Cold War) can push a democracy toward an active foreign policy of this sort.

Can one anticipate a shock or a threat coming from the territory of the former Soviet Union of such a magnitude that it would energize U.S.

foreign policy and outweigh the negative domestic side effects of a more active U.S. involvement in Eurasia? Such a prospect seems very remote. True, the U.S. public can be shocked by the slaughter of civilians in Tajikistan, war crimes in Abkhazia and Nagorno-Karabakh, or political terrorism in Crimea, especially if these tragedies are magnified by the media. But such shocks can easily be overshadowed by other shake-ups; in the case of Somalia the picture of a soldier's body being dragged through the streets of Mogadishu was enough to turn a large part of the U.S. public against continuing involvement in the country.

Likewise, experts and officials of the Clinton administration can speculate about various real or potential threats to U.S. security coming from the vast Eurasian landmass: a resurgence of Russian nationalism and expansionism, an explosion of Islamic fundamentalism in Central Asia, the Russian mafia spreading to U.S. soil, etc. Or else, they might warn against the proliferation of nuclear weapons, uncontrolled arms trade, millions of refugees fleeing from trouble spots in the former USSR, numerous Chernobyl-type accidents at insecure nuclear power plants in Eurasia, and other sinister symptoms of the coming Apocalypse. But none of these dangers and challenges can be compared in their mobilizing power with the overwhelming and hypnotizing threat that Soviet communism posed.

If an active U.S. policy toward the Russian "near abroad" does not look very likely, the idea of a "collective Western leadership and responsibility," cherished by the U.S. president, is even less convincing. While U.S. isolationism is moderated by an American messianic zeal, a version of the Manifest Destiny, West Europeans and Japanese have not kept much of their messianic heritage and, as recent events show, are not very eager to share with the U.S. the burden of building a "new world order," especially in dangerous and unpredictable places like the Russian (or non-Russian) "near abroad." The former Soviet republics might need resolute Western leadership more than ever before, but the West is less than ever prepared to provide it. From Canada to Germany to Japan, Western states are undergoing dramatic domestic political changes that paralyze their foreign-policy activism. At least for a decade most of America's partners will be governed by very fragile and unstable political coalitions predisposed to isolationism instead of internationalism, regionalism instead of globalism, and risk avoidance instead of risk taking. And this is exactly the decade during which the fate of the newly independent states of Eurasia will be decided.

These trends cannot but have a profound impact on the coming "new world order." Instead of a harmonious system of global and regional security structures, the world is much more likely to see a multiplication of autonomous power centers in different regions in the world, a fragmentation of the global security space into regional and sub-regional pieces.

The least costly strategy, politically and financially, is not to settle local conflicts but to prevent their horizontal and vertical escalation by limiting arms transfers to all parties to the conflict, imposing embargoes, and building stable regional balances of power. Some modest level of violence in the Caucasus, Central Asia, even Moldova (as well as sub-Saharan Africa or Central America) might be politically acceptable for the United States. Another question is whether such conflicts have a marked impact on the stability of the international system and whether they affect the vital interests of key players in world politics.

The territory of the former Soviet Union will clearly not be the top priority area for the United States. In case of a more aggressive Russian policy toward its "near abroad," one could expect a lot of critical rhetoric to come out of the White House, but not too much action or alternative strategies. The most sensitive issue is the future of the Baltic states; here a Russian imperialist policy might provoke a tough U.S. response. Otherwise, one could expect that even a gradual reabsorption by Russia of some of the other successor states—provided it takes place with a minimum of violence and regional instability—would be met with a good deal of indifference if not understanding by the United States. Both sides would then exchange ritual accusations and reproaches: Washington charging Moscow with aggression and imperialism, and Moscow accusing Washington of hypocrisy and a refusal to participate in building stability in Eurasia. The subsequent deterioration of Russian-U.S. relations would be practically inevitable but not fatal.

Notes

1. See, for example, Aleksandr Tsipko, "The Drama of the Russian Choice," *Izvestiia*, October 1, 1991.

2. As Kozyrev put it: "There can be no blueprint. What exist are reactions to specific situations, and those reactions display Russia's national interests. No country has an official description of its national interest." *Nezavisimaia gazeta*, April 1, 1992, pp. 1, 3.

3. Thus Suzanne Crow noted in early 1992 that "while Russia's leaders declared that the CIS states took top priority on Russia's foreign policy agenda, evidence to the contrary abounded. Russian Foreign Minister Kozyrev traveled to Western Europe, North America, Africa, the Middle East, and the Far East before setting out on his first visit to the CIS states in early April [of 1992]." Suzanne Crow, "Russia's Relations with Members of the Commonwealth," *RFE/RL Research Report*, Vol. 1, No. 19 (May 8, 1992), p. 8.

4. The Russian Inter-Agency Foreign Policy Commission reminded many of the old Soviet institution with a similar name. The composition of the new Commission, which included along with the Minister of Foreign Affairs the Ministers of Defense, Interior, and Security, reflects a return to the old Soviet-style bureaucratic decision-making.

5. For example, at a round-table discussion hosted by the liberal *Moscow News* in December 1991 almost all the participants expressed the hope that the Minsk agreement would prove a step toward the reintegration of the former Soviet republics. Yeltsin adviser Galina Starovoitova said that it offered hope for "a future confederation", while the head of Russian television's First Channel, Yegor Yakovlev, spoke of "the contours of a new Union." (*Moskovskie novosti*, No. 51, 1991.)

6. In a roundtable discussion published by the liberal weekly *Moscow News* in late December 1991, its editor-in-chief Len Karpinsky emphasized the importance of the CIS in keeping Russia, Ukraine, and Belarus in some kind of a union. According to him, there would have been disastrous consequences for Russian national consciousness, had these three Slavic nations been split up. Karpinsky was referring to the fact that, for Russians, the history of Rus' has its roots not in Moscow but in the Kievan state founded in the ninth century and that until the twelfth century Kiev (described as "the mother of Russian cities" in the Russian Primary Chronicle) was the political, economic, and cultural center of Rus'. Moscow, by contrast, was not settled until the twelfth century and did not acquire the status of a separate principality until 1301. Accordingly, Karpinsky argued, "Millions of Russians are convinced that, without Ukraine, it is impossible to speak not only of a great Russia but of any kind of Russia at all." (*Moskovskie novosti*, No. 51, 1991.)

7. In 1992 only a handful of liberals continued to emphasize the principle of self-determination, arguing that a possible disintegration of Russia was not necessarily an apocalyptic scenario. True, some radical democrats even claimed that such a future was preferable because it would create a more stable balance of power within the CIS and thus facilitate future integration on the territory of the USSR. The vast majority, however, opted for the territorial integrity of the Russian Federation as a key element in building a new state. This evolution in thinking did not necessarily mean that liberals abandoned their initial principles for the sake of a "united and indivisible Russia." It was in large part the tragic Yugoslav experience of 1991–1992 that made them change their attitudes toward national self-determination. Such a change affected not only liberal approaches to secessionist inclinations in Tatarstan, but also assessments of the Georgian-Abkhazian and Nagorno-Karabakh problems. In both cases most Russian liberals argued against changes in the territorial status quo.

8. One may note that the disintegration of the Soviet Union did not lead to a comparable disintegration of the Soviet foreign policy community. The latter has always been concentrated in Moscow, with very few academics, journalists and politicians engaged in international affairs living in the Soviet periphery. This is why the Russian Federation inherited the core of the Soviet foreign policy community with all the differences of opinion within it. After the creation of the CIS, a number of Moscow-based scholars and diplomats of non-Russian national-

ity went to their respective republics to assume high positions there within the newly-created Foreign Ministries and Presidential Councils, but this was not a massive outflow.

9. Liberals often did not distinguish between a defensive alliance and a collective security system; the structure they advocated was a hybrid of NATO and CSCE.

10. Kazakhstan's President Nursultan Nazarbaev remarked in January 1992: "Each republic has begun to act on its own and has been putting up barriers in the way of goods traffic and is establishing various quotas and licenses." Interfax, January 16, 1992.

11. Thus Khasbulatov argued: "After a while we should come to the realization that we need a supranational parliament" and "we must preserve our common citizenship within the confines of the CIS." (*Rossiiskaia gazeta*, September 18, 1992, p. 1.)

12. TASS, December 27, 1991. A similar "pro-Soviet" view was expressed by the Russian Christian Democratic Movement led by Viktor Aksiuchits. "We are told that the Commonwealth will lead to the unification of people," Aksiuchits stated. "But in my opinion it will lead to the opposite—to the complete separation of all Union republics and especially of the three Slavic ones. Why? Because it suits only nationalistic regimes." (*Pravda*, January 12, 1992.)

13. *Izvestiia*, December 19, 1991.

14. "It has to be admitted that in Alma-Ata something took place that the putschists failed to achieve in August: the legally elected president of the country was toppled while the constitution and the law were violated.... If one follows the logic by which the CIS was set up, one cannot rule out the possibility that, one day in the near future, the presidents of Tatarstan, Chechnia, Bashkiria, and other autonomous regions will get together somewhere in a farmhouse near Uriupinsk and proclaim the disbanding of the Russian Federation because they find the behavior of the federal leadership unsatisfactory. Still following precedent, they will telephone Bush and, after securing his blessing, inform Yeltsin that the post of president of the Russian Federation has been abolished and he himself has been awarded an appropriate pension." (*Moskovskie novosti*, No. 52, 1991.)

15. *Russkii vestnik*, No. 12 (March 18–25), 1992, p. 8.

16. *Russkii vestnik*, No. 15 (April 8–15), 1992, p. 3.

17. Among the more visible leaders of the movement are Sergei Baburin, Mikhail Astaf'ev, Viktor Alksnis, Nikolai Pavlov, Ilia Konstantinov, Viktor Anpilov, Viktor Aksiuchits, Gennadii Ziuganov, Aleksandr Sterligov, Viktor Filatov, and Albert Makashov.

18. It would be tempting to suggest that the struggle between the "confederalists" and imperialists follows the more general political and philosophical division between Westernizers and Slavophiles. However, such a hypothesis would be a clear oversimplification. The modern post-Soviet Slavophiles embrace a wide variety of political groups and ideas ranging from very liberal ecological-oriented movements to radical nationalistic and anti-Semitic parties. Some of them would undoubtedly prefer a "Eurasian confederation" to a revived Russian Empire. On the other hand, not all the Westernizers are necessarily devoted to Western democracy and Western concepts of international law. Some of them

argue that the only way for Russia to catch up with the West is by an authoritarian regime capable of handling inevitable social tensions and instabilities during the transition period as well as defending Russian interests in the "near abroad" by various means—including military, if need be.

19. The Seventh Congress of People's Deputies, which met in December 1992, issued an appeal to the parliaments of the former Soviet Union to consider "creating a confederation or another framework for bringing together the independent states of Europe and Asia that were formerly republics of the USSR, whose peoples are expressing a desire for unification." (Radio Rossii, December 14, 1992.)

20. Marshal Evgenii Shaposhnikov argued that "as a result of the present instability and lack of coordination among CIS member states, grave anxiety is replacing the interest [the West] used to have in what we are doing. NATO is giving serious thought to the establishment of peacekeeping forces for use, among other things, in the CIS. Now that the USSR has collapsed, the influence of certain states such as Turkey, Iran, Pakistan, and others is increasing....That is precisely why—along with a number of other reasons—the United States is stepping up its attempts to design a monopolistic system of world administration in which it would have the decisive role. Other centers of power are also gaining ground. All this, taken together, has to be borne in mind by CIS states, and above all by Russia if, of course, it does have geostrategic interests." (Radio Rossii, December 11, 1992.)

21. *Nezavisimaia gazeta*, January 19, 1994, p. 1.

22. "I was opposed to the breakup of the Union and believe that the consequences of the Belovezhskaia [Minsk] accord were not correctly calculated. But to return to the pre-Belovezhskaia situation is impossible." *Rossiia*, No. 47 (November 18–24), 1992, p. 5.

23. "As the internationally recognized legal successor to the USSR, the Russian Federation's foreign policy must be based on a doctrine that proclaims the entire geographical space of the former Union a sphere of its vital interests (following the example of the U.S. Monroe Doctrine in Latin America). Furthermore, it is necessary to obtain from the world community an understanding and recognition of Russia's special interests in this space. Likewise, Russia must secure from the international community [approval of] the role of political and military guarantor of stability on the territory of the USSR. It is therefore necessary to obtain the support of the G-7 countries for those functions of Russia, up to and including hard-currency subsidies for rapid-response forces (Russian 'blue berets')." (*Izvestiia*, August 7, 1992.)

24. *Nezavisimaia gazeta*, August 19, 1992, p. 4.

25. ITAR-TASS, March 1, 1993.

26. On March 17, 1993, in his address to the CIS leaders, Yeltsin declared: "First of all, we need real instruments to eliminate 'hot spots' and the means to prevent the buildup of new tension. Such mechanisms, including collective peacekeeping forces, ought to be started as soon as possible. Here the experience of international operations in keeping the peace, especially direct support for our joint efforts by the UN, the CSCE, and other organizations, will also be useful. In my opinion, we should strive to set up an effective security system within the

structures of the CIS, which would become an important factor in sustaining peace in the entire Eurasian region. Pooling our efforts in this area would also allow each state to cut its defense spending while maintaining the necessary level of security." (*Nezavisimaia gazeta*, March 18, 1993, p. 1.)

27. The decline of the Ottoman Empire and the divergent approaches of the great powers of Europe to this process led to political crises in 1832–1833, 1839–1840, 1885, 1908, the Crimean and the first world wars, and the Balkan wars of 1875–1878 and 1912–1913. See M.S. Anderson, *The Eastern Question 1774–1923* (New York: Macmillan, 1966); as well as Rene Albrecht-Carrie, *A Diplomatic History of Europe Since the Congress of Vienna* (New York: Harper and Row, 1958), pp. 40–55, 84–92, 167–177, 196–197, 259–272, 280–286, 321–334.

28. William Eckhardt, "Wars and War-Related Deaths, 1945–1989," in Ruth Leger Sivard, ed., *World Military and Social Expenditures 1989*, 13th ed. (Washington, D.C.: World Priorities, 1989), p. 22.

29. Erik Whitlock, "Obstacles to CIS Integration," *RFE/RL Research Report*, Vol. 2, No. 27 (July 2, 1993), p. 35. Vladimir Mashits, the chairman of the State Committee for Economic Cooperation with Members of the CIS, gave even higher figures of the Russian surplus for 1992: 3 trillion rubles or 14% of GDP. (ITAR-TASS, February 18, 1993.)

30. *Rossiiskie vesti*, February 26, 1993.

31. The most radical, if caricatured, manifestation of the latter position can be found in statements of Vladimir Zhirinovsky. Speaking to an Armenian paper on how to resolve the Caucasian conflicts, he declared: "What have you got? Peaches?... Eat your peaches! But how will you manage without Russian timber and metal? ... I am neither a Russian tsar nor a Bolshevik. I won't send a single soldier into your area. I'll wait while you kill each other. I'll come in only after the place is empty." (*Golos Armenii*, September 25, 1991.) During the 1993 election campaign Zhirinovsky went even further. Not only did he threaten to cut all economic ties with the "near abroad" to make them join Russia as "gubernii," but he also proposed a program of ethnic cleansing: "The flow of refugees is easy to stop. It's enough to threaten the regions pushing out the Russians that we'll treat their nationals in Russia the same way. Take, for instance, Azerbaijan. Five hundred thousand Russians used to live there. Now there are 100 thousand left. And how many Azeris are on the loose in Russia? A million. So, to start with, we should deport from Russia to Baku 400 thousand Azeris. And if you still dare to touch the Russians, the whole million will be deported. And the same should apply to all the regions." (*Izvestiia*, November 30, 1993, p. 4.)

32. *Novoe zarubezhie i shansy rossiisko-amerikanskogo partnerstva* (Moscow: Rossiiskii Nauchnyi Fond, 1993), p. 15.

33. *Ekonomika i zhizn'*, No. 19, 1993.

34. The problem with the use of economic relations for political or military purposes is that to be effective economic policies have to be very selective. For example, Russia should be able to "punish" Ukraine for inappropriate political behavior by raising prices on oil, but at the same time it should be in a position to "reward" Belarus for keeping in line by fixing low prices on oil going to this country. Yet the level of economic integration between Ukraine and Belarus is so high that Russia is unable to prevent a large-scale re-export of oil from Belarus to

Ukraine. Besides, the government in Russia no longer controls all the oil exports. Under the circumstances, any economic sanctions would be extremely difficult to implement.

35. Numerous critics underscored the point that the decision to protect the Tajik-Afghan border had been taken in the absence of any relevant military or political doctrine, or any defined Russian national interest, nor had the way to defend such interests been properly analyzed. Russia had been sucked into a military conflict with unreliable communication lines, in the absence of powerful local allies, and in the face of hostility on the part of a large part of the Tajik population. The Russian involvement was also very difficult to justify on economic grounds: Tajikistan lacks marketable resources and can hardly present any economic value for Russia even in the long term; on the other hand, the republic was readily accepted into the ruble zone and promised large-scale credits. The need to protect the Russian minority in Tajikistan was hardly convincing: at the current migration rates, by 1996 there will be no Russians in the country at all.

36. Some leaders in this region have more ambitious plans. Former Lithuanian President Vitautas Landsbergis persistently put forward the idea of the so-called Black Sea-Baltic confederation including Ukraine, Belarus, and the three Baltic states. Such a union, if created, would have at least an implicitly anti-Russian content.

37. It should be noted that new security arrangements in the European part of the former Soviet Union would make sense only if they formed an open, not a closed, system. Thus the Baltic states, in order to balance the Russian military might, would have no choice but to create some kind of Nordic sub-regional security system with the Scandinavian countries. Ukraine would do its best to establish a special partnership with Poland or Germany. Russia would be likely to try to reach over its next-door neighbors to make special arrangements with Central and West European countries as well as with European transnational institutions. Furthermore, the "near abroad" states, feeling betrayed by the West and considering Russia to be the prime threat to their security, might try to circumvent "finlandization" by forging an anti-Russian alliance of their own, without Western participation. Finally, the current political instability in Russia puts in doubt, for the West, any long-term strategic compromises with Moscow. These compromises, even if reached, could be unilaterally rejected or revised by a new Russian leadership.

6

Demilitarization and Defense Conversion

David Holloway and Michael McFaul

The past weighs heavily on the new Russia. This is especially true of the Soviet military legacy. Reducing defense expenditures, establishing mechanisms for subordinating the military to Russia's new democratic leaders, working out a new defense doctrine, and converting defense industries to civilian uses have greatly complicated Russian politics in the three years since the August 1991 putsch.

The Soviet Union was a highly militarized state in several ways. First, the Communist Party leadership ascribed to military power a central place in its foreign policy. Military rivalry was the focus of its relationship with the United States, for example, and military power underpinned Soviet domination of Eastern Europe. Second, the Party—especially in the Brezhnev years—tried to instill military patriotism into the society at large by recalling the victory over Germany in World War II as the greatest triumph of Soviet power. Third, the Party leadership gave top priority to military power—only by devoting a very large part of its GNP to defense was the Soviet Union able to compete with the economically much stronger United States during the Cold War.

Although the USSR was a highly militarized state, the military remained under civilian control. The Party claimed primacy, and an extensive network of Party and KGB controls maintained that primacy. The military chafed against these controls and asserted its professionalism in military affairs, but it never challenged the principle of civilian control.

Gorbachev tried to move away from the traditional Soviet emphasis on military power in domestic and foreign policy. His "new thinking" rejected the ideological view of the world in which the militarization of

Soviet policy had been embedded. By stressing "general human values" rather than the conflict between capitalism and socialism, he provided the conceptual framework for better relations with the West. He made a determined effort to ease the external pressure on the Soviet Union by pursuing arms control and by improving relations with the United States, Western Europe, China, and Japan.[1]

Military expenditure continued to grow in the mid–1980s, but it was clear by 1988 that Gorbachev wanted to reduce the defense budget and to convert part of the defense sector to civilian production. In December 1988, he announced a unilateral reduction of 500,000 men in the Soviet Armed Forces, and in the following month he stated that defense spending would be cut. Discussion of military reform started at about this time, and the press began to publish unprecedented criticism of the Armed Forces. The first signs of serious draft resistance began to appear, and mothers began to protest against the maltreatment of their sons in the Army. A process of gradual demilitarization appeared to be under way.[2]

As the political crisis in the Soviet Union grew more acute in 1989–1991, the military became increasingly politicized. Members of the High Command were openly critical of Gorbachev for weakening the Soviet Union and pursuing policies that threatened to lead to its disintegration.[3] But the military was not united in its political views; like other Soviet institutions, it was affected by divisions within the political elite, and split by the crisis through which the country was passing. The situation recalled Trotsky's comment that the Red Army was "a copy of society and suffers from all its ills, usually at a higher temperature."[4]

Divisions in the military proved crucial in August 1991, when leading figures in the Army, the military-industrial complex, the government, and the KGB—the institutions that made up the core of the Soviet system—tried to seize power in order to preserve the Soviet state as they knew it. Although Marshal Dmitrii Yazov, the Minister of Defense, was one of the coup's leaders, key elements in the Army proved unwilling to take action against Boris Yeltsin and those who rallied around him to oppose the coup. The split in the Army was a major cause of the coup's failure.[5]

The coup precipitated the very thing that the putschists had tried to prevent—the breakup of the Soviet Union and the collapse of communist rule. Boris Yeltsin, who had been elected president of Russia by popular vote in June 1991, now had the opportunity to carry through economic and political reform, and to define a new place for Russia in world politics. Inevitably these reforms included a military element: with the Soviet Union gone and the Cold War over, what kind of army did Russia need?

How should the Army be adapted to a democratic state? How could the defense sector be converted to civilian production? How would the Army influence the outcome of the revolutionary change through which Russia was passing?

The Founding of the Russian Army

The August putsch did not lead at once to the breakup of the Soviet Armed Forces. Gorbachev, as president of the USSR, still hoped to hold the Union together. But Yeltsin too, it is worth recalling, proposed in early September 1991 the creation of a "Union of Sovereign States," which would preserve a single "defense space" and maintain joint armed forces. A draft Treaty of Collective Security was prepared in Moscow.[6]

The overwhelming vote for independence in the Ukrainian referendum of December 1 ended the hope of creating the Union envisaged by Yeltsin. On December 8, Russia, Ukraine, and Belarus agreed to set up the Commonwealth of Independent States. Article 6 of this agreement stated that the member states of the Commonwealth would "maintain and support a common military-strategic space under a joint command, including unified control of nuclear weapons." This commitment remained when eleven of the former republics (all except the three Baltic states and Georgia) signed the Alma-Ata Declaration on December 21.[7]

The Soviet Armed Forces had already passed through a very difficult period by December 1991. In the late 1970s, they occupied a privileged position in Soviet society and were regarded abroad as an invincible military machine. The war in Afghanistan, however, dented their reputation. Then Gorbachev's policies began to squeeze the defense budget, and glasnost opened them up to unprecedented criticism. Armed Forces' involvement in domestic public order operations made them the focus of political controversy, while the collapse of Communist rule in Eastern Europe forced their withdrawal from the region and caused severe housing problems for the Army at home. With the breakup of the Soviet Union, a once-great army was being further weakened.

The Soviet High Command very much wanted to keep the Armed Forces intact. The newly appointed Chief of the General Staff, General V. Lobov, stated categorically in an interview on September 9, 1991 that only unified armed forces were acceptable. He gave two reasons for this view: first, the more separate militaries there were, the greater the danger of conflict between the former republics; second, it was important to retain unified control of nuclear weapons.[8] The High Command hoped that the Soviet Armed Forces might be preserved as a single entity, in spite of the breakup of the Soviet Union. In January 1992, General Y.

Shaposhnikov—the new Commander-in-Chief of the CIS—and General K. Kobets, an adviser to Yeltsin, proposed to Yeltsin that the Soviet Armed Forces be put under Russian control "until a comprehensive agreement on their further role is reached with Ukraine and other former Soviet republics."[9]

It quickly became apparent, however, that these hopes were illusory, and that the disintegration of the Soviet Union entailed the breakup of the Soviet Armed Forces. Several of the newly independent states wanted to create their own armies. Most importantly, President Kravchuk of Ukraine—in line with earlier commitments he had made—issued a decree on December 12, 1991 ordering the creation of the Armed Forces of Ukraine.[10] Yeltsin did not oppose these moves, since opposition would have brought conflict with the new states. By March 1992, the Russian government accepted that the Soviet Armed Forces could not survive without the Soviet state. On May 7, 1992, Yeltsin signed a decree establishing the Armed Forces of the Russian Federation. At the time of its founding, the Russian military was therefore in a state of considerable disarray and demoralization. General Pavel Grachev, the new Minister of Defense, complained in December 1992 that Russia had inherited the "ruins and wreckage" of the military might of the Soviet Union:

> The systems of communication, command and control, of intelligence, of early warning of ballistic missile attack, of air defense, of ensuring the viability of forces, had been destroyed. ... The units that were most combat ready and best equipped with new weapons remained outside the Russian Federation. ... Discipline dropped sharply. There was fertile soil for thievery and corruption. The number of legal transgressions began to grow catastrophically."[11]

Establishing the Armed Forces of the Russian Federation was difficult for other reasons as well—the military assets of the Soviet Union had to be divided up and military relations with the former republics worked out; a new military doctrine had to be elaborated to provide guidance for defense policy; new arrangements for civil-military relations had to be devised. Moreover, these tasks had to be accomplished in a drastically changed economic environment.

At the beginning of 1992, the Russian government made a determined effort to cut government expenditure in order to reduce the budget deficit. Defense spending was badly hit. In 1992 funding for military procurement was cut by 68%, and for military research and development by 50%, by comparison with 1991.[12] These cuts not only shook the defense economy (see below); they also signalled a further loss of priority for the Armed Forces.

The Development of a New Military Doctrine

The Russian government cut defense expenditure for economic reasons, not because it had formulated a new concept of Russia's security needs. But Russia's security interests were obviously different from those of the Soviet Union, if only because the territorial dimensions of the state and its geostrategic position had changed. The premises underpinning foreign policy had also changed with the end of the Cold War. Finally, military policy had to be adjusted to the state of the country's economy. Without a conception of Russian security interests—of the nature of the threats to Russian security and of the wars that Russia might have to fight—it was impossible to decide what armed forces Russia needed. Hence it was important to elaborate a new military doctrine as a guide for policy-makers.[13]

On November 2, 1993, Yeltsin adopted a new military doctrine by decree, "The Basic Provisions of the Military Doctrine of the Russian Federation."[14] Worked out by an interagency group and reviewed by the Security Council (the top policy-making body for national security), the document was designed, according to its authors, for a transitional period in which Russian statehood would be established, democratic reforms carried out, and a new system of international relations formed. More specifically, it was intended to define the purpose of the Armed Forces.

In fact, however, the document is couched in very general terms and does not provide the kind of specific guidelines that could help policy-makers. It does not give a clear picture of the most likely sources of danger for Russia; nor does it indicate in even the vaguest terms what criteria might be used for deciding on the peacetime strength of the Armed Forces. And finally, the new doctrine fails to take serious account of the country's economic circumstances.

Nevertheless, the doctrine does contain some important points. First, it marks a break with the Soviet past by asserting that Russia does not regard any state as its enemy and that Russia will not use its Armed Forces except in defense of itself or its allies. This does not mean, of course, that Russia takes no interest in its strategic environment. It has sought to develop good relations with China, in the military as well as other spheres. Russia has also made it clear that the military-political evolution of the former Warsaw Pact countries is a matter of vital interest. It has objected—so far successfully—to the extension of NATO membership to the countries of East-Central Europe. Russia has joined NATO's Partnership for Peace (PFP), which was established in January 1994 to provide for cooperation between NATO and the other countries of Europe. The decision to join the PFP was a controversial one in Russia, but Yeltsin accepted the argument put forward by the Ministries of Defense and Foreign Affairs that refusal to join would leave Russia isolated strategically. It remains to be seen how far Russia will pursue cooperation within the PFP, and to what extent it will use its influence to prevent cooperation. It is clear, however, that Russia intends to have a major say in the construction of a new security system for Europe.

Second, the new doctrine elaborates a concept of nuclear deterrence without reiterating the traditional Soviet pledge not to use nuclear weapons first. Russia will not have the kind of conventional forces that the Soviet Union had and will rely heavily on nuclear deterrence for its security, especially in its relations with the other great powers. The strategic nuclear forces are to be restructured within the framework of START (Strategic Arms Reduction Treaty) I and II. START II, which was signed by Presidents Yeltsin and Bush in January 1993, provides for the reduction of strategic nuclear warheads on each side from about 10,000 to 3,000–3,500 by the year 2000. It has not yet been ratified by either side. Ratification will be controversial in Moscow, because critics have argued that the agreement is unfair to Russia.[15]

Third, the new doctrine pays great attention to the "Near Abroad." This is apparent in the stress on ethnic and religious conflicts as a source of danger, and in the statement that the presence of foreign troops in neighboring countries, without Russian agreement, would constitute a threat to Russia. The Ministry of Defense is creating new mobile forces that can be transported quickly to conduct operations in any region where a threat to Russian security may arise. The stress on mobile forces reflects the current perception that the greatest threat to Russia's security comes from conflicts on its southern borders.

The new doctrine lacks the emphasis on large-scale strategic offensive operations so characteristic of the Soviet Armed Forces and the Warsaw Pact. It gives priority to nuclear deterrence and to the development of mobile forces. The Ministry of Defense has adopted a plan of staged withdrawal of forces to Russia and gradual reduction of the Armed Forces to a level of 1.5 million troops (though General Grachev has more recently spoken of a level of 2.1 million troops). But this plan will be difficult to implement. Officers and their families withdrawn from Eastern Europe and the former Soviet republics have to be housed, a problem that affects hundreds of thousands of families and is a cause of great demoralization and disaffection in the officer corps. In addition, the system of conscription has broken down almost completely, and as a result there are now as many officers as enlisted men in the Russian Army. The Ministry of Defense is introducing a mixed (volunteer and conscript) system of recruitment, but it will take some time for the system to work properly. It will therefore be some time before the Russian Army is an effective fighting force.

Military Relations with the Near Abroad

In the Cold War the central focus of Soviet military policy was the confrontation between NATO and the Warsaw Pact; the priorities of post-Soviet Russia have been less clear-cut. The strategic relationship with the United States remains vital for Russia, and military relations with the other great powers are at the center of Russia's policy. But the most complex set of military issues facing Russia are with the "Near Abroad": the military assets of the Soviet Union have had to be disposed of; security arrangements have had to be worked out among the newly independent states; and Russian forces have become involved in local conflicts outside the Russian Federation.

Dividing up the assets of the Soviet Armed Forces among the new states has proved to be a complex problem, involving not only people and weapons but also infrastructure such as Early Warning radars. Most of these issues have been resolved peacefully through negotiation, but two have been politically very sensitive: the Black Sea Fleet and nuclear weapons. In spite of several attempts to resolve the issue, Russia and Ukraine have still not agreed on the future of the Black Sea Fleet, whose home port is Sevastopol in the Crimean peninsula. What is involved is not merely the division of the ships, but whether Russia will continue to base its ships in Sevastopol. The issue is complicated by the claim of Russian nationalists (though not of the Russian government) that Crimea belongs to Russia, and by the desire of many Russians living in Crimea to be reunited with Russia. The Black Sea Fleet has thus acquired symbolic importance in relations between Russia and Ukraine, making the dispute more difficult to resolve.

The future of Soviet nuclear weapons has also been a source of conflict between Russia and Ukraine. Even before the breakup of the Soviet Union, the Soviet government had taken the precaution of beginning to move its tactical nuclear weapons from the republics to Russia. This process was completed in 1992. Three countries apart from Russia still had strategic nuclear forces on their territory, however: Belarus, Kazakhstan, and Ukraine. This has been a matter of great concern to the United States. Washington does not want nuclear proliferation to be speeded up by the creation of four nuclear-weapon states in place of one, while it also wants to move ahead with ratification of START I and II. Russia was recognized as the successor to the Soviet Union for the purposes of the

Nuclear Non-Proliferation Treaty (NPT)—i.e., it was recognized as a nuclear-weapon state—and the three other states came under pressure to give up their nuclear weapons. Belarus ratified START I (Strategic Arms Reduction Treaty I) and became a non-nuclear-weapon-state party to the NPT in 1993; Kazakhstan ratified START I in 1992 and became a party to the NPT in 1994. Both countries are transferring the nuclear weapons on their territory to Russia.

The Ukrainian case has been more contentious. Ukraine declared at the time it achieved independence that it would be a non-nuclear state, and committed itself in May 1992 to signing START I and acceding to the NPT as a non-nuclear-weapon state. As Russo-Ukrainian relations deteriorated, however, opposition grew in Ukraine to handing over the nuclear weapons to Russia. It looked as though Ukraine might try to gain operational control of the weapons on its territory and thus acquire a nuclear force of its own. But a combination of domestic problems and international pressure led President Kravchuk to sign, in January 1994, a Trilateral Agreement with Presidents Yeltsin and Clinton committing Ukraine to eliminating all nuclear weapons on its territory. The Ukrainian parliament ratified START I in 1994, but Ukraine has not yet acceded to the NPT. It started to transfer its warheads to Russia early in 1994. Progress has thus been made, but Ukraine could still change its mind and opt to retain some nuclear weapons.[16]

A second important aspect of Russian policy in the "Near Abroad" has been the effort to create new security arrangements among the members of the CIS. When Russia set about creating its own Army in May 1992, it also signed a Treaty of Collective Security with some of the other CIS states.[17] The Treaty provided for consultation and for coordination of defense policy, but several key states, notably Ukraine, did not sign. The Treaty, moreover, did not provide an effective basis for joint Commonwealth Armed Forces. In August 1993, the position of Commander-in-Chief of the Joint Armed Forces of the CIS was abolished, and the CIS High Command was turned into a Coordinating Staff for Military Cooperation under the CIS Council of Defense Ministers. The same meeting decided not to create Joint Armed Forces, although a multinational force was formed to maintain security on the Tajik-Afghan border.

The idea of creating joint CIS forces has not been abandoned completely. In April 1994, General Grachev spoke of the possibility of forming such forces in the near future, though it is clear that not all members of the CIS would agree to take part. Russia is evidently eager to form a system of collective security on the territory of the former Soviet Union, and to deepen military ties to such a degree that it is possible to speak of a single military-strategic space.

When the Soviet Union ceased to exist, there were units of the Soviet Armed Forces in all the former republics. In some of the new states—for example, in Ukraine—these units became part of new national armies. Other units—for example, in the Baltic states—are being withdrawn to Russia. In other cases, Russia has negotiated the right to retain forces and bases in the new states. Delays in withdrawing forces have caused tension between Russia and the Baltic states, Estonia and Latvia in particular, and raised fears that Russia wants to maintain garrisons there. In Moldova, the Commander of the Russian 14th Army, General Aleksandr Lebed, has actively supported the Russian minority that set up the autonomous Trans-Dniestr republic. In Georgia, too, the Russian Army has intervened by supporting the Abkhaz rebels with arms and equipment. It remains unclear, however, whether local commanders have acted primarily on their own initiative, or whether they are acting on orders from the Ministry of Defense in Moscow or the Russian government. Whatever the case, the Russian Army has been an important political force in the "Near Abroad."

Russian military involvement in the "Near Abroad" extends beyond the dilatory withdrawal of Russian forces and the activities of local commanders. Russia has also become involved in peacekeeping operations in Tajikistan and Georgia. It has sought from the United Nations and from the CSCE (Conference on Security and Cooperation in Europe) recognition of its role as guarantor of peace and stability on the territory of the former Soviet Union. Neither the UN nor the CSCE has acceded to Russia's request, but discussions are taking place in the CSCE about possible arrangements for peacekeeping. Russia wants its role in the "Near Abroad" legitimated by international organizations, and it is possible that some such legitimation will be forthcoming. But if it is, Russia will have to abide by certain rules and not disregard the sovereignty of the new states.

Civil-Military Relations

The Army was praised after the August 1991 putsch for not turning its weapons upon the people. However, the coup drew the Army further into politics by showing that Army support was crucial for claimants to political power. In December 1991, before the collapse of the Soviet Union, both Gorbachev and Yeltsin made outright bids for the Army's support. On December 10, Gorbachev met high-ranking military officials and asked them to support him as Supreme Commander-in-Chief of the Soviet Armed Forces. He urged them to endorse his plans to preserve the Union and lectured them on Soviet patriotism. The following day Yeltsin met the same group of officers. He reminded them that he had recently raised their pay by 90% and promised to do what he could to help them. The military threw its weight behind Yeltsin, and Gorbachev's last-minute attempt to save the Union failed.[18]

The trials and tribulations of the Army have created widespread dissatisfaction among the officer corps and potentially fertile ground for political opponents of Yeltsin. Yeltsin has been aware of this and has attempted to secure the loyalty of the military by raising pay and treating its demands seriously. He has always been conscious of the crucial role that the Army could play in politics.

In spite of the turmoil and dissatisfaction in the military, the Russian High Command has shown no desire to seize power or to act as king-maker, deciding who should rule. General Grachev made it clear that he wanted to stand aside from the conflict between Yeltsin and the Congress of People's Deputies in 1992 and 1993. He told the Congress of People's Deputies in December 1992 that

> in the name of stability, in the name of Russia's rebirth, we propose to the various political forces and groupings to declare a kind of moratorium on drawing the Army into politics. To exclude any playing of the 'Army card' from the arsenal of permissible means of political struggle. ... I think it is time once and for all to state whose side the Army is on. The Army was and will be on the side of the people, on the side of the law, on the side of the Constitution. The Army serves the Fatherland, it is an instrument and attribute of the state, and that says it all.[19]

Grachev's intention seems clear enough, even though political conflict between the president and the parliament deprived his statement that the Army was on the side of the Constitution of much of its meaning. Grachev's point was that the Army should stand above party politics and leadership conflicts. He was not successful in achieving this goal, however. In October 1993, he came to Yeltsin's aid by shelling the White House, though he did so only reluctantly.

The Army's reluctance to be drawn into politics springs in part from the Russian and Soviet tradition of military subservience to civilian authority. A more important reason may be that, given the splits within the military, involvement in politics might destroy the Army. The officer corps is profoundly dissatisfied with the government for its failure to solve the Army's problems; this disaffection was reflected in the high proportion of officers who voted for Zhirinovsky in the December 1993 election.[20] But the Army might find it more difficult, if not impossible, to solve its problems if it pursued an active role in leadership politics. The Army appears to be fearful of being manipulated by politicians.[21] Its political role has resulted more from political leaders' desire to draw the

Army into politics than from any ambition on the part of the High Command to seize political power. The future role of the Army in politics will depend very largely, therefore, on the actions of politicians, and on the stability of the institutions established by the new Constitution.

But the Army's desire to avoid involvement in leadership conflicts is only one part of the story. The Army clearly wants to occupy a powerful place in the new Russian state. It has a considerable interest in acquiring political influence in order to solve the many problems with which it is faced. The Army's corporate interests, which militate against its involvement in leadership politics, nonetheless encourage it to seek political influence and support. A contradictory dynamic has thus been set up in which the possibility of military intervention in leadership is useful to the Army as it seeks to win concessions from the government, even though actual intervention might be very damaging to the cohesion of the Army as an institution.

The influence of Russian nationalism has grown in Russian politics since the election of December 1993. This is evident in Russian foreign policy, which is more forthright in its assertion of Russian national interests. The Army has benefitted from this shift, and perhaps also from its support for Yeltsin in October 1993. The version of the new military doctrine adopted in November 1993 was the Ministry of Defense's version. Yeltsin also heeded military advice in opposing the extension of NATO membership to the countries of East-Central Europe. In this context Russian military activities in the Near Abroad might assume a more sinister aspect as the instrument of a new imperial policy.

It would be a mistake, however, to exaggerate these trends. Russian military policy in the Near Abroad is not necessarily a sign that Russia intends to create a new empire within the borders of the former Soviet Union, but can be seen as the assertion by a great power of its interests in unstable and conflict-ridden neighboring states. The long-term trends in Russia's military relations with the Near Abroad are not yet clear. Besides, the politics of defense in Russia is very different from what it was in the Soviet Union. Even though political leaders have to pay attention to the Army's interests, the government's priorities are more open to question than they were in the Soviet period. There is now debate about military policy in parliament and in the press. Economic constraints on defense policy are now much more stringent. The Ministry of Defense has pressed very hard in the spring of 1994 for a major increase in the defense budget, but Yeltsin and the government appear to be standing firm. There is strong countervailing pressure from other lobbies; and restraints on government spending are essential if hyperinflation is to be avoided. Although the new military doctrine ignores economic constraints, a process of adjustment is now taking place in which the

Russian military is having to accustom itself to a less privileged position than it enjoyed in the Soviet past. But this process is complex and difficult, as the efforts at defense conversion show.

Demilitarization of the Russian Economy

Russia inherited, as Gorbachev put it, "the most militarized economy in the world and the largest defense expenditures."[22] The Soviet military industrial complex (MIC) was not simply a part of the Soviet economy— it was the Soviet economy. All economic activity was organized to support it, and all of the Soviet Union's most talented scientists and engineers served it. Military enterprises, especially those involved in the development of strategic technologies, enjoyed almost unlimited access to financial credits, natural resources, equipment, and machinery.[23] Moreover, budgets for the Soviet economy were structured to meet its needs. All allocations for the military industrial complex were specified first during the preparation of every annual budget; remaining funds were then rationed throughout the civilian economy.

As a result, by the end of the 1980s the Soviet MIC accounted for over 20–25% of Soviet GDP. While the rest of the Soviet economy approximated Third World standards, the Soviet military industrial complex propelled the USSR to superpower status. Of this mammoth Soviet military industrial complex, 70% was located in the Russian Republic.

Given the scope and scale of this inheritance, marketization could not proceed in Russia without a radical reorganization of the military sector as a whole, along with a major restructuring of individual military enterprises. This transformation cannot occur organically. The institutional setting that structured and governed the MIC did not collapse with the Soviet state. On the contrary, Soviet practices regarding weapons acquisitions and state orders, the interface between military enterprises and the Ministry of Defense, the vertical integration of military industries, and the organization and allocation of assets at the enterprise level continue to guide the behavior of Russian military enterprises. Until these institutions are changed, Russian military enterprises will remain beyond the influence of the market and will pose a major impediment to reform more generally.

From Planned Conversion to State Collapse

Gorbachev's efforts to reform the Soviet economy that began soon after he assumed power in 1985 made changing the balance between civilian and military production a top priority for the Soviet leadership. Initially, Gorbachev sought to reduce the rationale for military expenditures by improving U.S.-Soviet relations.[24] To ease the transition from military to civilian production, a conversion plan, first announced in 1988, did not reduce budget allocations to individual enterprises. Rather, each enterprise was required to reduce its military production and increase civilian production.[25]

During the last three years of Gorbachev's rule, budget allocations for weapons procurement did decrease from 32.6 billion in 1989 to 24.8 billion rubles in 1991, while money devoted to military research and development fell from 15.3 to 10.2 billion rubles during the same time period.[26] New factories devoted solely to the production of consumer products were not opened, however, and no military enterprises were closed. Consequently, the basic organization of the military industrial complex, or its centrality to the Soviet economy as a whole, changed little.

The disintegration of the Soviet Union after the aborted August 1991 coup, however, changed a great deal. Most dramatically, state expenditures devoted to weapons procurement decreased over 80% in 1992.[27] Commensurately, the volume of output from the military industrial complex decreased by approximately 23% in that same year.[28] The collapse of the Soviet state and the creation of several independent states also destroyed the centralized integration of the military industrial complex. Suddenly, Russian factories had to import airplane engines from Ukraine or bolts from Belarus, while other enterprises had to seek ways to receive payments for their exports to other newly independent states of the former Soviet Union.

Finally, the new Russian state's commitment to creating a market economy challenged the norms, rules, and procedures of production practiced by the military industrial complex. Of all sectors of the economy, military enterprises were the least inhibited by hard budget constraints and were the most isolated from the ways of the market, especially the international market.[29] After the coup, these enterprises were suddenly compelled to pay market prices for their inputs, acquire their own contracts, balance their books, and produce and sell competitive goods in a market economy.[30]

The resultant crisis was exacerbated by the newly-independent Russian government's initial strategy for encouraging conversion and the economic restructuring of military enterprises generally. In the fall of 1991, President Yeltsin appointed Yegor Gaidar as deputy prime minister (he later became acting prime minister) to coordinate economic reform. Launching an ambitious program of reform in January 1992, Gaidar and his team of young economists were militantly committed to macroeconomic stabilization—a policy that began with price liberalization, followed by privatization in the context of a tight monetary policy.[31]

Gaidar's government initially rejected the idea of a government industrial policy.[32] By maintaining restrictions on credits and promoting austerity more generally, Gaidar believed that the forces of the market—the invisible hand—would compel state industries to undertake the necessary restructuring to survive. Those that did not restructure would be forced into bankruptcy.

Defense enterprises were especially threatened by this laissez-faire strategy. Dependent on the state as their sole customer, military factories could not adapt immediately to the production of competitive consumer goods. And even if they could, the Russian market was only emerging, which made decisions based on projections of market demand virtually impossible. Immediately following the collapse of the Soviet Union, the newly formed Russian Ministry of Defense assured military enterprises that it intended to maintain some level of military procurement. The lack of a clearly defined military doctrine, however, delayed and sometimes stalled indefinitely the allocation of these state orders, forcing military enterprises to find new methods of survival.

In recognition of the special conditions facing military enterprises, the Russian government established a series of incentives for promoting conversion, including tax concessions, long-term and low-interest loans for conversion projects, accelerated amortization of fixed capital assets, subsidies for conversion projects related to agro-industry, and a 95–billion-ruble conversion fund for new equipment and technical assistance needed for conversion projects.[33] The government declared a special interest in financing those projects that utilized the high-technology expertise already developed at many military enterprises.[34]

Consistent with their messianic doctrine of neoliberal economics, however, Gaidar's government minimized state involvement in the planning or coordination of the conversion process.[35] The Law on Conversion of the Defense Industry, initialed by Boris Yeltsin in May 1992, specifically delegated actual decisions about conversion projects to the enterprise directors themselves.[36] The result was spontaneous conversion—that is, conversion neither planned by the state nor dictated by the market.[37]

Strategies of Conversion

In the broadest sense, conversion is "industrial demilitarization and the construction of a viable, industrial, market-driven economy that utilizes some of the technology, personnel, and assets of the military production complex."[38] This general objective can be pursued in different ways. The lack of strategic directive from the Russian state, combined with poorly defined market institutions, has left military enterprises to their own devices in seeking ways to convert to civilian production. Consequently, a wide range of conversion strategies have been attempted by Russian military enterprises during 1992–1994.

Diversification

Most Russian military enterprises were already involved in the production of non-military products well before 1991. Rather than convert to civilian production only, Soviet military enterprises were instructed to diversify their production lines so that each enterprise would produce some percentage of both civilian and military goods. The simplest strategy for conversion, then, is to increase the capacities of these civilian production lines, and decrease or phase out military production. Saratov Aviation Plant (SAP), for instance, used to produce both fighter aircraft and cruise missiles as well as commercial airplanes. As late as 1988, roughly 55% of the Plant's production was devoted to military products. When it became apparent that contracts for their military aircraft would be curtailed, SAP managers began to phase out their fighter aircraft production lines and focused instead on expanding production of their civilian passenger plane, the Yak-42. By 1992, military production constituted less than six percent of SAP's total output.[39]

While the most logical and straightforward approach to conversion, this strategy is viable only for the small number of military enterprises that were involved in the production of attractive and profitable civilian goods. Moreover, production for the consumer market at most plants was based on auxiliary capacity. By-products or scrap materials from military production were utilized to produce consumer items, while lesser trained employees were assigned to these civilian production lines. The phasing out of military orders would undermine the raw material inputs for this kind of civilian production, at the same time eliminating the jobs of the most talented workers as well as those of the less qualified.

Undisciplined by market forces, this kind of auxiliary production was rarely rational. For instance, scrap titanium from the production of submarine hulls was used to make sled rails, while individual enterprises often produced dozens of different products.[40] As these military enterprises are compelled to pay market prices for inputs, such production becomes unprofitable. Finally, directors of high-tech enterprises have little interest in producing low-tech consumer goods. Aerospace engineers have little difficulty in switching from working on fighter aircraft to passenger planes, but will rocket scientists want to make baby carriages?[41]

Reapplication of Dual-Use Technologies

A second conversion strategy being pursued by Russian military enterprises is the application of military technologies to civilian purposes. Largely prohibited during the Soviet era, commercial application of tested and developed military technologies has tremendous potential. The redeployment of intercontinental ballistic missiles for civilian launches, for instance, promises to secure at least one sector of the Russian military industrial complex a market share in a lucrative and growing world industry. Moscow's Khrunichev Enterprise, the producer of the Proton rocket, has formed a joint venture with the American defense firm, Lockheed Corporation, to market launches of satellites and other space-bound payloads.[42] The former producers of the SS-25 have created a new company, START, which also seeks to compete in the satellite-launching business.[43] For smaller payloads, the consortium of enterprises formerly involved in the production of the mobile SS-20 have also begun seeking foreign partners.[44] These rockets and launching systems are reliable, roughly half the cost of Western launches, and do not require major capital investments for reconfiguration for commercial uses.[45]

Enterprises involved in telecommunications are a second Soviet military industry with vast commercial potential. Vympel Corporation and Almaz Corporation, two enterprises formerly involved in the Soviet Union's SDI program, have launched multi-billion-dollar projects aimed at capturing a market share of the world telecommunications industry.[46] Similarly, the Russian Space Agency has sought to commercialize parts of "Glonass," the Soviet equivalent to the American Global Position Satellite (GPS) system.[47] Energiia Corporation, the producer of the MIR space station, has made bids on contracts involved in the American space station, Freedom. Russian companies have even found a commercial demand for espionage photos.[48]

Another form of conversion, closely related to the reapplication of dual use technologies, is the modification of military products and technologies for civilian use. This kind of conversion, probably the most pervasive, is practiced by enterprises that formerly produced electrical equipment for tanks, planes, or communication systems, but now manufacture electrical engines for hair dryers, computer chips for personal computers, or receivers for ham radios. Included in this category are tank factories now producing tractors, nuclear weapons labs now developing radiation equipment, research and development institutes now writing commercial software, and naval cruiser production facilities now producing high-speed ferries.

This method of conversion, in all its variations, is the most attractive one for directors of Russian military enterprises because it takes advantage of already developed and sophisticated technologies and allows the enterprise to continue to employ its most highly skilled staff. This kind of conversion usually requires that the enterprise as a whole be maintained, avoiding the painful and difficult process of breaking up large enterprises into smaller companies and/or downsizing the labor force.

Unfortunately, only a small number of Russian military enterprises possess the kinds of technologies needed to make this kind of transition. While it is the one most commonly associated with the idea of conversion, this strategy has enjoyed limited success even in developed capitalist economies.[49]

Development of New Product Lines

A third strategy for conversion involves the initiation of a completely new kind of operation or product line that bears little relation to previous activities at the factory or institute. For instance, Leninets in St. Petersburg, one of Russia's largest defense enterprises specializing in the production of avionics, has recently begun to produce Gillette razor blades. Similarly, the Sverdlovsk Ammunition plant received credits from the state to produce medicines and synthetic fibers used for pantyhose, while a Voronezh factory previously involved with space vehicles had now begun to produce bricks.[50] In Komsomolsk-na-Amure, an aviation production association used proceeds from the sale of SU-27 fighter aircraft to purchase a color television production line from a South Korean company.[51]

This conversion strategy offers enterprises not endowed with world-class technologies the opportunity to manufacture competitive consumer products. Because it often involves the licensing of Western technologies or investment by a Western firm, production initiated by this kind of conversion promises to be more rational and more sensitive to market demand than are those consumer product lines that were established at military enterprises during the Soviet era. The involvement of Western entrepreneurs also insures some level of intellectual transfer regarding enterprise organization in a capitalist economy.

At the same time, rationalization of production undertaken to maximize profits contradicts other objectives considered important to military factory directors. To ensure that a new product line will be profitable, especially if a Western investor is involved, requires the reorganization of the enterprise as a whole. According to the standard model for such conversion ventures, one production line is separated from the mother enterprise and is then incorporated as an independent private company, often with an equity stake reserved for the outside investor. This smaller company then attracts the most talented workers and managers from the mother or host enterprise, which often is still state-owned. New production at this company is indirectly subsidized by the host enterprise in the form of free rent or the use of the host enterprise's equipment, but all profits remain with the parasite company. While profitable for some, this conversion necessarily splits up the original enterprise, a sacrifice that many directors are not willing to make. Like the first method of conversion outlined above, this strategy in most cases also diverts the military enterprise away from the production of highly sophisticated, capital intensive technologies.

"Converting" Individual Employees: Spin-Offs and Start-Up Companies

While often not considered conversion at all, conversion of individual employees—that is, the movement of labor from military enterprises to commercial firms—is the most common in the West and promises to be the most pervasive in Russia's defense conversion as well. In the United States, for instance, when an enterprise loses a contract or set of contracts from the Department of Defense, the most common business response is to downsize. A portion of the work force is laid off. These unemployed workers then seek new employment with other companies that may or may not be involved in defense work.

A similar phenomenon already has begun in Russia. While still emergent, nascent, and unstable, Russian commercial structures are nevertheless forming at a rapid rate. These new economic entities demand talented labor and can pay wages that are considerably higher than those offered at military enterprises. Experienced managers and engineers are in high demand in certain sectors of this emergent capitalist economy, while talented bookkeepers and accountants are needed by almost every new business operation. Given the wage differentials, even highly educated scientists and engineers are quitting their technical jobs at military enterprises to work as janitors or word processors for triple the wages in commercial companies.

A rarer but more attractive conversion of individual employees has occurred when a consortium of scientists or engineers from a military institute or enterprise join together to create new companies. Low state wages coupled with the uncertainty about the viability of conversion and privatization of large military enterprises has compelled talented defense workers to experiment with this method of conversion rather than relying solely on the successful conversion and privatization of their state enterprise. Typically, these new companies employ less than fifty people, produce high-technology products (and usually intellectual products rather than serial production), and still maintain a relationship with their state institute or enterprise.

These kinds of new companies are particularly successful if they can secure contracts from Western companies.[52] The computer company, Sun Microsystems, for instance, has concluded a series of agreements with Russian scientists to write computer programs. Sun has deliberately not signed contracts with the actual state institutes affiliated with Russia's military industrial complex.[53] Rather, they have contracted with individuals or small companies formed by a group of scientists.

Closely related to the Sun model is the emigration of Russia's most talented scientists and engineers. With little opportunity to continue doing research or development in Russia, many of the top former scientists of Russia's military industrial complex have sought employment with Western companies, universities, and research institutions. The potential destabilizing consequences of this brain drain of nuclear scientists to Third World countries even prompted the creation of a U.S.-sponsored research center in Russia to entice these individuals to stay in Russia.[54]

Ironically, the movement of labor in the military industrial complex appears to be the one allocative mechanism that is governed by market forces. In 1992 alone, one million workers left the military industrial complex to seek work in other sectors of the economy.[55] Prime Minister Victor Chernomyrdin has called this loss of jobs from military enterprises a major tragedy, as nuclear scientists now work as translators while rocket engineers drive cabs. Without question, the unique dynamics of Russia's transitional labor market will place thousands of people in jobs for which they are overqualified. That this process so far has happened spontaneously—that is, employees in military enterprises are leaving voluntarily to take less skilled, but better paying jobs—suggests that it may be the only practical "conversion" mechanism available to most enterprises in the long run.

Bankruptcy

Bankruptcy is the most radical form of conversion. If military enterprises cannot develop a plan to become financially solvent according to the new conditions of a market economy, they must be closed.[56] As Deputy Prime Minister Boris Fedorov declared, it is "better to shut down an enterprise ... than to continue churning out products which nobody needs."[57] International financial institutions have estimated that as many as half of all Russian military enterprises should already be bankrupt according to Western standards.[58]

In the United States, bankruptcy is one of the most common forms of defense conversion. Bankruptcy and laws governing bankruptcy compel enterprises to reorganize assets according to the demands of the market. As Yeltsin remarked, "For the Russian economy, for many enterprises, a bankruptcy will not be the end, but the start of a healthy operation. One should not treat it as a disaster."[59] The potentially explosive social consequences associated with this restructuring strategy, however, have impeded bankruptcy declarations.[60] To date, only one Russian military enterprise has officially declared bankruptcy.[61]

"Economic Conversion"

A final conversion strategy, developed by presidential advisor Mikhail Malei, is the promotion of arms exports for hard currency. Given that the Russian government has no money to finance conversion projects, Malei and others have argued that defense companies must generate funding by themselves. These hard currency earnings would then be used to finance conversion projects at the enterprise level.[62] Theoretically, this strategy would eventually lead to the phasing out of arms exports as civilian production lines become viable. According to Malei, "economic conversion means turning the military-industrial complex into an export sector for a transitional period. ..."[63]

This strategy has gained increasing support from politicians and directors of military enterprises frustrated with other conversion strategies. Strapped for hard currency, Russian government officials see the arms market as one of the few in which Russian enterprises are already competitive. They have argued that Russia needs to recapture the market share once controlled by the Soviet Union. According to Yegor Gaidar, the former acting prime minister, the Soviet Union recorded annual sales of over $50 billion in arms exports during the 1980s, whereas Russian sales in the 1990s averaged less than $3 billion a year.[64] Victor Glukhikh, Chairman of the Russian Committee for Defense Industries, has estimated that Russia could earn $11 billion a year with a successful export campaign.[65] To achieve these kinds of earnings, Russian government officials and individual military enterprises have both renewed old contacts with traditional customers in Eastern Europe, the Middle East, and India, and also begun to court new customers—customers with cash—including Turkey, Malaysia, South Korea, and even the United States.[66] In 1993, Russia organized massive military shows in Siberia and in Abu Dabi, at which over 370 different weapons systems were displayed.[67] The message at these arms fairs was clear; the Russian military industrial complex is open for business.

When pressed about the political and strategic implications of this "conversion" strategy, Russian government officials have responded that they have no other choice. According to Malei, real "conversion makes a loss, not a profit."[68] Arms export, on the other hand, is perceived as one of the only profitable endeavors available to Russia's collapsing economy. As Boris Yeltsin said, "Today, trading in arms is a necessity for us."[69]

Moreover, when confronted by Western government officials, Russian leaders have pointed out the hypocrisy of the West's position. As Malei retorted, "Arms are exported by highly moral Germans and Americans concerned about human rights."[70] Similarly, Foreign Minister Kozyrev has urged that Western acquiescence to Russian arms exports is a form of Western economic assistance.

> I would say to the U.S. and other Western countries: consider as a political decision giving a place to Russia in these markets. This is the same as economic assistance, it is economic assistance. ... If we sell MiG-31s or Sukhoi-27s to someone, it is earned money and will be less humiliating for Russia. The money would be used for conversion, and (some of it) for consumer goods and new machinery.[71]

That proceeds from arms exports abroad will be used to finance conversion projects is not guaranteed, however. If a military enterprise (re)acquires a market for its weapons system that earns hard currency profits, why would this enterprise have an interest in funding conversion projects aimed ultimately at replacing this profitable business? The more likely outcome is that "economic" conversion will produce a revitalized arms export industry.

Privatizing Military Enterprises

Issues of privatization are closely related to conversion of military enterprises and demilitarization of the Russian economy. Conversion and privatization strategies carried out in parallel can be mutually reinforcing.[72] If directors have an economic stake (either as owner or employee of a privatized firm) in the kinds of conversion projects pursued, they will select profit-maximizing, market-oriented projects. Conversely, as the experience in "Soviet" conversion starkly demonstrated, conversion projects that are insulated from market forces result in poor quality products not demanded by consumers. The Russian government originally decided to postpone the issue of privatizing military enterprises until 1993 and thereby exempted most military plants and institutes from the 1992 privatization program. This policy elicited two divergent responses from enterprise directors in the military industrial complex. Some directors viewed the government's exemption list as a form of discrimination. This group, consisting of directors at enterprises with market potential, wanted to join their civilian counterparts in escaping control of the state ministries and acquiring equity shares in their companies.[73] Consequently, directors of some large, politically powerful enterprises used their lobbying influence to gain special permission to privatize.[74] At military enterprises where the Ministry of Defense would not allow privatization, directors have set up parasitic companies that use the assets of the state enterprise but channel profits to the private company.

Other military directors, however, were threatened by the specter of privatization. Having spent their careers shrouded in the secrecy of the Soviet military industrial complex, these directors had little knowledge of or exposure to market principles. Instead, they preferred to cultivate the more familiar terrain of state orders. Directors of enterprises that produced unfinished goods were especially wary of potential disruptions in the highly structured hierarchies of defense industries caused by privatization. Officials in the Ministry of Defense and the Committee for Defense Industries also expressed concern about the deleterious strategic consequences of "spontaneous" privatization within the military industrial complex.[75] This group of directors, in cooperation with their government allies, have organized into associations such as the League of Defense Enterprises to pressure the Yeltsin government to adopt a more "planned" and slower strategy for privatization of military enterprises.

The Reemergence of the Russian State

The confluence of two years of rapidly falling production, exploding debt, chaotic conversion, and spontaneous privatization within the Russian military industrial complex eventually precipitated a renewed effort from the Russian state to reestablish a coherent relationship between the state and the military industrial complex regarding conversion and privatization. First and most significantly, the Committee for Defense Enterprises, chaired by Victor Glukhikh, was created to coordinate all MIC-related policy within the government. This Committee immediately assumed a veto power over any privatization proposal submitted to the Committee of State Property (the GKI) by a defense plant. According to Glukhikh, "those enterprises whose operation directly affects Russia's combat readiness will be retained in state ownership."[76] Glukhikh's Committee has also established a policy of retaining "golden shares"—shares with veto power over all major decisions—in firms that are allowed to privatize but still considered vital to Russia's defense needs.[77] Special privatization procedures also have been established whereby the design bureau of a military scientific-industrial association (NPO) remains state-owned, but the rest of the enterprises can be privatized.[78] The Committee also has fostered the creation of gigantic holding companies whereby all enterprises in particular defense industries will have some fraction of their ownership retained in a holding company.[79] According to Andrei Kokoshin, these new efforts by the state are causing many enterprises to reconsider the value of privatization. As he observed, "Increasingly often we are coming across examples in which enterprises are inclined to remain state-owned but to act according to the laws of the market."[80]

The Committee for Defense Industries, in close cooperation with the Ministry of Defense, has also recentralized conversion efforts. Most importantly, a comprehensive conversion program was released in 1993 that delineated the kinds of conversion projects that will be promoted and discouraged.[81] Above all, the program aims to retain the scientific potential of the military industrial complex.[82] According to Russian defense ministry officials, this new conversion program will be closely coordinated with Russia's new military doctrine. Under the new doctrine, production of specific weapons systems will not be spread between several enterprises. Rather, sole suppliers will be cultivated, and previous suppliers will be encouraged to pursue conversion strategies. This policy will preserve Russia's defense production base, eliminate uncertainties about future state orders, reduce state defense expenditures, and also focus conversion efforts.[83] As for "economic" conversion, the Committee for Defense Enterprises, the Ministry of Defense, and Exportoboron, have worked closely to reestablish state control over but also promote Russian arms exports.[84]

Both the "October events" and the results of parliamentary elections in 1993 served to bolster and further consolidate this new relationship between the state and the military industrial complex. In securing the military's loyalty and participation in the "October events," Yeltsin had to grant a series of concessions to the Defense Ministry, including a promise not to make further cuts in defense spending. The perceived two-year assault on the Russian military was over.

Even more important for defense enterprises was the voter rejection of the liberal reformers in the December elections. After the election, the composition of Russia's government changed dramatically. Deputy prime ministers Yegor Gaidar and Boris Fedorov resigned, leaving only one of the original reformers, Anatolii Chubais, in the government. In their place, Prime Minister Victor Chernomyrdin has installed Soviet-era bureaucrats with little expressed commitment to market reforms. In firmly asserting himself as the head of the government, Chernomyrdin has rejected "shock therapy" and proclaimed an end to "the age of market romanticism."[85] Instead, Chernomyrdin already has indicated that he will increase government credits and subsidies to ailing state enterprises, including first and foremost the military industrial complex.[86] In his first ever "state of the federation" address to parliament in February 1994, Yeltsin appeared to support Chernomyrdin's pledges of support for military enterprises when he stated that "producers that are highly competitive in the world markets ... must be given normal state support over the next few years."[87]

The departure of liberal reformers and the total control of the government by former Soviet bureaucrats completes a process of re-statization of the Russian economy that began with Gaidar's first departure from the government in December 1992. Especially with reference to military enterprises, the lines between private and public are becoming increasingly blurred once again. For a significant minority of directors at military (or former military) enterprises who are confident in their ability to perform and prosper in a market economy, this turn toward state consolidation is threatening. For the majority of military directors, however, this new political environment offers a new opportunity to escape the hard choices and uncertain future associated with the transition to a market economy. Whether this new policy is a temporary reprieve or the beginning of a long-term trend remains to be seen.

Notes

1. See David Holloway, "Gorbachev's New Thinking," *Foreign Affairs*, Vol. 68, No. 1, 1989, pp. 66–81; Coit D. Blacker, *Hostage to Revolution: Gorbachev and Soviet Security Policy, 1985–1991* (New York: Council on Foreign Relations Press, 1993).

2. See David Holloway, "State, Society, and the Military under Gorbachev," *International Security,* Winter 1989/90, pp. 5–24.

3. An interesting account of the evolution of the views of Marshal Yazov, the Defense Minister, is given in L.G. Ivashov, *Marshal Yazov (Rokovoi avgust 91–go)* (Moscow: Biblioteka zhurnala "Muzhestva").

4. Leon Trotsky, *The Revolution Betrayed* (London: New Park Publishers, 1967), p. 222.

5. For the best account in English see John B. Dunlop, *The Rise of Russia and the Fall of the Soviet Empire* (Princeton: Princeton University Press), 1993, pp. 247–250.

6. Dunlop, *The Rise of Russia*, pp. 266–267.

7. *Izvestiia*, December 9 and 23, 1991.

8. Interview in *Pravda*, September 9, 1992.

9. Pavel Felgengauer, *Nezavisimaia gazeta*, January 8, 1992, p. 1.

10. The text is in *Nesokrashimaia i legendarnaia: V ogne politicheskikh batalii 1985–1993 gg.* (Moscow: Terra, 1994), pp. 259–260.

11. Speech at the VII Congress of People's Deputies, December 5, 1992, in *Krasnaia zvezda*, December 8, 1992.

12. Adam N. Stulberg, "The High Politics of Arming Russia," *RFE/RL Research Report*, December 10, 1993, p. 1.

13. In Russia, "military doctrine" refers to the general framework of military and political ideas that guide the formulation of national security policy.

14. Discussions about a new military doctrine had gone on since the late 1980s. A draft document on doctrine was published in May 1992 in the journal *Voennaia Mysl'*. The "Basic Provisions" document is in *Izvestiia*, November 18 , 1993.

15. See Konstantin E. Sorokin, *Russia's Security in a Rapidly Changing World* (Center for International Security and Arms Control, Stanford University, 1994), pp. 59–79.

16. *Nuclear Successor States of the Soviet Union*, No. 1 (Monterey: The Monterey Institute of International Studies, 1994), pp. 2–4.

17. On May 15, 1992, five countries signed the treaty (Russia, Armenia, Kazakhstan, Kyrgyzstan, Uzbekistan); Tajikistan joined in November 1992, and Belarus in April 1993.

18. Pavel Felgengauer in *Nezavisimaia gazeta*, December 12, 1991, p. 1.

19. *Krasnaia zvezda*, December 8, 1992.

20. ITAR-TASS, December 23, 1993, in FBIS-SOV-93-246, December 27, 1993, p. 2.

21. Sorokin, *Russia's Security*, pp. 42–43.

22. Mikhail Gorbachev, *Izvestiia*, February 6, 1991, cited in Sergei Rogov, ed., *Defense Expenditure Trends in the USSR and the Commonwealth of Independent States*, Brookings Discussion paper (Washington, DC: Brookings Institution, October 22, 1992), p. 1.

23. Christopher Mark Davis, "The Exceptional Soviet Case: Defense in an Autarkic System," *Daedalus*, Fall 1991, pp. 113–134; Peter Almquist, *Red Forge: Soviet Military Industry since 1965* (New York: Columbia University Press, 1990); interview with Major General Vladimir Tsarkov, President of the State Center of Conversion for the Aerospace Complex, in V. Khrustov, "Tsentr konversii: Ot pervykh proektov k natsional'noi programme," *Rossiiskie vesti*, No. 22 (191), February 3, 1993, p. 3. This kind of resource allocation was confirmed in the author's interviews with Nikolai Ryzhkov, former Soviet prime minister (Moscow, June-August 1992).

24. Military expenditures, however, did not begin to decline until 1989, four years into Gorbachev's rule.

25. Well before Gorbachev, almost all Soviet military enterprises devoted some fraction of their production to consumer goods. This meant that rocket factories also produced bicycles, airplane plants made silverware, and enterprises which produced anti-ballistic weapon systems also made televisions. Gorbachev's plan simply required these enterprises to increase civilian production already underway.

26. These figures are in constant, not current prices. See Julian Cooper, "Defense Industry Conversion in the East: The Relevance of Western Experience" (manuscript, 1993), p. 3. See also Sergei Rogov, ed., *Defense Expenditure Trends in the USSR and the Commonwealth of Independent States*, Brookings discussion paper (Washington, DC: Brookings Institution, October 22, 1992), p. 18; and Julian Cooper, "Military Cuts and Conversion in the Defense Industry," *Soviet Economy*, Vol. 7, No. 2, April-June 1991, p. 123.

27. Sergei Rogov, ed., *Defense Expenditure Trends in the USSR and the Commonwealth of Independent States*, Brookings discussion paper (Washington, DC: Brookings Institution, October 22, 1992), p. 40.

28. "God nazad VPK poluchil silneishyi [pokdaun]. Teper' on vykhodit iz sostoianiia groggi," *Moskovskie novosti*, January 10, 1993, p. B8.

29. In addition to the high levels of secrecy at all defense plants, the Soviet defense ministries created a whole archipelago of secret cities devoted solely to military production. Without state orders for military products, the economies of these cities will collapse.

30. Price liberalization has been especially devastating for military enterprises, where prices during the Soviet era were subsidized for those economic entities associated with the military industrial complex.

31. See Anders Aslund, *Post-Communist Economic Revolutions: How Big a Bang?* (Washington, DC: Center for Strategic and International Studies, 1992).

32. Erik Whitlock, "Industrial Policy in Russia," *RFE/RL Research Report*, Vol. 2, No. 9, February 26, 1993, pp. 44–45.

33. *Rossiiskaia gazeta*, April 27, 1992, p. 6, as cited in FBIS-SOV-92-083, April 29, 1992, p. 30; Sergei Rogov, ed., *Defense Expenditure Trends in the USSR and the Commonwealth of Independent States*, Brookings discussion paper (Washington, DC: Brookings Institution, October 22, 1992), p. 41. This fund was increased in 1993 to 150 billion rubles to keep up with inflation. See Mikhail Glukovskii, "Conversion Voronezh Style," *Delovye liudi*, May 1993, p. 20.

34. Yegor Gaidar, ITAR-TASS, November 18, 1992, in Yekaterinburg, in FBIS-SOV-92-224, November 19, 1992, p. 21.

35. For a critical retrospective assessment of this strategy, see the interview with Major General Vladimir Tsarkov, President of the State Center of Conversion for the Aerospace Complex, in V. Khrustov, "Tsentr Konversii: Ot Pervykh Proektov k Natsional'noi Programme," *Rossiiskie vesti*, No. 22 (191), February 3, 1993, p. 3. Oblasts such as Leningrad, Sverdlovsk, Kaluga, and Tula, in which military enterprises comprised the majority of all economic activity, eventually stepped in to develop their own local conversion programs. "Tratit' valiutu ne obiazatel'no," *Moskovskie novosti*, January 10, 1993, p. B8.

36. *Rossiiskaia gazeta*, April 27, 1992, p. 6, as cited in FBIS-SOV-92-083, April 29, 1992, p. 29.

37. For a critique of this spontaneous approach to conversion, see the comments by A. Shulunov, President of the League of Defense Enterprises, in "Ekonomika, Konversiia, Predprinimatel'stvo," *Ekonomicheskaia gazeta*, No. 22, May 1992, p. 6.

38. David Bernstein, "Conversion," in Michael McFaul, ed., *Can the Russian Military Industrial Complex Be Privatized? Evaluating the Experiment in Employee Ownership at the Saratov Aviation Plant* (Stanford, CA: Center for International Security and Arms Control, 1993), p. 7.

39. See John Battilega, "The Saratov Aviation Plant," in McFaul, ed., *Can the Russian Military Industrial Complex Be Privatized?*, p. 42.

40. In contrast, according to Arthur Alexander, President of the Japan Economic Institute of America, 70 percent of all American plants manufacture a single product, 15 percent manufacture two products, and only 7 percent manufacture four or more products. See Arthur Alexander, "Perspectives on Russian Defense Industry Conversion," manuscript, December 1992.

41. Aircraft factories seem to have initiated the transition to civilian production most successfully. In addition to the Saratov Aviation Plant, see Paul Betts,

"Russian Aerospace Group Looks for Western Partners," *London Financial Times*, October 2, 1992, p. 1.

42. Jeffrey Lenorovotz, "Lockheed, Khrunichev to Market Proton Launcher," *Aviation Week & Space Technology,* January 4, 1993, p. 24. Motorola has also signed a separate agreement with Khrunichev regarding launches of its satellites, while Martin Marietta and Hughes Aircraft are also pursuing deals. (Author's interviews with managers at Khrunichev Enterprise, July, August & October 1992. See also "Dorogoi, no poleznyi proekt," *Nezavisimaia gazeta*, February 11, 1993, pp. 3–4 of special section on conversion; and "Razrabotchiki i proizvoditeli 'protona' soedineny v [odnoi firme]," *Moskovskie novosti*, No. 26, June 27, 1993, p. 11B.

43. Anatolii Zak, "Pasmurnaia zima Baikonura, *Nezavisimaia gazeta*, February 9, 1993, p. 1 of special section on conversion; "SS-25 na kommercheskoi orbite," *Rossiiskie vesti*, January 28, 1993, p. 5; Daniel Green and Leyla Boulton, "Fight for the Final Frontier," *Financial Times*, February 2, 1993, p. 14; and "Start-1 Vykhodit na Start," *Delovye liudi*, December 1992, p. 11.

44. See Leyla Boulton and Daniel Green, "Moscow Invites Pretoria to Missiles Talks," *Financial Times*, January 19, 1993, p. 3.

45. A launch of a modified SS-20, for instance, costs $10 million, compared to $40 million for a comparable launch conducted by a Western company. See Leyla Boulton and Daniel Green, "Moscow Invites Pretoria to Missiles Talks," *Financial Times*, January 19, 1993, p. 3.

46. Sergei Protasov, "Vympel: Turning Over a New Leaf," *Delovye liudi*, April 1993, pp. 24–25.

47. Anatolii Zak, "Kosmicheskaia Programma Rossii," *Nezavisimaia gazeta*, February 11, 1993, pp. 3–4 of special section on conversion.

48. William Broad, "Russia Is Now Selling Spy Photos From Space," *New York Times*, October 4, 1992, p. 10.

49. See Arthur Alexander, "Can Russia's Closed Cities Convert to Non-Defense Economies?" manuscript, May 1992, p. 2.

50. Domenick Bertelli and John Tepper Marlin, "Defense Conversion in Russia: Progress, Prospects, and Recommendations for U.S. Aid" (New York: Council on Economic Priorities, March 1993), p. 20; and Mikhail Glukovsky, "Conversion Voronezh Style, *Delovye liudi*, May 1993, p. 21.

51. Radio Rossii Network, May 18, 1993, in FBIS-SOV-93-096, May 20, 1993, p. 51.

52. See, for instance, Clive Cookson, "Russian Scientists on Market," *Financial Times*, January 15, 1993, p. 4.

53. In contrast, the Lawrence Livermore National Laboratory has contracted Russian institutes to undertake research for the American lab.

54. William Broad, "In Russia, Secret Labs Struggle to Survive," *New York Times*, January 15, 1992, p. C1.

55. See "Draft Program on Defense Conversion," *Delovoi Mir/Business World*, Vol. 2, No. 23(68), July 2, 1993, p. 2.

56. Anders Aslund, *Post-Communist Economic Revolutions*, p. 80.

57. UPI, January 13, 1993.

58. See European Bank for Reconstruction and Development, *Privatization, Restructuring, and Defense Conversion*, Vol. II, Selected Case Studies (London: EBRD, 1993), p. 37.

59. Yeltsin, speech to the Russian Union of Industrialists and Entrepreneurs, Moscow Russian Television Network, November 14, 1992, in FBIS-SOV-92-221, November 16, 1992, p. 24.

60. The lack of attention devoted to creating a social net (unemployment benefits, job retraining, job placement offices, a welfare system, etc.) is one of the primary impediments to proceeding with bankruptcies. Without a social net to support, retrain, and help reemploy workers, the state has instead continued to subsidize inefficient enterprises. On the necessity of a social net, see Adam Przeworski, "Economic Reforms, Public Opinion, and Political Institutions: Poland in the Eastern European Perspective," in Luiz Carlos Bresser Pereira, Jose Maria Maravall, Adam Przeworski, *Economic Reforms in New Democracies* (Cambridge: Cambridge University Press, 1993).

61. Leyla Boulton, "Bankruptcy Law Claims First Victim," *Financial Times*, September 17, 1993, p. 3.

62. See Minister Kozyrev's remarks in John Lloyd, "Russia Offers US Arms Sales Deal," *Financial Times*, February 16, 1993, p. 3.

63. Interview with Mikhail Malei, in *Rossiiskaia gazeta*, February 28, 1992, pp. 1–2, as cited in FBIS-SOV-92-043, March 4, 1992, p. 43.

64. UPI, June 23, 1993, p. 1; see also *RFE/RL Daily Report*, No. 224, November 20, 1992.

65. Richard Boudreaux, "Strapped Defense Industry Adopts Capitalist Strategy," *Los Angeles Times*, February 12, 1993, p. 3.

66. On old customers, see Jim Mann, "Russia Boosting China's Arsenal," *Los Angeles Times*, November 30, 1992, p. 1; Michael Gordon, "Russia Selling Submarines to Teheran's Navy," *New York Times*, September 24, 1992, pp. 1, 9. On new customers, see "Mig-17 'Hips' Set for Turkey," *Jane's Defence Weekly*, November 21, 1992, p. 12; Kiernan Cooke, "Malaysia May Buy $700m Mig Fighters," *Financial Times*, March 3, 1993, p. 4; See Thomas Lippman, "U.S. Wary on Purchases From Russia, Hill Told," *Washington Post*, March 26, 1992, p. 30; Petr Aven, Minister of Foreign Economic Affairs, *Moscow Russian Television Network*, December 15, 1992, in FBIS-SOV-92-242, December 16, 1992, p. 18.

67. John Kampfner, "Russia Takes Shot at Arms Market with Big Display at Mideast Show," *Washington Times*, February 11, 1993, p. 7; and "Sekretnye zavody ustroili vystavku-iarmarku," *Izvestiia*, March 19, 1993, p. 6.

68. Interview with Mikhail Malei, in *Rossiiskaia gazeta*, February 28, 1992, pp. 1–2, as cited in FBIS-SOV-92-043, March 4, 1992, p. 43; and interview with Malei, "Oboronyi kompleks mozhet ne razoriat', a kormit'," *Izvestiia*, March 31, 1992, p. 2.

69. Quoted in Fred Hiatt, "Russia Boosts Weapons Sales to Aid Economy," *Washington Post*, February 24, 1992, p. 1. See also Yeltsin's remarks about the potential benefits of arms exports in "Za gosudarstvennye oshibki vinovnykh nado privlekat' k otvetstvennosti," *Rossiiskie vesti*, February 5, 1993.

70. Quoted in Bruce Nelan, "An Army Out of Work," *Time*, December 7, 1992, p. 48. See also Leyla Boulton, "Russia Wants Arms Market Access," *Financial*

Times, December 5–6, 1992, p. 3; and Rutskoi's remarks as quoted in *Pravda*, November 21, 1992, p. 2, in FBIS-SOV-92-226, November 23, 1992, p. 33.

71. See Minister Kozyrev's remarks in John Lloyd, "Russia Offers US Arms Sales Deal," *Financial Times*, February 16, 1993, p. 3.

72. William Perry, *Soviet Defense Conversion—Problems and Opportunities* (Stanford, CA: Center for International Security and Arms Control, September 19, 1991), p. 3.

73. See Vitaly Naishul, "Institutional Development in the USSR," *Cato Journal*, Vol. II, No. 3 (Winter 1992), p. 496.

74. Energiia, Svetlana, and Leninets are famous examples. Similarly, even before the Yeltsin government, the Saratov Aviation Plan and the Saratov Electromechanical Unit received special permission from then prime minister Ryzhkov to privatize.

75. See Natalia Kalinichenko, "Gluboko zakonspirovannye otkrytyi aktsionernyi obshchestva," *Kommersant*, No. 5, February 1–7, 1993, p. 20; and the remarks of Andrei Kokoshin, First Deputy Defense Minister, ITAR-TASS, June 29, 1993, in FBIS-SOV-93-123, June 29, 1993, p. 37.

76. Glukhikh, quoted on Moscow Radio Rossii Network, in FBIS-SOV-93-092, May 14, 1993, p. 33.

77. See *RFE/RL Daily Report*, No. 222, November 17, 1992, p. 3.

78. Viktor Glukhikh, "Still an Arms Race," *Delovye liudi*, April, 1993, p. 22.

79. The activities of the Russian Space Agency, Aviaprom shareholding company, Aviaexport foreign trade association, and the Military-Industrial Investment Corporation (VPIK) are examples. See Natalia Kalinichenko and Pavel Krizhevskii, "Chif-Chif-Chif! Ptichka po zernyshku klyuet, Chif VPK—po vaucheru," *Kommersant*, No. 17, April 26–May 2, 1993, p. 20.

80. Interview with Andrei Kokoshin, in *Rossiiskie vesti*, July 23, 1993, p. 2, in FBIS-SOV-93-142, July 27, 1992, p. 34.

81. "O proekte gosudarstvennoi programmi konversii oboronoi promyshlennosti," mimeo, 1993, pp. 1–19.

82. See the remarks of Andrei Kokoshin, First Deputy Defense Minister, ITAR-TASS, June 29, 1993, in FBIS-SOV-93-123, June 29, 1993, p. 37.

83. Interview with Andrei Kokoshin, in *Rossiiskie vesti*, July 23, 1993, p. 2, in FBIS-SOV-93-142, July 27, 1992, p. 33.

84. *The Wall Street Journal*, March 11, 1993, p. A11; Viktor Glukhikh, "Still an Arms Race," *Delovye liudi*, April, 1993, p. 23.

85. See Mikhail Berger, "Konets epokhi rynochnogo romantizma," *Izvestiia*, January 18, 1994, p. 2; and comments by Sergei Yushenkov in INTERFAX, January 27, 1994, in FBIS-SOV-94-019, January 28, 1994, p. 18.

86. Chernomyrdin, quoted in INTERFAX, January 21, 1994, in FBIS-SOV-94-015, January 24, 1994, pp. 22–23. See the candid accounts of this shift in policy by Mr. Chernomyrdin's former chief economist, Andrei Illarionov, in Leyla Boulton, "Money Oils Old Russian Machine," *Financial Times*, February 10, 1994, p. 2. For Gaidar's harsh evaluation of these shifts, see Yegor Gaidar, "Novyi Kurs," *Izvestiia*, February 10, 1994, pp. 1, 4.

87. Quoted in *RFE/RL Daily Report*, No. 39, February 25, 1994. While Yeltsin did not single out military enterprises for this support, arms trade is one of the few markets in which Russian goods are competitive.

7

Aid to Russia: What Difference Can Western Policy Make?

George W. Breslauer

The question of "assistance" to Russia is frequently discussed in U.S. newspapers and foreign-affairs journals. Most commentators agree that the West should help Russia, by some means or other, to weather the transition from communism. Any disagreement revolves around the desirability of various amounts and types of assistance; the goals to be pursued (democratic capitalism, authoritarian capitalism, free-market capitalism, regulated capitalism); the mix of Western "altruism" versus self-interest;[1] the extent to which aid and conditionality should be based on sympathy (or lack thereof) for various class, gender, national, and religious interests within Russia and the former Soviet Union; and the relative parts to be played by Western governments versus nongovernmental organizations in assisting Russia.

In both scholarly and journalistic discussions, more often than not, it is taken for granted that the goal is to assist in the creation of a free-market democracy; that Western assistance is largely benign, if not benevolent, in impact, and altruistic in intent; and that the transition's painful impact on varied groups and strata, while regrettable, is a necessary condition for success.

Most published discussion, therefore, concentrates on questions of feasibility: what would "work" in the circumstances of Russia today, and

I am grateful to the Carnegie Corporation of New York for support during the period in which this chapter was conceived and written. I am also grateful to many individuals for comments on earlier drafts of the chapter: Michael Burawoy, James Chavin, Gregory Grossman, Ernst Haas, Dwight Jaffee, Gail Lapidus, Jason McDonald, Joel Ostrow, Richard Temsch, Edward Walker, Steve Weber, and John Wilhelm.

what is "affordable" given political and resource constraints in the West. As Sergei Khrushchev put it:

> Nobody needs convincing that Russia needs help. But *whom* to help and *how* to help to good effect are more difficult to say. ... As things stand now, foreign aid ...would most likely disappear without a trace into the secret accounts that Russian bureaucrats and industrial managers hold in Western banks ... leaving behind only the problem of repaying Russian debts.[2]

Or as Leslie H. Gelb wrote, "Throwing money at a trillion-dollar economy that's sinking in political anarchy, waste and corruption is not a brilliant idea."[3]

These observations remain as relevant in Spring 1994 as they were when written in Spring 1993, even though the surprising electoral strength of Vladimir Zhirinovsky greatly raises the stakes involved in Russia's transition. With the specter of fascism in Russia, assistance to that country's peaceful transition to market democracy suddenly appears both more urgent and more problematic. What would help in a situation of such political polarization, administrative disintegration, widespread corruption, and social anomie?

This chapter assumes that the goal of U.S. policy is to assist in creating a free-market democracy in Russia and that the transition to such a social order cannot but be painful. The discussion therefore concentrates on matters of on-site feasibility—how best to assist Russia in its transition.[4]

What contribution can a social scientist make to policy discussions? The evaluation of discrete, often technical, programs is better left to experts in those specific policy realms, such as staff and consultants of the World Bank, the IMF, and other organizations. As a social scientist and a Russia specialist, I address here the general nature of the "Russia problem" and ways of thinking about the matter of Western assistance. My analysis therefore is cast at a level that is sufficiently concrete to avoid abstractions devoid of policy implications, but sufficiently general to avoid narrow program evaluation. It yields both statements of feasibility and general prescriptions for policy.

Specifically, this chapter proposes a governmental strategy of selective engagement, and a nongovernmental strategy of comprehensive engagement. Most of the chapter focuses on governmental policy, though it addresses nongovernmental policy as well. Ernst Haas first suggested the term "selective engagement" in the early 1980s,[5] as a prescription for moderating but maintaining U.S. containment policy toward the USSR. I use the term here as a prescription for a U.S. policy of cooperation with post-Soviet Russia. My definition is deliberately broad, and it begs for specification of the criteria for selectivity and the forms and scope of engagement—which are outlined below. In sum, it requires that we need be wary of overcommitment but determined to get involved.

Rules of Thumb for Specifying Selective Engagement

I begin with a point that is obvious, but that needs to be stated, precisely because it is a "first principle": we must base the strategy on realistic goals for the region. It is axiomatic, for example, that contemporary West European levels of affluence, democracy, liberalism, and stability are unachievable in Russia for at least the next three decades, if then.[6] Moreover, it is likely that the process of transformation, if it is not derailed entirely by fascism, will take place in fits and starts, over a rocky road, at best, rather than a smooth or even unilinear one. Thus, progress will have to be measured over long stretches of time; and the outcomes of the process, if it is successful, will likely be variants of democracy, market, and nation-state that are less liberal, more collectivist, and more statist than the United States in the 1990s. All of which means that selective engagement cannot be based upon an effort to force Russia onto a track that is faster and more far-reaching than its body-politic can bear.

A second rule of thumb is modesty in expectations of the magnitude of the difference official Western policy can make. As Barton Kaplan has put it, U.S. influence is "limited [but] not negligible."[7] To be sure, this conclusion is but another intellectual way-station toward specifying the scope and limits of possible influence; but it is worth bearing in mind as one devises strategy, for it suggests the need to distinguish those realms in which transformative processes are more and less likely to be susceptible to external influence. I return to this later, arguing that nation-building processes are likely to be only marginally influenced by external governmental "assistance" (though they can of course become militarized by external threat).

A third rule of thumb is sensitivity to the conditions under which the transition to market democracy will be derailed completely. The social sciences have developed some conditional generalizations that are applicable to the transition from Leninism, however novel this phenomenon. Sustained hyperinflation, for example, will hinder economic recovery and, thus, scuttle privatization and marketization. Large-scale bloodshed (as in the Caucasus and Yugoslavia) will overwhelm efforts to build a democratic political community; assuming neither side simply conquers the other, some form of partition is the only practicable solution, once violence between groups reaches these levels. Strategies of selective engagement must be conceived with these limits in mind. A policy that "works" under conditions of peace is not likely to work under conditions of hyperinflation or civil war.

A fourth rule of thumb guiding selectivity and engagement is to recognize the limits of our knowledge. What is happening in Russia is an unprecedented historical experiment, set within a country with a unique history. Moreover, even were the project and the terrain more familiar, we would still face the reality of the overwhelming role of unintended consequences in human affairs. (Lenin himself was dizzy at the thought that the Bolshevik revolution had actually succeeded; less than a year earlier he had assumed he would not live to see the victory.) To some extent, then, we implement selective engagement by a process of trial and error, hoping that the errors are not so large as to derail the entire project. These propositions, however, suggest more than just the need for modesty and prayer—they also suggest a conscious strategy of moderating risks by avoiding overcommitment.

All efforts to specify strategies will be subject to an epistemological tension between "understanding" and "prediction." Stephen Toulmin has properly warned that the primary goal of the social scientist is understanding, by which he means an appreciation of the main causal interactions at work in a situation, "a number of general notions and principles which make sense of the observed regularities, and in terms of which they all hang together."[8] In the post-Soviet case, this would require ways of conceptualizing the situation that capture the nature of the interaction between the liberal and anti-liberal forces at work after the collapse of communism.

This search for understanding, however, is insufficient for policy prescription. The policymaker does not have the luxury of eschewing prediction. All policy choice is based, implicitly or explicitly, on a prediction about the ways in which the stimulus (policy) is likely to interact with the situation to produce a desired outcome. The social scientist may prefer to dwell on the analytic task of fathoming the nature of the situation; the policymaker or the social scientist acting as policy advisor must venture a predictive guess. The comparative advantage of specialists lies in their understanding of the situation; when understanding is lacking, prediction is merely a "lucky guess" when it happens to come true. But the duty of the policy-maker is to do all three: understand, predict, and prescribe.

These three tasks (understanding, prediction, prescription) can be treated as logically sequential. Engagement that is selective, then, must be based *initially* on an appreciation of the situation in Russia today. Let me tackle this task before returning to policy prescriptive considerations.

Understanding the Situation

Talk of transition to a market democracy is an exceedingly narrow shorthand for what we hope Russian leaders are trying to accomplish. It is misleading on two major scores: it understates the breadth of the national goals being pursued by those currently (Summer 1994) in power; and it bears little relation to the nature and intransigence of the transitional reality in which Russia finds itself.

Would-be "market democrats" in Russia today are indeed attempting a transformation that is simultaneously economic and political. In the economic realm, they have been seeking to stabilize, marketize, privatize, demonopolize, demilitarize, and restructure the Soviet economy, and thereby to set it on a new path toward sustained growth. In the political realm, they have been trying to build democratic institutions, political parties, voluntary associations, an effective state structure, constitutional, judicial, and legal systems appropriate to the tasks of governing a market democracy, and a popular, civic culture supportive of liberalism and democratic procedure. These are mammoth tasks; it is little wonder that progress is spotty and slow and that relatively few individuals are committed to pursuing all of these economic and political goals, much less all of them simultaneously. Nor is it surprising that, in the wake of the elections of December 12, 1993, Boris Yeltsin and his administration have shown some signs of losing their nerve to keep pushing forward on these fronts.

But excessive focus on progress toward these goals obscures the fact that three other tasks are being tackled as well, and most participants in Russian politics today probably consider them to be more important than marketization and democratization. These tasks are nation-building, state-building, and constructing a new role for Russia in the international arena.

Nation-building is the effort to create a political community based on a distinctive identity, be it ethnic ("Russianness"), civic ("citizen of Russia"), or an amalgam of the two. We hope the result is more civic than ethnic in emphasis,[9] and is compatible with democratic politics and international cooperation. But we also know that all "nationalism" is self-serving, and that even a friendly Russian government will define its "national interests" in ways that will often conflict, or at least compete, with the national interests of other states, including those of the United States.

State-building is the process of constructing authoritative institutions of governance and public administration, of defining the scope of their territorial reach, and of defining authority relations among them. This is mostly what the constitutional crisis in Russia has been about. The task overlaps, of course, with the process and goal of democratization but is not identical to it. The issue of statehood in Russia today is focused on both horizontal and vertical authority relations: among the main branches of the federation's government, and between the federal, regional, and local organs of state power. The outcome of this struggle may determine whether Western assistance is directed to Russia, or to smaller entities that are parts of Russia.

The *construction* of a new role for Russia in the international arena is the foreign-policy counterpart of the construction of a national identity. Current Russian leaders (and citizens) are trying to come to terms with both the loss of empire and the loss of global power status. They must redefine Russia's role in the world, according to what is both desirable and feasible. And they must cope with pressures to demonstrate that they are neither "selling out" Russian national interests to outside powers nor abandoning Russian nationals in the new states of the former Soviet Union, nor forsaking ethnic or religious brethren still farther from their borders (as in Serbia, for example).

Glib talk of "building a market democracy" obscures not only the complex tasks facing Russian leaders but also the context within which these multiple transitions are taking place. Whether as a result of the Leninist legacy, the collapse of the USSR, or the policies pursued by Gorbachev and Yeltsin, the context is hardly propitious for either competitive markets or competitive politics. In its economic life, Russia is in a phase marked by supply-side depression, high open inflation, and corruption as a way of life, with widespread rackets,[10] speculative "merchant capitalism,"[11] radical redistribution of wealth, theft of state property, and vast capital flight.[12] Under these circumstances, the question is not whether Russians can make the transition from "plan" to "market," but whether they can break out of the grip of organized crime, protectionist tendencies, and monopolistic networks that currently dominate and cannibalize much of the economy. To be sure, there are other tendencies at work in the slowly expanding, productive private sector, and in sectors decisively influenced by foreign investors; but it remains to be seen whether these will prove strong enough to resist the obstruction of those who oppose them. A strong state and a corps of "Untouchables" were required to battle mafia control of portions of the Chicago economy in the 1920s, with mixed results. Such a strong state does not exist in Russia, and it is questionable whether it could be created in the foreseeable future.

Politics at the national level is marked by weak, or nonexistent, democratic institutions (parties, interest groups, an independent judiciary) that are ill equipped to mediate between the branches and levels of government and between citizens and their representatives. Personalities and referenda therefore dominate federation politics; it remains to be seen whether the constitution adopted in December 1993 succeeds in structuring political relations in ways that balance legitimacy and effectiveness.[13] At the local levels, the picture is somewhat different but no more "democratic." There, the old guard has frequently managed to retain its hold over the bureaucracy and the new institutions of governance, leading provincial politics more often to resemble New York City's Tammany Hall, or Mississippi in the 1930s, than democratic pluralism, liberalism, and accountability. As in economics, so in politics, the question is whether monopolistic tendencies consolidate their grip or, alternatively, are broken through on the way to further democratic development.

The task of constructing a new national identity is made difficult by the fusion of Russian with imperial identity under the Tsars and in the Bolshevik period. It is also complicated by the simultaneous loss of status as a global power. Russians are being asked, for the first time in their modern history, to define an identity for themselves and their state that is both nonimperial and nonglobalist. In the past, even moderates equated "Russianness" with empire; likewise, today, even among liberals and democrats, the liberation from Soviet repression is offset to some degree by the disorientation caused by having to come to terms with the loss of "ancestral" lands (e.g., Kievan Rus' to independent Ukraine). The disorientation is compounded by guilt toward the twenty-five million Russians living as minorities in newly independent states of the former USSR. And all these emotions are intensified by a sense of humiliation that Russia has come to be viewed internationally as a supplicant rather than a supplier of aid. (Vladimir Zhirinovsky has played cleverly on these sentiments.) In sum, the search for national identity and a new relationship with the outside world touches upon emotions that are intense and basic.

These tasks are being tackled simultaneously, and they interact with each other. For example, the democratic project, and the pace of demonopolization of the economy, may be hostage to the ability of moderate forces to steer the search for national identity away from xenophobic channels. Their ability to do so will also determine the prospects for regional and international peace. Less obviously, the construction of a strong state to support a nationwide market economy, or to prevent the fragmentation of Russia itself, might have to be based upon a normative glue that legitimizes the building of such a state. As things stand today, the only available normative message with sufficient power to provide such a glue may be an ethnically intolerant form of Russian nationalism.

Many other interaction effects could be cited, and still more will become visible to outside observers with time. It is likely that the results of the interaction of complex but contradictory social processes are inherently unpredictable. If this is the case, the observation has profound implications for policy prescription, which must be based on some prediction or other. At a minimum, these conundra must temper both our expectations as to how much is achievable and our strategies for influencing the situation in desirable directions. Tempering our strategies in the name of selective engagement means avoiding overcommitment to a policy that might prove counterproductive. The more one commits to a *comprehensive* strategy that attempts simultaneously to transform the economic, political, military, and foreign policies of Russia, the more one is hostage to untested theories of marketization, democratization, nation-building, state-building and international relations (which were derived largely from the West European experience) and to assumptions about the interaction among these processes. These theories may be elegant in their exposition, but they are likely to be misapplied in practice, for we have no propositions even remotely specific and relevant enough to guide policy in the unique circumstances of a post-Leninist, post-imperial power attempting simultaneously to tackle all five tasks.

How, then, can one logically proceed? If synoptic planning is impossible because interaction effects are unpredictable given the current state of our knowledge, what can be the basis for policy prescription? Let me suggest that we begin by distinguishing between *short-term ameliorative goals* and *long-term transformative goals* in each of the realms of policy discussed above. The distinction is elementary, but it can help us prioritize our goals. Selective engagement, I would argue, calls for much greater Western *governmental* concentration on short-term amelioration than on long-term transformation, and for a concentration on tasks that have shorter, more predictable, and more controllable lines of causation.

Short-term Amelioration

We know what we want to avoid: anarchy, fascism, economic collapse, civil war, and warfare between Russia and its neighbors. We also have a sense of what conditions or eventualities might be symptomatic or predictive of these outcomes. In the socioeconomic realm, these conditions would include prolonged hyperinflation, a foreign debt that precluded economic progress, mass destitution, lawlessness, epidemics and ecological catastrophes, and collapse of the basic infrastructure of an industrial economy (energy, transportation, and telecommunications).

In the sociopolitical and military realms, the most dangerous conditions would include a mass in-migration of ethnic Russians from former Soviet republics and of demobilized soldiers, who live in impoverished conditions and who seek scapegoats for their sudden deprivations; the mobilization of interethnic resentments and the cultivation of a pogrom mentality; wildcat strikes in industries, capable of paralyzing the economy; nuclear accidents associated with reactors, waste storage, or weaponry; and nuclear proliferation. All these conditions already exist in Russia, to one degree or another. The danger lies in their prospective, sharp intensification. With respect to nation-building and inter-state relations, the condition to avoid is the rise to power of xenophobic, chauvinistic, and neo-imperialist forces, such as those represented by Vladimir Zhirinovsky.

Western states may try to prevent "the worst" by a variety of policies, many of which are currently being implemented. Debt relief or rescheduling, trade credits, humanitarian assistance, direct investment in upgrading the technological standards of nuclear reactors, construction of housing for demobilized soldiers, employment and retraining programs for scientists and military personnel, reduction or abolition of CoCom restrictions on high-technology transfers (for example, fiber-optic cables for upgrading telecommunications), governmental encouragement of direct investment in the Russian energy industry—these and many other programs are already in place or being negotiated.[14] It is too early to measure their effects.

To be sure, tactical problems abound, some of which may negate the intended impact.[15] How should aid be delivered so as to serve the intended purpose?[16] How much assistance, and of what kinds, is needed and affordable to the West? How should conditionality be defined and enforced?[17] How should Russian pride be protected in conditions of dependency?[18]

These are the types of questions on which entire essays could be written, each devoted to addressing that question with respect to a specific program. Many of the controversies hinge on highly technical evaluations of conditions, which would not be appropriate in this chapter. One way to evaluate programs, however, would be to ask whether they are sensitive to the realities of the racket economy, machine politics at the local level, the disorientation and identity vacuum in Russia today, the lack of a strong central state, and the possible interaction among economic, political, nation-building, and foreign policy agendas.

In this vein, let me therefore suggest another general rule of thumb that can guide the search for programs that are likely to supply the greatest benefit per dollar:[19] *We should seek programs that stand at the intersection of multiple interrelationships within the society, economy, and international order, and that are therefore likely to supply simultaneous social, economic, political, and international benefits.* This is less ambitious than a comprehensive transformative strategy, but more ambitious than a sector-specific, ameliorative strategy. Let me give a few illustrations.

The Soviet-German agreement of July 1990 was an example of precisely such a program. The Berlin Wall had fallen, East Germany was collapsing, and the preference in both Bonn and Washington was for the reunification of Germany within NATO. This prospect had been denounced emotionally in Moscow but, short of military intervention, would be difficult for the USSR to prevent. The Soviets, however, did still have some 300,000 troops in East Germany, whom most Germans wanted to see go home in the context of reunification. A rapid withdrawal of those troops, though, would create immense social dislocation in the USSR. Given these dilemmas, West German Chancellor Helmut Kohl and Soviet President Mikhail Gorbachev worked out a deal whereby Moscow would accept German reunification within NATO and would agree to withdraw its troops, in exchange for which Soviet troops would be withdrawn over a four-year period; Germany would invest 7–8 billion dollars in the construction of high-quality housing for returning Soviet soldiers and their families, and would pay the costs of Soviet troop maintenance in eastern Germany in the interim; Germany would assume East Germany's trade commitments to the USSR, and would fulfill them at *West German* standards of technological quality; and Germany would release humanitarian assistance drawn from West Berlin's emergency stocks of food and medicine.

Here, then, was an agreement that simultaneously addressed economic, social, military, and international problems. It facilitated Gorbachev's "selling" of German reunification to domestic audiences, marginally assuaging the fury of those who saw this as rolling back the Soviet victory in World War II.[20] It mitigated the economic disruption caused by the collapse of East German-Soviet trade relations. It was aimed at minimizing the resentment of returning Soviet soldiers and their families, as well as the social and economic disruption of a precipitous withdrawal, and it promised to help (at least some) Soviet citizens cope with the forthcoming winter. The value of this model is the attention to varieties of interrelationships on which it was based.

In a parallel vein, Czech President Vaclav Havel once suggested that the West invest in development of the Russian oil industry, on condition that the countries of Eastern Europe and the former Soviet Union receive oil supplies from the Russians at subsidized prices, as used to be the case under the old system. This approach would simultaneously help develop a key sector of the Russian economy on which Russian hard currency earnings depend, would promote (though not guarantee) economic recovery and political stability throughout the region, and would diversify world energy sources.[21]

Complex programs designed to provide multiple benefits need not be as wide-ranging as these examples have been. Programs could address

problems in key sectors, the collapse of which would reverberate dangerously throughout the economy and society, and the further development
of which would be highly beneficial to economic recovery and development. Energy is one such sector; transportation and telecommunications
are others. Nor need such programs be expensive. If short-term cost is
the consideration, the West could accomplish much by simply dropping
CoCom restrictions on the transfer of fiber-optic technology. Western
companies have been eager to sell this technology to Moscow to modern-
ize Russian telephone systems. The result would presumably facilitate
the use of both telephones and fax machines throughout that vast
country, and thereby increase the attractiveness of private foreign investment in Russia.[22]

Thinking through interrelationships and interdependencies is never
easy, especially when these are not confined *within* the economy and
must take account of unknowable sociopolitical reactions. Brainstorming
among groups of Russia specialists drawn from several disciplines might
highlight interconnections that are not immediately obvious to more specialized or casual observers. For example, George Soros once suggested
that Western financing of a social safety net within Russia would be quite
inexpensive given the galloping devaluation of the ruble, would head off
mass destitution, and would have the added benefit of setting off a "virtuous circle" of economic improvements.[23] More recently, Andrei Schlei-
fer has argued that Western financing of a non-enterprise based social
safety net would "put the enterprises out of the business of providing
crucial social services," and thereby facilitate the bankruptcy of ineffective firms.[24]

In a similar spirit, Andrei Kortunov (personal communication) points
out that U.S. credits for Russian purchase of U.S. grain have deprived
Ukraine of markets in Russia for Ukrainian grain, and of leverage on
Russia for negotiation of an energy-for-grain swap. Whether technically
accurate or not, this example highlights a key issue in the pondering of
interrelationships: How many countries' interests should one seek simultaneously to advance? This question is partly normative: With which
countries or peoples does one identify? But it is partly analytical: How
do interconnections among events in different countries impact on the
prospects for catastrophe in Russia? For example, pogroms against Russians in neighboring countries might well trigger a militarist restoration
in Moscow.

A strategy of short-term amelioration, therefore, should not be predi-
cated on the interconnections among events within Russia alone.[25] Selective engagement must be less selective than that, while not being so
comprehensive as to try to reconcile the interests of all the states of the
region. Such reconciliation is probably impossible, anyway; but even if it

were possible in principle, devising a strategy that anticipated the inter-action effects among events and tendencies within so many countries would surely defy human capacity for calculation.

A strategy of selective engagement for purposes of short-term amelio-ration must also be based on prudence. In the economic realm, this means avoiding overexposure to risk of total loss and searching for novel and reliable means of channeling assistance. It means searching for low-cost solutions that might have large impact.[26] In the other realms, it means preparing fallback positions should events spin out of control. An overcommitted strategy of selective engagement would tempt the outside power to deepen its commitments rather than cut its losses.

Avoiding Fascism: Politics in Moscow

So far, we have focused on programs of amelioration that are largely in the economic and technical realms but that might have some predict-ably beneficial sociopolitical impact. We also have noted that the failure of amelioration could produce social conditions conducive to the rise of fascism, anarchy, or civil war. The analysis has emphasized what the West can do to avoid such conditions. There is one additional prescrip-tion, however, that is of the "don't" variety, and that has been borne out by experience. Western hostility, or condescending dictation of terms, would likely have a negative impact on democratic state-building and nation-building. As Edward Walker has put it,

> Outside threats have historically probably done more to foster the creation of a sense of national identity than anything else. …Likewise, outside threats have done an enormous amount to stimulate an increase in the size and reach of the state, and probably were responsible for the very emergence of the state.[27]

Avoiding fascism, then, is a matter of both policy and style. Ameliora-tion of economic and social conditions requires policy choices that are largely technical in nature. And while building a democratic nation-state is largely beyond the control of our governments' policies, we do have great capacity to facilitate the ambitions of those who prefer a fascist state. This could result from a posture of hostility (whether directly threatening or by refusal to offer technical-economic amelioration) or from a style that fuels xenophobic sentiments in Russia.

For example, we must avoid overreacting to the Russian search for a national identity and national interest. If the Russian radical democrats do not embrace Russian nationalism, they will cede this function to more intolerant forces. Building a nation requires a definition of the political

community that differentiates it from other communities. However tolerant and non-invidious the definition they embrace, it will demand policies that will often not coincide with U.S. definitions of national interest.
We may wish to treat Russia as an ally, but we should bear in mind that
allies disagree on many, many things.

Similarly, if we wish to avoid having a negative effect on the nation-
building process, we should avoid deepening Russian humiliation by
making triumphal, interventionist demands for the application of our
own doctrines to Russia's foreign and domestic policies.[28] Because
democratization and nation-building are *emotional* processes, Western
postures that do not deepen the humiliation already widespread in
Russian political circles are something for which to strive.

Of course, as Russians seek to redefine their role in the world and to
legitimize new roles, they can be influenced also by the traditional means
of international diplomacy, both bilateral and multilateral. Western states
can reduce the transaction costs of post-Soviet regional cooperation by
offering services as mediators, facilitators, peacekeepers, fact finders, and
the like, in regional disputes. A more ambitious Western policy could
reward peaceful conflict resolution, urge respect for existing borders (or
their peaceful renegotiation), and help to foster intra-regional economic
cooperation (the Havel plan for the Russian oil industry comes to mind
again); but the more ambitious the schemes for stage-managing the creation of regional order, the more likely they are to fail, and then to create
backlashes both in the West and within Russia. Instead, we should select
modest forms of engagement that foster a context that will undermine
the credibility of Russian right-wingers.

Accordingly, I am skeptical of the wisdom of a proposal recently
advanced by Zbigniew Brzezinski.[29] Alarmed by the strengthening of
neo-imperial tendencies in Russian policy and politics, Brzezinski calls
for a new Western policy of building counter-weights to Russian power
on the Eurasian landmass. In particular, he would seek to bolster Ukrainian power and independence through "substantial economic assistance" and "political assurances for Ukraine's independence and
territorial integrity," while encouraging the admission of East European
countries into NATO. Measures would be taken simultaneously to reas-
sure Russia of the West's benevolent intent, such as a treaty of cooperation between the enlarged NATO and Russia.

This is an example of precisely the kind of stage-managing that is
likely to have the opposite effect from that intended. The plan is likely to
further strengthen fascist tendencies within Russia, for the reassurances
pale in comparison with the implicit or explicit threats. The undefined
"political assurances" to Ukraine, moreover, will either be ineffectual for
lack of credibility (if weak) or provocative (if strong); in the latter case,

they would likely escalate the disputes between Russia and Ukraine, while dragging the United States into the defense of Ukraine against Russia.

Other components of Brzezinski's plan, such as the use of United Nations peacekeeping forces in the Caucasus, are less objectionable, and indeed are already being advocated by some officials of the Clinton Administration.[30] Certain features such as the goal of opposing Russian neo-imperialism are already components of Western diplomacy, and are being pursued in a low-key fashion; but a new strategy of continental containment of Russia is probably beyond U.S. capacity to prosecute at acceptable levels of cost and risk.

Long-term Transformative Goals

Is it sufficient to pursue short-term ameliorative goals? Or must Russia simultaneously make progress on transformative goals to prevent eventual breakdown? I would argue that amelioration without transformation is a prescription for failure. It is a finger-in-the-dike approach, when construction of a new system of dikes is required—at some point we are bound to run out of fingers, as new holes get punched in the defenses. However, while one could argue that short-term amelioration is partially hostage to Western governmental assistance, long-term transformation is largely hostage to Russia's internal politics and social forces. This conclusion naturally leads to a tacit, low-key conditioning of Western ameliorative assistance on Russian transformative initiatives.

But whether these initiatives come principally from Russians or the West, a common epistemological problem arises. Designing policies that are likely to foster progress toward transformative goals strains the limits of our knowledge of what would work. Policy prescription for long-term transformation requires more than "just" an understanding of the situation in Russia today; it also requires dynamic theories of system-transformation and nation-building, rather than static identification of interrelationships. And it is precisely such dynamic theories that are in shortage in the social sciences today.

For example, it is obvious that reliable distribution of antibiotics can alleviate a public health crisis, or that improved telecommunications make for a more attractive business environment. We also know how to upgrade the technical safety requirements of nuclear reactors, and how to clean up or avert environmental disasters. But it is not obvious how to build capitalism at a price that Russian elites and other social groups will be willing to pay. Nor is it obvious how to resolve, or even manage, the contradictions among the major transformative tasks being tackled—

marketization, democratization, nation-building, state-building, and the redefinition of Russia's role in the world.

In each of these realms, disputes rage over the theoretical underpinnings of alternative strategies for building capitalism, democracy, and a new, post-imperial nation-state. Economists debate "shock therapy" versus "evolutionary" strategies of transformation.[31] Political scientists debate "presidentialism" versus "parliamentarism," proportional representation versus winner-take-all electoral rules, the requisites for elite cohesion, political tolerance, and civic culture, strategies of nation-building and state-building, federalism versus confederation, and the relevance of lessons from other locales.[32] International relations theorists debate the requisites of peace in the region.[33]

Most daunting, however, is the indeterminacy of any of these realm-specific theories in light of the unprecedented and comprehensive nature of the task. Because the context is post-Leninist, and because all these challenges are being tackled simultaneously, it is unclear that any realm-specific theory can provide deductive guidance to policy.[34] Nor can highly generalized theoretical debates about human nature, often called "rationalist" versus "culturalist" theories, decide the issue.[35] At best, one could argue that if the market incentives are set correctly and maintained long enough, then cultural aversions, predilections, and "meanings" may eventually be adjusted in the directions indicated by the incentives. But at best this applies to economic relations only, as sociopolitical relations are more cultural and identity-driven than rational-materialist. When dealing with the interaction among these tasks, we will not have the luxury of embracing either rationalist or cultural theories to the exclusion of the other.

As time goes on, we will surely learn more about how these interaction effects condition the generalizability of specific theories developed in other locales; but in the meantime, the question of how Western policy might affect those interactions remains an open one.

A prudent strategy of selective engagement therefore would approach the question with a certain measure of agnosticism. In turn, this would call for tolerating the policies of a relatively broad range of political forces. In Russia today, as in many post-Leninist societies, the political spectrum has been occupied by three main tendencies: liberal, centrist, and reactionary. Depending on the country and the issue, the labels will vary. Andrew Janos conceptualizes these in Eastern Europe as "liberal," "technocratic nationalist," and "populist nationalist."[36] In Russia, these camps are called the "radical-democrats," the "centrists," and the "Red-Browns" or "fascists," though during 1994 the communists appear to be dividing into centrists and reactionaries.

Short-term amelioration strategies should be oriented toward avoiding a victory for the populists or fascists, since these are the groups that feed on catastrophe. Long-term transformation strategies should facilitate the eventual victory of liberals and democrats; but given our confusion over which strategies are likely to eventuate in such a victory, Western governmental strategy should give priority to avoidance goals. That is, Western policy, and the conditionality attached to Western aid, should be tolerant of both leftism and centrism, but unambiguously intolerant of reactionary tendencies. Conditions in different countries may dictate the tolerable speed and form of change; as long as centrists are not "stand-patters," and foster movement (however slow) toward market democracy, they should be treated as a legitimate force to be accommodated.

This approach stems naturally from the understanding that, in contrast to ameliorative goals, most progress toward transformative goals is largely outside Western control. Western policy can be facilitative, and can provide selective material, diplomatic, and military inducements; but the long-term trajectory of development in the economic, political, and nation-building realms will mostly be determined by Russians. And it is appropriate that it be so. Within the context of a commitment to building a peaceful market democracy, basic choices will have to be made about the balance between equity and efficiency, collectivism and individualism, social security and individual achievement, nationalism and cosmopolitanism, statism and liberalism, federalism and decentralism, exclusivism and inclusivism. These are *character-defining* issues. And such issues are among the least susceptible to dictation by non-members of the political community, especially in a country with the size, power, and imperial traditions of Russia. Even if such dictation were successful in the near term, it would not be likely to "stick" for very long, as the body-politic and body-societal would likely reject, deflect, or absorb alien patterns of behavior.

Centrists who eschew reactionary programs will likely disagree with radicals about the desirable and feasible balance among these conflicting imperatives. But that does not necessarily make a given centrist anti-market or anti-democratic. A prudent strategy of selective engagement calls for efforts to facilitate and reward, but not dictate, the formation of center-left coalitions, as well as for patience about the time frame for measuring "success."

While most of the structural transformation of the Russian economy and polity will be products of political will and state capacity within that country, Western policy can facilitate transformation in a number of ways that would cost little. A Peace Corps of retired government and business executives to teach the skills required in a market economy can have an important microeconomic impact, while fostering cosmopolitan attitudes if the executives do not behave like "ugly Americans." Tax and trade treaties, the accordance of Most Favored Nation status, and changes in anti-dumping laws all can facilitate Russian access to U.S. and West European markets, thus encouraging but not bankrolling the development of export oriented sectors of the Russian economy.[37]

Similarly, a (materially) low-cost change in the Foreign Corrupt Practices Act would make it easier for would-be U.S. investors to do business in Russia.[38] Western governments might use their influence also to pry loose from secret bank accounts the billions of dollars that have been illegally diverted from Russia's economy by corrupt officials and their underworld allies. Elimination of CoCom restrictions would allow Russia to import advanced information-processing technologies for building a modern banking system. Though potentially more risky and expensive, one can recommend an expansion of OPIC (Overseas Private Insurance Corporation) insurance for selected private ventures in sectors of the Russian economy that are likely to develop an international niche or a domestic market. Then, too, joint projects between the U.S. National Aeronautics and Space Administration (NASA) and the Russian space program would reduce costs on both sides while salvaging a sector of the Russian economy that has export potential. There may be other projects that fit this model.

Some programs and policies could be costly to Western budgets, but would foster demilitarization of the economy and the growth of a private sector. Financial and technical assistance in dismantling Russian nuclear weapons is one such program, as is the partial funding of defense conversion efforts. Direct aid to, and investment in, the productive private sector, including assistance in institution-building (legal structures, small business associations, regulatory experience, managerial training), could nurture the growth of free enterprise—and the strengthening of a currently tiny entrepreneurial "middle class" to provide the political base for sustained reform. The decisions of the G-7 (the governments of the rich democracies) in 1993 to funnel aid toward the privatization of Russian state enterprises was made in the same spirit.[39]

Many of the programs I have suggested are already being undertaken at the initiative of Western governments, foundations, citizen groups, nongovernmental organizations, and multilateral institutions. I mention them not for the purpose of technical program evaluation, nor of exhaustive enumeration of Western initiatives, but rather as illustrations of programs that might have a limited but still significant impact on the course of economic transformation. We should have no illusions, however, that their impact will be decisive rather than merely facilitative.

When we look beyond economic transformation to the political projects of democratization, state-building, and nation-building, we should temper our expectations even further. These character-defining issues will be determined even more fully by internal considerations than will the economic ones. I have already argued that, with respect to short-term amelioration, salutary Western influence is more limited in these realms than in the economic or technical. With respect to long-term transformation, I assume it is even less than that. And given the theoretical uncertainties about which paths to a democratic nation-state "work" in a post-Leninist context, I would suggest that we again set our sights more on "avoiding the worst" (fascism) than on "imposing the best" (radicalism). Again, this means settling for center-left coalitions when internal forces within Russia bring them into being. It means fostering an international context that bolsters the credibility of claims advanced by both radicals and centrists and that discredits the claims of right-wing extremists.

Throughout this chapter, I have distinguished between governmental and nongovernmental assistance. Nothing I have written about the difficulty of knowing what will work in the realm of either short-term amelioration or long-term transformation should be read as an attempt to discourage Western social organizations (voluntary associations, churches, universities, foundations, and others) involved in assisting Russia. Such organizations can transfer concrete assistance of all sorts: material aid, knowledge, technology, ideas, and, importantly, a spirit of good will and concern. They can do so with more flexibility and grassroots contact than can governmental agencies, while avoiding the appearance of dictation by Western governments. Since fascism feeds on both catastrophe and stereotypical depictions of outsiders, these society-to-society efforts might diminish the credibility of fascist claims. Only history will tell us just how much of a difference they will make.

Conclusion

In thinking about ways in which Western policies might foster "progress" (as we define it) in Russia, I have concentrated in this chapter on general rules of thumb rather than specific program evaluations. I have borrowed the term "selective engagement" and argued that a strategy of assistance based on this precept can be usefully applied to both short-term ameliorative tasks and long-term transformative tasks. I have argued that, given the limits of our theoretical and contextual knowledge, Western policy should concentrate more attention and resources on the ameliorative tasks. Policy-makers should seek to identify core interrelationships which suggest policies that could have benefits that are simultaneously economic, socio-political, and/or international. Policies of this sort could be based on conscious linkage in a complex "deal" (as in the Soviet-German agreement of 1990), or on unregulated spillover or reverberation of policies from one realm into other realms (Soros' "virtuous circle," for example). Policy-making toward Russia, however, must be based upon an understanding of the agenda as something different from, and more than, "building market democracy."

Whether tackling ameliorative or transformative tasks, though, Western governmental influence is likely to be greater on economic and technical than on character-defining, sociopolitical issues. For all these reasons, I have argued that our general posture should be tolerant of centrist forces that seek coalitions (and compromises) with radicals. For, given the decisive role of internal factors in these transitions, we should concentrate our limited governmental influence more on trying to hold off or discredit the reactionary forces than on stage-managing the victory of the radicals. Leave to nongovernmental organizations, perhaps with governmental subsidy, the daunting task of facilitating the transformation of institutional and sociopolitical relationships, and of societal attitudes.

Notes

1. For example: should Western "aid" be structured primarily in ways that benefit Western economic interests (e.g. credits earmarked for purchases of grain and technology from the United States)?

2. *The New York Times*, March 19, 1993, p. A17.

3. *The New York Times*, March 14, 1993, p. E17.

4. Thus, I will not be discussing the political feasibility in Washington, D.C., of enacting the measures I propose.

5. Ernst B. Haas, "On Hedging Our Bets: Selective Engagement with the Soviet Union," in Aaron Wildavsky, ed., *Beyond Containment: Alternative American Policies Toward the Soviet Union* (San Francisco: ICS, 1983), pp. 93–124.

6. I could as easily have written "four or five decades, if then." I resist excessive pessimism in the realization that, thirty years ago, South Korea was dirt poor; and the same was true of Italy and Japan forty years ago. By West European levels, I am referring to the more affluent of these states, not to Portugal or Greece, with which Russia could conceivably converge more quickly.

7. Barton Kaplan, "U.S. Assistance to the Former Soviet Union," *Occasional Paper No. 3* (Monterey: Monterey Institute of International Studies, Center for Russian and Eurasian Studies, March 1993), p. 15.

8. Stephen Toulmin, *Foresight and Understanding* (Westport: Greenwood, 1961), p. 33.

9. On civic versus ethnic orientations, see Ken Jowitt, *New World Disorder: The Leninist Extinction* (Berkeley: University of California, 1992), pp. 319–326.

10. Stephen Handelman, "The Russian 'Mafiya'," *Foreign Affairs*, Vol. 173, No. 2 (March/April 1994), pp. 83–96.

11. See Michael Burawoy and Pavel Krotov, "The Rise of Merchant Capital:

Monopoly, Barter, and Enterprise Politics in the Vorkuta Coal Industry," *The Harriman Institute Forum*, Vol. 6, No. 4 (December 1992).

12. Alec Nove, "Economics of the Transition Period," *The Harriman Institute Forum*, Vol. 5, Nos. 11–12 (July–August 1992).

13. On this balance, see Stephen Holmes, "Superpresidentialism and its Problems," *East European Constitutional Review*, Vol. 2, No. 4 and Vol. 3, No. 1 (Fall 1993 and Winter 1994), pp. 123–126.

14. Useful summaries of U.S. and international assistance to the former Soviet Union appear in Kaplan, *U.S. Assistance*, and The Congressional Roundtable on Post-Cold War Relations, *Briefing Book on the Former Soviet Union* (Washington: Peace through Law Education Fund, 1993), Sections I, II. These sources, of course, need to be continually updated, as new initiatives of one sort or another are announced almost weekly.

15. As indicated in the quotations from Sergei Khrushchev and Leslie Gelb, reproduced at the beginning of this chapter.

16. For example, Leonid Khotin (personal communications) has argued that the only reliable conduit are the managers of large enterprises. Andrei Melville (personal communication) has argued for joint Russian-American soup kitchens, with American organizations subcontracted to deliver supplies. Others have argued that the Russian Orthodox Church, or specified local congregations, are the most reliable channels.

17. For example, Western policy cannot control Russian inflation, but Western aid of certain types can be conditioned on the Russians controlling their inflation. Jeffrey Sachs, in contrast, suggests that the G-7 offer noninflationary grants or loans to help finance the Russian government's budget deficit (Peter Passell, "Economic Scene: Needed: fresh ideas on how to dig Russia out of its mess," *The New York Times*, February 17, 1994, p. C2).

18. For example, S. Frederick Starr has proposed "a Pentagon-sponsored program for retraining former Red Army officers, using American businessmen and academics, and meeting at abandoned United States Army bases in Germany" ("Year One of Capitalism in Russia," typescript, January 1993).

19. Edward Walker, in personal communication, felicitously refers to this as a strategy of "minimizing the maximal damage."

20. A high Soviet foreign-ministry official told Strobe Talbott in 1990 that the collapse of East Germany made clear that the Soviet Union had lost the Cold War, but the reunification of Germany within NATO would make Russians feel they had lost World War II! See Strobe Talbott, "The Fear of Weimar Russia," *Time Magazine*, June 4, 1990, p. 36.

21. The issue, for my purposes, is not whether Havel's idea is technically sound. It is rather that it is the product of a thought process that seeks simultaneous beneficial impact in multiple realms. For another example of such thinking, see the proposal advanced in Roald Sagdeev and Michael Nacht, "Space Policy is Foreign Policy," *New York Times*, June 26, 1993, p. 15.

22. Of course, modernization of the entire Russian telephone system would take time, but short-term benefits would be available along the way. To be sure, improved telecommunications would not be a sufficient condition for making Russia attractive to foreign investors, but it is probably a necessary condition.

Most sufficient conditions are in areas that are largely the homework of Russian officials, such as contract enforcement and property rights protection. As this book went to press, the Clinton administration dropped the restriction on fiber-optics.

23. George Soros, "A Social Safety Net for Russia," *The Washington Post*, January 4, 1993, p. A21.

24. See Passell, "Economic Scene." The quoted phrase is Passell's.

25. Joseph Brandt, a doctoral candidate in the Department of Political Science, University of California at Berkeley, is conducting research on a doctoral dissertation that explores how Western policies affect the prospects for politicians "playing the ethnic card" in Estonia, Moldova, and Yugoslavia. In Estonia, he has found that the Council of Europe has had a demonstrable restraining influence on Estonian politicians' inclinations to disadvantage politically the local Russian population. To be sure, Russia may not be as easy to influence in this direction as Estonia has proven to be.

26. A simple linkage strategy that fits the spirit could be Western conditioning of economic assistance and credits on Russian enhancement of the safety of their nuclear arsenal, or on Russian compliance with nuclear reduction agreements, or on Russian abjuring of nuclear threats against former Soviet republics. Such a linkage of economic aid to nuclear issues might be dubbed "less bang for the buck."

27. Edward Walker, in a personal communication.

28. See Stephen F. Cohen, "U.S. Policy and Russia: Fallacies and Flaws," *The Nation*, April 12, 1993, pp. 476–485.

29. Zbigniew Brzezinski, "The Premature Partnership," *Foreign Affairs*, Vol. 73, No. 2 (March/April 1994), pp. 67–82.

30. Steven Greenhouse, "Georgian Asks U.S. to Back Peace Force," *New York Times*, March 8, 1994, p. A6.

31. The most substantial juxtaposition of these arguments is Josef C. Brada, "The Transformation from Communism to Capitalism: How Far? How Fast?," *Post-Soviet Affairs*, Vol. 9, No. 2 (April–June 1993), pp. 87–110; and Peter Murrell, "What Is Shock Therapy? What Did It Do in Poland and Russia?" in ibid., pp. 111–140.

32. Many useful articles and debates along these lines have appeared in *Journal of Democracy* (quarterly).

33. See, for example, articles by Robert Jervis, Jack Snyder, John Mearsheimer, and others in the quarterlies *Foreign Affairs*, *Foreign Policy*, and *International Security*.

34. For example, one major debate in both Russia and the West concerns the mutual compatibility of marketization and democratization processes in a post-Leninist context.

35. For a penetrating discussion of rationalist versus culturalist theories, see Harry Eckstein, *Regarding Politics* (Berkeley: University of California, 1992), chapters 1, 7, 11.

36. Andrew C. Janos, "The Domestic and International Contexts of Politics in Eastern Europe," paper presented at the Conference on the Political Economy of

Post-Communist Transformation, Center for German and European Studies, University of California, Berkeley, CA, February 11–13, 1993.

37. On the other hand, Richard Temsch, in personal communication, argues that Russia would be better served by a development strategy that emphasized sales to its domestic market, rather than an export-driven strategy of development.

38. Indeed, I am told that Henry Kissinger once proposed that Western investors put the local head of the Russian mafia on their board of directors! This may be risky. Richard Temsch, in personal communication, argues that this would compromise both capitalism and foreign investment in the eyes of the bulk of the population, which hates the "mafia's" control of many sectors of the economy.

39. See *New York Times*, July 9, 1993, p. 1.

8

Where Have All the Flowers Gone?

Alexander Dallin

Who does not remember the euphoria of liberation in the Soviet Union and Eastern Europe from 1989 to 1991? From Moscow to Prague, people rallied in the hundreds of thousands to demand civil and human rights, to protest against repressions, and to organize as they could not for generations. The Wall came down in Berlin, and East rejoined West. And when in August 1991 a motley assemblage of reactionaries sought to stage a coup to reverse the tide and take over the government of the Soviet Union, democracy prevailed—or so it seemed—with Boris Yeltsin atop a tank, proclaiming the defense of parliament. Soon the Communist Party was suspended, the Soviet Union itself dissolved into fifteen new national states, and the Cold War was over. All was aright in that vast part of the world that only a few years earlier had been described as the evil empire and the major threat to world peace and Western civilization. Now the Russians were our friends, communism was dead, and the good guys were in charge.

Less than three years later, it was hard to recognize the picture. The Russian economy was in serious trouble; GDP was dropping almost as fast as inflation was rising; corruption and violence had become pandemic; throughout the land people ignored laws and decrees issued in Moscow; the president felt obliged to dissolve a recalcitrant rump parliament and call out the troops to shell and seize it. In the elections that followed, the democrats—splintered into four parties—lost control of parliament to the neo-communists and to the super-nationalists, both anti-Western and authoritarian in orientation. The old institutions no

---

This chapter does not represent the consensus of views of the contributors to this volume but reflects merely the author's own opinions.

longer functioned, and no new ones had been erected in their place. Inter-ethnic strife was threatening peace within and among states, and Russia was once again demanding a hegemonic role in "its" part of the world. The wave of optimism about the future had yielded, it appeared, to confusion, lassitude, and widespread despair. And in February 1994, in a symbolic slap at Boris Yeltsin and what he stood for, the new parliament voted to amnesty and release from prison both the coup plotters of 1991 and the rebels and resisters of 1993.

How was all this possible? It will not do to dismiss the changes as the natural revolution of the wheel of history, where night follows day and light succeeds darkness. Nor will it do to throw up our hands and conclude that events in Russia defy rational explanation. While it may be too early to come up with definitive answers, we must at least sketch the range of alternative explanations and some of the arguments for and against them.

Did the Democrats Ever Have a Chance?

The pessimistic, or deterministic, perspective argues that the Russian democrats never had a chance. Indeed, where—and who—were the democrats? What criteria should we use to identify them? It is highly questionable whether any sizable number of people around Mikhail Gorbachev during the years of perestroika can properly be considered democrats; but even if we so label the reformers and liberalizers who came out of the leadership of the Communist Party of the Soviet Union, they were a thin layer of converts.

A second group of democrats consisted of those organized in coalitions such as Democratic Russia, which helped elect Boris Yeltsin president in June 1991 and played a part in the Supreme Soviet of the Soviet Union and later in the Congress of People's Deputies of the Russian Federation. There were also a number of democrats in key positions in the media, in the Russian Academy of Sciences, and scattered throughout the Russian government. All these people had a good deal of visibility and names well known to Western observers. There were also some self-styled democrats who organized locally and managed to win elections in individual towns and regions. Of course they all had some influence on what has happened in Russia since 1991.

And yet, the pessimists would argue, they (and we) failed to understand the scope and depth of resistance that the democratic reformers faced throughout the Soviet system, which Yeltsin's Russia inherited largely intact. Although the apex of the Communist Party had been shattered, both the elaborate bureaucratic institutions and the millions of incumbents, deeply entrenched across the land, dotted the political and economic landscape with invisible obstacles, as if they were hidden land mines. This after all was the huge network that had managed and controlled the Soviet Union—its politics, its ruling party, its economy, its society, its security arm, its armed forces, and its propaganda machine— for more than half a century. To them Yeltsin and the democrats constituted a mortal threat—not so much to their beliefs (there were few true believers left by the 1990s, though most of them were no doubt Soviet patriots) as to their power and positions. Amidst all the gloating about the downfall of communism, how could we have missed the fact that they all remained in place? Did anyone really believe that they would, or could, overnight change their convictions, their mindsets, or even their style of work?

Local party officials, plant managers, chairpersons of collective farms, officers of the KGB, personnel of the many state planning agencies and economic ministries—their many years of experience in the Soviet system had taught them how to keep quiet when they disagreed with official policy. Some of them no doubt remembered how they had gone underground during the Nazi occupation in the 1940s. What they needed was patience—and a tacit determination to drag their feet, sabotage or ignore orders they found threatening, and in some cases shift to other jobs with a more promising future. But otherwise it was astounding to what extent business—both government and privatized—continued to operate much as it had before. Indeed, in a striking number of cases, the old political nomenklatura became the new economic elite—for instance, managers of state enterprises privatizing them by selling them to themselves or to new joint-stock companies in which they had a major stake.

In a very real sense—which was not then fully apparent—the old regime was never overthrown. Or, more precisely, to quote Gavriil Popov, the former mayor of Moscow, "the democrats' victory over the coup plotters did not bring to power the democrats, who were totally unprepared to be in that position ... [The democrats'] main mistake was that they imagined they had taken power in Russia after the coup. Unfortunately, the people believed this, too."[1]

This point also addresses the contrary argument—that the democrats missed their opportunity. After the defeat of the coup and the enormous weakening of Gorbachev and his apparat, the Yeltsin democrats had their chance. In the following weeks there was no one in a position to oppose them, and Yeltsin was riding the crest of his popularity. Their failure to oust the incumbents and to launch meaningful reforms in the economy, the judicial system, the dismantling of the military-industrial sector—in brief, to complete the revolution—foreshadowed their subsequent disintegration and general failure as a political force. Some would blame it on their incompetence, on their inexperience, on their arrogance, or on their failure to create a national organization.

To these charges, the answer is essentially that they indeed did not know what to do: their seeming victory came too suddenly for them to be ready; they were accustomed to functioning as an opposition and lacked an action program; for the most part, they were not policy makers or administrators. As for ousting the existing officialdom, there was simply no one else with whom to replace the old communist cadres.

> When the coup occurred [Popov recalled in the same paper] the democrats were split by numerous schisms and were characterized by organizational weakness within individual blocs and the movement as a whole. Organizationally, the democrats were not ready to take power. Added to the organizational weakness was weakness in terms of programs. After all, for a long time we had acted on the assumption that we would be only an opposition. ... In all the main areas—nationalities policy, the state system, privatization, structural reorganization of the economy, micro-economic policy, agrarian reform, a social program for the USSR, foreign relations—we lacked concrete programs in versions that were suitable for practical application.[2]

One of the many complicating consequences that stemmed from the fact that virtually the entire society was serving the party-state was the absence of alternative cadres who could have replaced the old apparat. True, this later permitted some of the apologists for the Yeltsin policy to point with pride to the wise decision not to embark on witch-hunts or purges of Soviet-era officials. But in fact the crucial consideration was—with a few individual exceptions—simply the absence of competent replacements.

The democrats—in particular, the democrats' leadership—consisted in overwhelming part of intellectuals, particularly of members of the cultural elite in Moscow and St. Petersburg, and some academics—at best policy analysts, but virtually without any administrative or organizational experience. Moreover, they had no stable or organized support, no cohesive socio-economic base or interest group to lean on. Their strength, for a time, came from their ability to convene mass rallies, at which—especially in the capital—literally hundreds of thousands would turn out to demonstrate their support. Soon, however, the population was exhausted. Other issues—food, corruption, prices, crime—came to the top of their agenda. No wonder the democrats' support appeared to be more volatile than that of their various rivals.

Another facet, which Popov hints at, is the fact that before the coup attempt, "democrats" were defined largely by their opposition to the existing order, not by a common set of values. This helps explain both their unpreparedness after the coup and the lack of cohesion in the democratic camp, which soon began to fall apart.

In the terminology of the comparative transitions literature, the result after August 1991 was a tacit pact of the new, "victorious" elite with part of the old bureaucratic and economic elites: each needed the other. The pact was never formalized or made explicit. By the same token, the democrats who, of necessity, accepted their coexistence with the old-timers did not realize that this tactical stance would ultimately prove to be a suicide pact for them. But if many of the constraints within which they were henceforth compelled to operate were structural, situational, or beyond their reach, this does not account for some of the subsequent organizational, policy, and communication failures for which the democrats must bear responsibility.

A major source of disorientation for the "victors" was the traumatic impact of the disintegration of the old Soviet Union—not so much of the system of government as of the state and the great power that it stood for—the state they had all lived in, all their lives, and, whatever their politics, had been proud of. Not only the "patriots" but many of the liberals soon experienced a profound sense of loss, confusion, and even a sense of guilt for having been present—if not complicitous—at the termination of the Union.

And if the "winners" failed to act in the weeks and months following the August 1991 crisis, then the going was bound to become even harder with the passage of time. Inevitably, the initial euphoria soon began to wane. The surviving functionaries began to assert themselves, at first cautiously and later brazenly. If the hope had been that the bureaucrats who remained in office would be those who had the most progressive outlook or who favored a democratic system of government, this expectation proved to be naive.

Anti-reformist and anti-democratic sentiment began to be translated into political organizations on the far right and far left flanks, with a fair measure of demagoguery and populism and with the support of high officials, from the vice president down. The democrats themselves—or better, those who had claimed to be democrats until then—divided in several ways; notably, Russians and non-Russians split as the union republics emerged as sovereign states; and among the Russians, too, "statists" and "anti-statists" pulled in different directions. Self-serving interest groups—for instance, managers of enterprises receiving government subsidies—began to function as powerful and sometimes corrupt lobbies. As economic conditions deteriorated across the country, and law and order became a priority concern, the initial enthusiasm for political action vanished. By 1993 electoral participation declined dramatically, and a general disappointment with "democracy" (and often with the United States as its symbolic surrogate) became apparent. Short of a new crisis, elite politics moved further and further away from the reformist end of the spectrum, and by 1994 the democratic ranks had pathetically shrunk.

In a comparative and historical perspective, this waning of euphoria is entirely normal and natural. Moreover, there were also good—objective and subjective—reasons why the alternative orientations gained a good deal of popular support: Russia experienced a national identity crisis once it became independent but no longer constituted the core of a superpower; economic conditions, law and order, and relations with neighboring states invited populism, demagoguery, and xenophobia of a sort from which the democrats shrank. There was much that had gone wrong in Russia, and it was natural—as happens elsewhere—to blame it on those in office. This was particularly true when the incumbents did not make a good case for their innocence in the resulting mess. In short, there were good and objective reasons why the democrats could not effectively consolidate their hold on power in 1991 or since. There were also serious sins of omission and commission by which the democrats themselves contributed to their failure to wield power, to become and remain a leading political force, to implement the reforms with which they were identified, and to capture the popular imagination.

Short of ousting the communist incumbents or the "super-patriots" in the armed forces and security services, short of refraining from the economic reforms with their inevitably destabilizing consequences, what could the democrats have done to consolidate the new order? A comparative perspective suggests that formation of a ruling political party, a "founding" election that would have provided an initial division of the political space, and a new constitution might have been important building blocks of a new political system. None of these things happened in 1991 or early 1992. When some of them did take place later on, the whole situation had seriously unraveled and deteriorated, probably beyond early repair.

Did the Economic Reforms Ever Have a Chance?

One of the circumstances that distinguished the Russian scene from other transitions from authoritarianism, such as the Latin American, Spanish, Philippine, or Greek examples, was the need to carry out a fundamental restructuring of the economy simultaneously with the reconstruction of political processes and institutions. Not only were there no autonomous economic institutions—the counterpart to civil society—in existence, but there was not even a blueprint for the "great leap backward" from a central command economy to a mixed market economy.

There is no question that, from the vantage point of 1994, the state of the economy is a major failure—if not the major failure—of post-Soviet Russia. While a new stratum of wealthy businessmen has emerged, a far larger part of the population has sunk below the poverty line (though estimates vary quite substantially); massive inflation has eaten up such savings as people had, and more; those on fixed incomes, such as pensioners and students, have in many instances been left destitute; and, whatever the reality, in popular perception economic insecurity—along with crime and corruption—has become probably the most serious grievance and source of destabilization for which the regime is held responsible. The parallel collapse of the public health system and the demographic catastrophe highlighted by the rise in mortality rates and the decline in birth rates only serves to dramatize the scope of the problem.

Was there a way of doing better? Could much of the pain and stress have been avoided? It is true but hardly helpful to say that we, and they, will never know. As so often, it was a matter of trade-offs, but surely things could not be left as they were. The central plan had in effect collapsed, national income was rapidly declining while inflation was rising at a dangerous rate, and the economy was in serious crisis even before Yeltsin took over. In a very real sense, in the economy, just as in political and social life, many of the problems encountered after the collapse of the Soviet Union were parts of the legacy of the ancien regime.

Essentially, the alternatives were to carry out the economic reforms more slowly than was attempted in an effort "to get them over with;" to implement them faster and with fewer compromises; to carry out a different sequencing of reforms, such as decontrol of prices, control of inflation, an end to government monopolies, and the conversion of defense-related enterprises; or to accompany the transition with a more comprehensive (and hence less painful but also more expensive) program of support and retraining, and a "social safety net" for those who were left to cope with the stressful consequences of reform. Economists will disagree over the desirability of alternatives, and politicians will contest the economic calculus of all.

The fundamental problem was that many of the needed preconditions for successful economic reform were missing. Nor did they emerge quickly, spontaneously, or cheaply. Thus an extensive institutional framework required for a market economy had not existed under Soviet conditions: this includes a modern banking system, a system of taxation (and its general acceptance by the business community and the population at large), a legal system including contract law, the assurance of property rights, a stock market and a commodity exchange, and the whole infrastructure for relations among different enterprises. No less important, what was sadly but inevitably missing were the attitudes of individual initiative, competition, and responsibility and the behavior that goes with them in a competitive society and economy.

A second major difficulty that went back to the Gorbachev years (and of course those preceding him) was the paucity of good economists with a sound grasp of non-socialist economics, beginning with elementary concepts such as supply and demand, the consequences of printing paper money, and how the market sets prices. The opposite difficulty was then the involvement—both by the Russian government's choice and by the not-so-subtle encouragement by the United States and the International Monetary Fund—of foreign specialists who, however brilliant as economists, had little or no feel for the Russian social or economic scene and essentially sought to apply recipes that had served well in Bolivia or at best Poland but could not be expected to work (or work as well) in Russia—and some Russians will argue that their homegrown equivalents, such as Yegor Gaidar, were equally out of touch with the lives of the rank and file across the land.

A further complicating factor of considerable magnitude was the vast size of the defense-related sector and its disproportionate weight, both in the economy and in political clout. In addition to its institutional role and the structural distortion it introduced, its net effect was, time and again, to undermine decisions taken by reformist decision-makers in the innocence of their cabinets.

Finally, supportive political conditions were essentially absent. Simply put, there was no strong or cohesive national government. Instead, there was the collapse of effective mechanisms for the implementation of central government orders. Laws, decrees, and regulations were roundly ignored with impunity. There was also a problem of governmental overload at a moment when the small and relatively inexperienced team of officials had to deal simultaneously with a wide range of problems, from wage bills to ethnic conflicts to foreign policy to bargaining with parliament to inquisitive media to massive theft and graft.

If this picture is accurate, it points to a tension between economic and sociopolitical priorities. There were several problems with the Yegor Gaidar-Jeffrey Sachs recipe. While it may have been theoretically sound, its sponsors were compelled to compromise when it was sabotaged by others in the Russian government whose true interests became more clearly apparent after the December 1993 elections and the triumph of the industrial and agrarian lobbies—what has been called "stagnation with a human face."

Secondly, the expected successes of what was erroneously labeled (but popularly perceived as) shock therapy were both exaggerated in advance and promised to be manifest in far too short a span of time. Furthermore, the pain that a speedy marketization was bound to inflict was underestimated and never explained, justified, or "sold" to the public as unavoidable.

There were no doubt good reasons why it would have been difficult to provide a more generous "social safety net" during the period of transition. As one economist remarked, its cost would have made Swedish welfare officials shudder. More particularly, many enterprises that should have been deprived of government subsidies in order to let them go bankrupt were kept alive, not only because of the lobbying of their managers but also because under Soviet conditions a large part of the social security package from housing to consumer goods and day care—was delivered through places of employment, which often became "company towns" in the sense of towns in the United States of a century ago.

And yet with effort and creativity it should have been possible to anticipate and minimize, if not totally to avoid, both the personal costs to the Russian population and the political costs to the incumbent government, to whom the elections of December 1993 administered a telling rebuke. It was simply not smart politically nor sufficiently compassionate to let the economists—who were not good politicians—do their thing. The generic failure to pay wages and salaries, in some cases for many months, in an effort to reduce the deficit, was characteristic of the disastrous attitude among those nominally in charge. A good case can be made that the calamitous state of public health should have been a priority concern. Nor was anything done to respond to the widespread, and not unfounded, perception that fundamental standards of social justice (in large part, products of the Soviet past) were being violated by the disparities between haves and have-nots under conditions in which the collusion between the new capitalists and the new "mafias" was more than accidental.

In any event, under the best of circumstances the successful and consistent transformation of the Soviet into some form of market economy would have exacted a cost and, most emphatically, would have taken a far longer period of time than was assigned to it. The experience of former East Germany—where the cost of reform, under much better conditions than in Russia, to every one's surprise turned out to be enormous—is instructive here, precisely in spite of the massive assistance provided by its Western twin. In any event there was in Russia neither a clear strategy of transformation, nor adequate incentives for people to work harder and better, nor time to grow a new generation of people with the ability and expectation to assume responsibility for their own behavior in an economic (as well as a legal) system with which they were unfamiliar. Once again, the objective difficulties were compounded by sins of omission and commission by the decision-makers on top. How much of this, if anything, Yeltsin understood is an open question.

Did a Moderate Foreign Policy Ever Have a Chance?

One of the principal reasons why the West cheered the transformations in the Soviet Union and its successor states was the fundamental changes they signalled in the international order.

The Soviet Union yielded its control of its "satellite" empire and espoused the "new thinking" that abandoned all unilateral or offensive ambitions, helped resolve regional conflicts from Cambodia to Namibia, withdrew from Afghanistan, and promised full cooperation in the international system. When Boris Yeltsin took over, the United States was reassured by the far-reaching arms control agreements that were signed, by the Russian desire to participate in the international economic system, and by the cooperative stance toward the United States adopted by the Russian foreign ministry under Andrei Kozyrev. Perhaps most important (though not often so stated) was the fragmentation of the Soviet Union that seemed to signal its end as a superpower, and the apparent weakness of the Russian Federation (and, a fortiori, of the other successor states) as an international actor. Washington spoke of a strategic alliance between Russia and the United States, cemented at ceremonial "summits" in Washington and Moscow, and before long exchanges and cooperation covered a vast and diverse universe, from mountain-climbing to Arctic fisheries, and the exchange of information concerning international terrorism to environmental pollution. All this was particularly welcome at a time of economic stringency in the United States, as it permitted the reduction, however modest, of American defense expenditures.

The United States had reason to be greatly relieved. So, it appeared, did Russia, given the substantial financial and technical assistance the West pledged to provide. American "culture" (using the term loosely), from fast food to loud music and from *Playboy* to CNN, was all the rage where only a few years earlier it had been proscribed and disparaged.

By 1994 the situation had begun to change in a highly troubling manner. It took no great skill to discover, sitting in Moscow, that American assistance had been far more meager than advertised, that it served in large measure to benefit American corporations or security interests and did little for the Russian economy at large. Comments from authoritative Russian sources hinted broadly that with the slowdown—or end— of economic reforms Western assistance had also become far more dispensable. This realization seemed to remove the constraints on the public expression of views that differed from American conventional wisdom.

Now a variety of issues began to sour relations—Russian arms sales to India that the U.S. objected to; Russian efforts to revise the terms of the treaty limiting the deployment of conventional forces in Europe; continued Russian intransigence over the "Northern Territories"—four trivial but symbolically significant islands that Japan wanted back. The two powers were at odds over NATO policy in Bosnia and elsewhere, but above all over the new Russian claim to hegemony in the region that had been the USSR. Moscow's posture vis-à-vis the "near abroad" (as detailed in another chapter) threatened to embroil it in serious controversy with its neighbors and with the Western powers beyond.

No less ominously, the whole tone of Russian foreign policy had changed, from the amiable search for accords in 1991–1992 to an acerbic national assertiveness in 1993–1994, which caused growing concern and alarm abroad. The emergence of the Zhirinovsky party, with a totally irresponsible foreign policy agenda (that was also espoused by other parties with greater moderation and decorum), in turn provoked the revival of a deep-seated anti-Russian animus from the Baltic to the Black Sea.

What accounts for this shift in Russian foreign policy? Several possible explanations have been advanced in Russia and in the West. One hypothesis is that the Yeltsin regime had always planned to pursue an assertive foreign policy and was merely biding its time until the circumstances became more propitious. On balance, this argument of protracted dissimulation makes no sense. Andrei Kozyrev had essentially inherited a "Shevardnadze orientation," which some of the personnel in the upper echelons of the new Russian foreign ministry seemed to absorb with apparent conviction. Kozyrev himself was often accused—not only by the far right but also by both successive chairs of the parliament's foreign affairs and foreign trade committee, Vladimir Lukin and Evgenii Ambartsumov—of an unduly pliant espousal of American views on world affairs; and on one occasion he delivered a "cold war" speech that was meant to give his audience a dramatic warning of what Russian foreign policy would again become if the Yeltsin-Kozyrev line was defeated and reshaped by the super-patriots in Moscow. More generally, many of those who have dealt with Russian diplomats and policymakers in recent years believe that the notion that Moscow was "faking it" is not credible. "They were simply not that clever, to begin with," one Russian scholar observed ungenerously. Moreover, the objective circumstances—beginning with Russia's military, political, and economic weakness—had scarcely improved between 1991 and 1994: Russia was in no better condition to flex its muscles.

If we exclude this explanation, several others deserve attention, and they are not mutually exclusive. One stresses the initial disorientation that followed the partition of the Soviet state, and the lack of any clear concept of Russian national identity and interest. Once an official doctrine was formulated, it would have been naive to expect it to be identical to the United States' perspective: Russia, after all, has its own geopolitical concerns, historical memories and perceived priorities.

A second hypothesis focuses on the subsequent disillusionment with Western assistance: once this was no longer an item of top priority, there was no need for Russian restraint. Moreover, the outside world now provided convenient and not implausible scapegoats for Russian failure. Indeed, a troubling view tends to impute to American policy-makers the intent to wreck the Russian economy, rather than mere ignorance or incompetence; it similarly sees American advice on conversion as a hidden effort to wreck Russian defense capabilities. A far more serious analysis encourages Russian initiatives abroad since it allows Moscow to count on the United States remaining indifferent or passive when it comes to events far from its shores.

Another hypothesis explains the shift in Russian foreign policy by pointing to the effect of changes in domestic politics which have served to shift the locus of decision-making in Moscow, to a far greater involvement of military personnel and the National Security Council, i.e., to actors with a distinctly "harder" approach; as well as the to weakening of those in the foreign ministry who were identified with a pro-Western orientation.

Finally, a fourth explanation sees the new foreign policy orientation as largely an effort of the foreign ministry establishment to overtrump the "super-patriots" in Moscow as they, and their views, gained greater salience and perhaps greater popularity in 1993–1994. In this view foreign policy becomes hostage to Russian domestic politics.

None of these four hypotheses can be firmly ruled out. It does not follow that they are of equal weight. Granting both the initial confusion regarding national identity and purposes as well as a subtle learning process during the subsequent years, this argument speaks to the process, not to the substance of the new policy articulation. Here one must take seriously a combination of imperial nostalgia for the past "greatness" of Soviet power, perhaps some compassion for and solidarity with Russian-speakers abroad, some sense of condescension toward other, weaker, smaller, and less developed states, a weakening of constraints that would have kept Moscow to its previous moderate, internationalist line, and a genuine sense of anger at what has befallen their country and its people.

There is no evidence of any aggressive or expansionist plans or inclinations beyond the borders of the former Soviet Union, on the part of either the government or the public at large, except for the lunatic fringe exemplified—how seriously, it is hard to say—by Vladimir Zhirinovsky. On the other hand, it is not clear what the popular attitudes would be in an "internal" conflict with, say, Ukraine or Kazakhstan, particularly if the circumstances—as might well happen—can be presented in ambiguous fashion. There is an abiding desire to avoid violence wherever possible. But the balance of the evidence suggests that Russian statesmen—notably, Andrei Kozyrev—have indeed evolved in all sincerity toward a significantly "harder" line toward other members of the CIS.

Such an evolution has to be understood in the context of Russian domestic politics, which by 1993 was centrally concerned with the allocation of blame for failure, in an atmosphere of growing bitterness. Under attack from the nationalist camp, the foreign minister found it easiest to find targets and scapegoats abroad. This was congruent with the more general perception that, while it would be hard to score great successes at home—be it on crime or standard of living or inter-ethnic relations—it would be considerably easier to look for victories in dealing with Russia's even weaker and more unstable neighbor states.

Russian Political Culture: Authoritarian or Democratic?

Political events in the late Gorbachev period—glasnost, elections, the failure of the attempted putsch, and the collapse of communism—all seemed to disprove the argument popular in the West that Russia was traditionally authoritarian and its people liked it that way. The events of 1993–1994 in turn seemed to reinforce the proposition that democratic sentiments had been a thin and transient veneer, which—much as in 1917—had proved to be an evanescent myth. Which was true?

Opinion in the scholarly community, and among diplomats and journalists as well, has long divided over the dominant political culture in Russia. A large, and perhaps the greatest, number of experts have held it to be traditionally authoritarian, as marked by the many centuries of domination by tsars and commissars, without representative institutions or political freedoms, and without the web of voluntary, intermediate associations which, in the view of some, are a necessary condition for civil society. Whether this is traced back to a continuity of "Muscovite folkways" or attributed to the idiosyncrasies of an Ivan, a Peter, or a

Dzhugashvili, whether it is found to be the product of climate, soil, and geography, or of the logic of empire, this view has typically interpreted popular attitudes as "oriental" and obedient.

A very different argument has stressed the existence, beneath the appearance of popular compliance and autocratic institutions, of both an ancient tradition of urban veche and village communalism, and the more recent experience of the zemstva and parliamentary institutions in 1905–1917. In this view, the appearance of verbal and demonstrative popular unanimity under Stalinist conditions was more indicative of people's survival skills than of their political values and convictions.

Still others have posited the existence of two rival political cultures or of a far more complex and sophisticated set of limited reformist impulses, or finally of the fluidity and malleability, rather than the invariability, of Russian political culture. Indeed, a historical approach would stress the fact that, at some point in the past, elsewhere in what are now solidly democratic polities participatory values and attitudes were well-nigh absent; and that the flourishing of democratic culture has typically been associated with socio-economic modernization, including urbanization and higher educational attainments. While such generalizations are open to many challenges (Hitlerite Germany was well "modernized," while democratic India is not), they do capture an important point: the need to approach the question of the present political culture in Russia without assuming that it must be the extrapolation of "traditional" values and attitudes.

Since the late 1980s, and especially in independent Russia, it has been possible to test some of these hypotheses against actual events and behavior, and to conduct survey research and public opinion polls of varying reliability and sophistication. Though by no means unanimous, the various polls point to some interesting conclusions.[3] While there is a growing sentiment in favor of an "iron hand"—primarily to deal with crime and corruption as well as other social problems at home, rather than with economic policy—there has been a fairly strong commitment to democratic values. It is true that it does not preclude expressions of intolerance or a lack of understanding of the rule of law or the scope of civil liberties, but that seems scarcely surprising. There is also, in a number of studies, a strong correlation between democratic values and youth as well as higher educational attainments—a distinctly hopeful sign.

How are we to reconcile the predominantly "democratic" orientation revealed by these surveys with other events, such as the December 1993 elections? Several alternatives come to mind.

One may wish to argue that the election results are a "snapshot" of opinions expressed in a constrained choice, where voters may have been more interested in "sending a message," expressing a protest (in itself, a democratic process, compared to going into the street to revolt), or compelled to choose among imperfectly differentiated alternatives, rather than voting their convictions, democratic or otherwise. Moreover, election and referenda results from 1989 until April 1993 would have rather consistently reinforced the strong (though by no means unanimous) "democratic" preferences.

But it is also possible to posit that the "democratic" values found in many of the surveys of 1989–1993 were only skindeep and were articulated when it was "politically correct" to do so, and that by the end of 1993 at least a substantial part of the Russian population—and one might specify particular demographic groups—either had shed such ideas or at least were confused about their validity. If accurate, these polls also suggest a curious paradox: many of those whose values an outside analyst may classify as at least partially democratic refuse to vote (or at least failed to vote, at the end of 1993) for candidates explicitly identified with a democratic program or nominated by a democratic party.

One may consider the possibility that the body of survey research is so unreliable as to produce not only inaccurate but simply erroneous conclusions. While much of the early opinion polling in Russia was open to serious and justified criticism, over time the surveys conducted have improved in professionalism and reliability, and the relative consistency of findings across a number of polling agencies, Russian and foreign, and over several years, strongly suggests that the problem with reliability must be located elsewhere. Probing for underlying attitudes and beliefs, nonetheless, is a problematic undertaking.

Finally, it is possible that the criteria for finding the respondents democratic were too simplistic, one-dimensional, or "American." Thus one survey correctly discovered that support for political reforms did not, in many instances, correlate with support for a reduced role of the state in economic or welfare functions. On the Russian scene that should hardly have been a surprise. Similarly, resentment of the growing gap between haves and have-nots is likely to be more natural—and more ominous—in a post-Soviet setting than in the West.

In any case, the experience of recent years has clearly dispelled the Orwellian specter. Despite generations of communist indoctrination, the vast majority of the population—and especially the younger groups—have no difficulty making political choices and standing up against the existing regime—whatever the regime. Virtually the entire political community has been prepared to accept the results of reasonably free and democratic elections. Only a rather marginal grouping advocates banning all political organizations and doing away with "pluralism" (as a Western, "un-Russian" concept). While no doubt there are strong vestiges of political instincts and assumptions dating back to pre-Gorbachev days, and while there are signs that the politics of nostalgia for a seemingly better past has attractions for some substantial portion of the population, the range of choices before Russia—both democratic and otherwise—covers a broad spectrum but hardly allows for any possible return to the old Soviet days. It would have been most surprising if, after three generations of communist rule, the Russian population in its vast majority had promptly and lastingly turned into convinced democrats. It is safe to say that, everything being equal, their political preferences will readily follow their living conditions.

The Prospects

What has been achieved in the tremendous transformations that Russia has experienced during the few event-packed years since the pathetic days of Brezhnev, Andropov, and Chernenko must not be forgotten as we contemplate the perplexing difficulties the country faces today. While there is little point in indulging the recent passion for alternative scenarios for the future, what is clear is that Russia will neither revert to a communist system nor find itself a stable democracy at an early date. To make responsible forecasts, we not only cannot foretell contingent events (such as the health of particular leaders) but more generally do not know enough about the future political orientation of the new business stratum, the vast but differentiated working class, or the military and security forces.

For the moment the democrats have been thoroughly outmaneuvered by their various rivals, left and right, and it is not now apparent where they could find the social basis of support for their program or for that matter charismatic candidates for national leadership. But then, this was equally true prior to 1985. Moreover, most of their political adversaries have no sound economic prescription to offer. Yet economic issues may turn out to be the crucial facet in future political campaigns. Along with the anchoring of the rule of law, stabilizing the economy and providing the proper institutions and incentives to assure its healthy growth may prove to be a greater challenge than securing political institutions and behavior. Surely the next generation could be counted on more readily in political than in economic affairs.

One circumstance that deserves special attention is the political diversity across Russia which has now, perhaps for the first time, become the subject of thorough study. The considerable and important variations in political and social preferences between center and periphery, by geographic regions, by generations, and by social groups, are just beginning to be documented and analyzed.[4] They reflect the growing emergence of grassroots politics and local self-management. They also suggest the considerable difficulty that future Russian governments will face in seeking to re-establish effective central authority and control—and for the foreseeable future these will be weak governments operating against myriad entrenched regional, economic, and other centrifugal interests, diverse public values, and networks of organized crime and corruption.

Russian practice has been far from a model democracy, even leaving aside the battle between executive and legislative branches. There have been abuses of public trust and authority, efforts to rule by decree, to control the media, to limit the right of political organizations, to postpone local elections, and to suspend or ignore particular provisions of the newly-enacted constitution. Yet among the achievements of the past decade we must count the disappearance of political fear and the creation of a firm foundation for reasonably free and independent media. The press and television—and perhaps the educational establishment—will need to assume a special responsibility for vigilance against the most dangerous of adventurers, the ugliest of bigots, and the most irresponsible of demagogues.

It is not unusual for transitional regimes to experience protracted periods of unconsolidated democracy or mixed systems with elements of both democracy and authoritarianism—in the Latin American setting they have received such fanciful labels as dictablanda and democradura. Neither is the retention of parts of the old elite—civilian and military—unusual under such conditions.[5] But this insight in itself is not necessarily reassuring about the system's future.

Transitions from authoritarianism to open societies, governed by law, do not often go smoothly. This one is likely to be particularly painful, protracted, and perverse. One can only wish its architects skill, faith, and perseverance. In time, the flowers will bloom again.

Notes

1. Gavriil Popov, "August 1991 g.," *Izvestiia*, August 21–26, 1992.

2. Ibid.

3. See Jeffrey W. Hahn, "Continuity and Change in Russian Political Culture," *British Journal of Political Science*, Vol. 21 (1991), pp. 393–421; James L. Gibson et al., "Democratic Values and the Transformation of the Soviet Union," *Journal of Politics*, Vol. 54 (1992), pp. 329–371; Gibson et al., "Emerging Democratic Values in Soviet Political Culture," in Arthur H. Miller et al., eds., *Public Opinion and Regime Change: The New Politics of Post-Soviet Societies* (Boulder: Westview Press, 1993), pp. 69–94; Ada Finifter and Ellen Mickiewicz, "Redefining the Political System of the USSR," *American Political Science Review*, Vol. 86 (1992), pp. 857–874; Russian Center for Public Opinion and Market Research, *Referendum Study: Exit Poll* (Moscow: TsIOM, 1993); Donna Bahry, "Society Transformed? Rethinking the

Social Roots of Perestroika," *Slavic Review*, Vol. 52, No. 3 (Fall 1993), pp. 512–554; Vtsiom (Moscow), *Informatsionnyi biulleten'*, Vol. 1–2 (1993–1994).

4. See, e.g., the doctoral dissertations of M. Steven Fish (Stanford University), Gavin Helf (University of California at Berkeley), and Katherine Stoner-Weiss (Harvard University).

5. Philippe C. Schmitter and Terry L. Karl, "The Conceptual Travels of Transitologists and Consolidologists: How Far to the East Should They Attempt to Go?," *Slavic Review*, Vol. 53, No. 1 (Spring 1994), pp. 173–185; Guillermo O'Donnell and Philippe C. Schmitter, *Transitions from Authoritarian Rule: Tentative Conclusions* (Johns Hopkins University Press, 1986). See also Russell Bova, "Political Dynamics of the Post-Communist Transition: A Comparative Perspective," *World Politics*, Vol. 44, No. 1 (October 1991), pp. 113–138.

Glossary

Agrarian Party: A successor to the former parliamentary faction Agrarian Union, the Agrarian Party was originally part of the Russian Unity movement. Headed by Mikhail Lapshin, the Party won 55 seats in the December 1993 elections. One of its leading figures, Ivan Rybkin, was elected the first Chairman of the State Duma in early 1993.

Aksiuchits, Viktor: Leader of the Russian Christian Democratic Movement (RCDM), a right-of-center political grouping.

Astafev, Mikhail: Leader of the Constitutional Democratic (Kadet) Party, a moderately right-of-center political grouping.

Baburin, Sergei: A right-wing former deputy of the Russian Supreme Soviet, Baburin was active in the National Salvation Front before it was banned by Yeltsin in the autumn of 1992.

Burbulis, Gennadii: A former State Secretary of the Russian Federation and Vice Premier (1991–November 1992), he was a member of Yeltsin's "inner circle" of economic and political advisors and a principal architect of the reform strategy adopted by Yeltsin at the end of 1991.

Centrists: In Russian political discourse, "centrists" are moderate reformers who have a less pro-Western orientation in foreign policy and who generally support a slower, less comprehensive economic transition than "radical reformers." Centrist groups include the Civic Union (which formed in mid-1992 as a result of a union of the Russian Union of Industrialists and Entrepreneurs under Arkadii Volsky, the People's Party of Free Russia under then Vice President Aleksandr Rutskoi, and the Russian Democratic Party under Nikolai Travkin); the Women of Russia group; and some Yeltsin government members, including Viktor Chernomyrdin, Aleksandr Shokhin, and Georgii Khizha.

Chernomyrdin, Viktor: Prime Minister of Russia since December 1992, replacing Yegor Gaidar. A centrist, he was originally appointed to the government in the summer of 1992 as a representative of the industrial lobby.

Commonwealth of Independent States (CIS): The name given to the loosely organized political entity created after the demise of the USSR in December 1991. The CIS originally encompassed 10 of the former union republics of the USSR. Georgia and Azerbaijan have since joined; the Baltic states have never participated.

Communist Party of the Russian Federation: First organized in February 1993 and considered a successor of the CPSU, it claims 500,000 members and won 64 seats in the party list vote for the State Duma in December 1993. It is headed by Gennadii Ziuganov.

Congress of People's Deputies of the RSFSR (later the Russian Federation): Modeled on the USSR Congress of People's Deputies (see below), this body was created in 1990. Elections to the RSFSR Congress, however, which took place in March 1990, were more competitive than the March 1989 elections for the USSR Congress. They nevertheless took place at a time when Article 6 of the Soviet Constitution was still in effect. At its first session in the early summer of 1990, the RSFSR Congress of People's Deputies elected Boris Yeltsin as its Chairman.

Congress of People's Deputies of the USSR: The 2,250-member legislative body was created in the Gorbachev era and convened for the first time in the summer of 1989 following partially-competitive elections in March 1989. The Congress had considerable legislative powers, including the power to amend the constitution. It in turn elected a smaller, standing legislature, the Supreme Soviet of the USSR.

Council of the Federation: The upper house of the new bicameral legislature created by the constitution adopted in December 1993, the Council of the Federation consists of two representatives from each of Russia's regions and republics.

Democratic Party of Russia (DPR): The DPR is a centrist party that received 18 seats by party slate in elections for the State Duma in December 1993. It is headed by Nikolai Travkin.

Federal Assembly: The name for the new bicameral legislature of the Russia Federation provided for by the constitution adopted in December 1993. The houses of the new parliament are called the State Duma and the Council of the Federation. Elections for the Federal Assembly took place on December 1, 1993, the same day that the new constitution was ratified.

Fedorov, Boris: Russia's special representative to the International Monetary Fund and western financial institutions, he was considered one of the radical reformers allied with former Prime Minister Gaidar. He resigned as finance minister in January 1994, claiming that reforms were blocked by the conservative economic program of Prime Minister Viktor Chernomyrdin and by the inflationary monetary policies of the Chairman of the Central Bank, Viktor Gerashchenko.

Gaidar, Yegor: Russian Finance Minister in early 1991, Gaidar was the architect of Russia's economic reform program and the price liberalization of January 1, 1992. He later became Minister of the Economy and then Acting Prime Minister from June 1992 until December 1992. In 1993 Yeltsin again appointed Gaidar Minister of the Economy. Also in 1993, Gaidar helped found "Russia's Choice," a political movement that won a plurality of seats (94) in the State Duma's first elections in December 1993.

Gerashchenko, Viktor: The chairman of Russia's powerful State Bank, his credit policies to ailing state industries have been blamed by western economists for fueling inflation.

Khasbulatov, Ruslan: The chairman of Russia's Supreme Soviet from October 1991 to October 1993, he was arrested and imprisoned for refusing to disband the legislature and for inciting violence. Khasbulatov was released from prison in an amnesty in March 1994.

Khizha, Georgii: A member of the centrist Directors' Lobby, he was appointed Deputy Prime Minister during the summer of 1992.

Kozyrev, Andrei: Russia's Foreign Minister since July 1990, he presided over the pro-Western foreign policy of the Yeltsin government. Despite criticism from conservatives, Kozyrev remained in office after Russian foreign policy became increasingly assertive of Russia's perceived national interests, in late 1993.

Liberal-Democratic Party: An extreme nationalist party led by Vladimir Zhirinovsky, it won the second largest bloc of seats in the December 1993 elections and came in first in the party list vote, with 24%.

Lobov, Oleg: First Deputy Prime Minister, appointed by Yeltsin in the spring of 1993, Lobov is considered moderately right-of-center and a supporter of the program of the Civic Union.

Lukin, Vladimir: Yeltsin's ambassador to the United States until his election to the Federal Assembly in December 1993, he was once chairman of the Russian Supreme Soviet's Foreign Affairs Committee. Lukin became one of the principals in the Yavlinsky-Boldyrev-Lukin Bloc (Yabloko) political group that formed to compete in the December 1993 parliamentary elections.

National Salvation Front (NSF): Created in 1992 and subsequently banned by Yeltsin, this right-wing group favored Yeltsin's ouster, the reversal of economic and political reforms, the preservation of Russia's former superpower status, and the restoration of the Soviet Union.

"Near Abroad": A controversial term used by Russian analysts and political figures since 1991 to refer to the former republics of the USSR. It is rejected by many because of what they perceive as its neo-imperial implications.

Party of Unity and Concord: This moderate pro-reform party, led by Sergei Shakhrai, won 22 seats by party slate in the newly elected State Duma in December 1993.

Pavlov, Valentin: A former Prime Minister of the USSR who, together with then Soviet Vice President Gennadii Yanaev and others, was one of the leaders of the unsuccessful coup against Soviet President Gorbachev in August 1991.

Poltoranin, Mikhail: Formerly head of the Federal Information Center of Russia, which was responsible for government policy on the media, he is a strong ally of Yeltsin and was elected to the State Duma in December 1993.

Popov, Gavriil: An economist, former mayor of Moscow, and former head of the Russian Democratic Reform Movement, he is considered a radical reformer. After the elections of December 1993, Popov broke with Yeltsin and became a critic of the president from the democratic camp.

Red-Browns: A term used mostly by Russian democrats to describe the extreme anti-democratic opposition, including communists (the reds) and extreme nationalists (the browns, after Hitler's Brown Shirts). Reds and Browns tend to share a common opposition to economic reform, democratization, and the pro-western Russian foreign policy of Yeltsin.

Regions and Republics: Twenty-one of the 89 territorial units of the Russian Federation are ethnically defined (e.g., Tatarstan) and are called the "republics" in Russian political discourse. The remaining sixty-eight are referred to as the "regions."

Right and Left: In Russian political discourse, "right" refers to nationalist-patriotic forces as well as to pro-communist forces, while the "left" refers to capitalist-oriented and democratizing forces.

Russia's Choice: The largest bloc of parliamentary deputies (94) elected by party slate to the State Duma in December 1993; headed by former Prime Minister Yegor Gaidar, it is considered the leading champion of radical reform.

Rutskoi, Aleksandr: The Russian Vice President between July 1991 and his arrest in October 1993, he led a reformist faction of the Communist Party of the RSFSR in early 1991. Yeltsin chose him as his running mate in the elections for the Russian Presidency in June 1991, and Rutskoi gave Yeltsin important support during the failed coup of August 1991. However, relations between the two began to deteriorate soon thereafter, and by early 1992 Rutskoi had come out openly against Yeltsin. During the crisis of September-October 1993, the Supreme Soviet declared Rutskoi acting Russian president after it "impeached" Yeltsin for ordering its dissolution. Rutskoi was arrested and imprisoned for his role in the violence of October 3, but was released in an amnesty issued by the State Duma in March 1994.

Shakhrai, Sergei: Leader of the regionally-oriented Russian Party of Unity and Accord, his Party won 22 seats by party slate in the newly elected State Duma in December 1993. Shakhrai was formerly Yeltsin's legal advisor and played an important role in preparing Yeltsin's draft constitution. He later became Chairman of the State Committee on Nationalities and the Federation.

Shevardnadze, Eduard: Foreign Minister of the USSR until his resignation from the government and the Communist Party in December 1990. He became president of Georgia in 1992, leading Georgia's entry into the Commonwealth of Independent States in the fall of 1993.

Shokhin, Aleksandr: A centrist and former Deputy Prime Minister, Shokhin became Minister of the Economy in January 1994, replacing the radical economic reformer Yegor Gaidar.

Shumeiko, Vladimir: First Deputy Chairman of the Russian government under Prime Minister Chernomyrdin, and a Yeltsin ally, he was elected Chairman of the Council of the Federation in the new Federal Assembly in 1994.

Skokov, Yurii: Appointed by Yeltsin to be Secretary of Russia's Security Council in June 1992. Skokov broke with Yeltsin in March 1993 after refusing to support a Yeltsin decree declaring a state of emergency.

Starovoitova, Galina: Former member of the USSR Congress of People's Deputies and the Russian Supreme Soviet, Starovoitova was also a former advisor to Yeltsin on nationality affairs. Considered a radical reformer, she was dismissed by Yeltsin in late 1992.

State Duma: The lower house of the new legislature created by the constitution adopted in December 1993.

Union Republics, Autonomous Republics (ASSRs), Autonomous Oblasts (AoSSRs), and Autonomous Okrugs (AokSSRs): The hierarchy of ethnically-defined territorial units in the Soviet federal system. There were fifteen union republics in the USSR, the largest of which was the RSFSR.

Volsky, Arkadii: A former Chief of Department in the Central Committee of the CPSU and aide to CPSU General Secretary Yurii Andropov, Volskii became the leader of the Russian Union of Industrialists and Entrepreneurs and later a leader of the centrist alliance Civic Union.

Women of Russia: Headed by Alevtina Fedulova, this economically centrist party won 24 seats by party list in the December 1993 elections to the State Duma.

Yabloko: One of the reformist, pro-democracy parties that competed in the December 1993 elections for the State Duma, it won 28 seats in the party list vote. The term means "apple" in Russian, and is derived from the names of the party's leaders: Grigorii Yavlinskii, Yurii Boldyrev, and Vladimir Lukin. Although it is pro-reform, it has often distanced itself from the policies and decisions of the Yeltsin administration. It is considered less radical in its approach to economic reform than Russia's Choice (see above).

Yeltsin, Boris: President of Russia since June 1991, when he received 58% of the vote in the first direct and genuinely competitive election for chief executive in Russian or Soviet history. A former party leader in Sverdlovsk oblast, Yeltsin was a member of Gorbachev's Politburo until he was expelled after publicly criticizing conservatives in late 1987. He subsequently joined the democratic opposition to Gorbachev and became a leading member of the Interregional Group of Deputies of the USSR Supreme Soviet and Congress of Peoples' Deputies.

Zhirinovsky, Vladimir: Head of the extreme nationalist Liberal Democratic Party, he received nearly seven million votes (8%) for president in 1990, while his party won 24% of the party list in the December 1993 elections to the State Duma.

Ziuganov, Gennadii: Head of the Communist Party of the Russian Federation, which won 64 seats by party slate in the new State Duma.

Zorkin, Valerii: Chairman of Russia's Constitutional Court, Zorkin resisted Yeltsin's attempts to introduce emergency presidential rule in March and September 1993. He was accused by Yeltsin's supporters of politicizing the Constitutional Court created in 1992. Yeltsin dismissed Zorkin from his position on December 1, 1993, because of his role in supporting Yeltsin's opponents during the September–October 1993 crisis in Moscow.

About the Book

In this book, distinguished U.S. and Russian scholars analyze the great challenges confronting post-communist Russia and examine the Yeltsin government's attempts to deal with them. Focusing on problems of state- and nation-building, economic reform, demilitarization, and the definition of Russia's national interests in its relations with the outside world, the authors trace the complex interplay between the communist legacy and efforts to chart new directions in both domestic and foreign policy. They give special attention to the defeat of liberal reformers in the latest parliamentary elections and to the implications of that shift for Russia's domestic and foreign policy in the years ahead.

About the Contributors

George W. Breslauer is Professor of Political Science, Chair of the Political Science Department, and Chair of the Center for Slavic and East European Studies at the University of California at Berkeley.

Alexander Dallin is the Spruance Professor of International History and Professor of Political Science, and Chair of the Center for Russian and East European Studies at Stanford University.

Richard E. Ericson is Professor of Economics and Director of the Harriman Institute at Columbia University.

David Holloway is Professor of Political Science and Co-Director of the Center for International Security and Arms Control at Stanford University.

Andrei Kortunov is Head of the Foreign Policy Department of the Institute for U.S.A. and Canada Studies in the Russian Academy of Sciences in Moscow, and is President of the Russian Science Foundation.

Gail W. Lapidus was Professor of Political Science at University of California at Berkeley and Chair of the Berkeley-Stanford Program in Soviet and Post-Soviet Studies during the preparation of this book. She is currently Senior Fellow at the Institute for International Studies at Stanford University.

Michael McFaul has worked as a research associate at the Center for International Security and Arms Control at Stanford University and is currently Assistant Professor of Political Science at Stanford.

Lilia Shevtsova is Director of the Center for Political Studies and Deputy Director of the Institute for International Economic and Political Studies of the Russian Academy of Sciences.

Edward W. Walker is Executive Director of the Berkeley-Stanford Program in Soviet and Post-Soviet Studies.

Victor Zaslavsky is Professor of Sociology at Memorial University in Newfoundland, Canada.

Index